2ND EDITION

FOR ORGANS, PIANOS & ELECTRONIC KEYBOARDS

E-Z PLAY TODAY

112

BEST OF THE

80 OF THE BEAT

MW01133953

ISBN 978-0-7935-2285-9

HAL•LEONARD®
CORPORATION
7777 W. BLUEMOUND RD. P.O. BOX 13819 MILWAUKEE, WI 53213

Visit Hal Leonard Online at
www.halleonard.com

CONTENTS

4 All My Loving	104 If I Needed Someone
6 All You Need Is Love	106 In My Life
2 And I Love Her	108 Julia
9 And Your Bird Can Sing	112 Lady Madonna
14 Back in the U.S.S.R.	114 Let It Be
16 Because	116 The Long and Winding Road
18 Birthday	122 Love Me Do
24 Blackbird	124 Lucy in the Sky with Diamonds
26 Can't Buy Me Love	128 Magical Mystery Tour
28 Come Together	119 Martha My Dear
30 A Day in the Life	130 Michelle
34 Day Tripper	132 Mother Nature's Son
21 Don't Let Me Down	134 Norwegian Wood (This Bird Has Flown)
36 Eight Days a Week	140 Nowhere Man
38 Eleanor Rigby	142 Ob-La-Di, Ob-La-Da
40 Fixing a Hole	146 Paperback Writer
46 The Fool on the Hill	148 Penny Lane
48 Get Back	150 Please Please Me
43 Good Day Sunshine	152 Rocky Raccoon
50 Good Night	154 Run for Your Life
52 Got to Get You Into My Life	156 Sgt. Pepper's Lonely Hearts Club Band
54 A Hard Day's Night	137 She Loves You
56 Hello, Goodbye	160 She's a Woman
60 Help!	162 Something
62 Helter Skelter	164 Strawberry Fields Forever
66 Here Comes the Sun	170 Taxman
70 Here, There and Everywhere	172 This Boy (Ringo's Theme)
72 Hey Bulldog	174 Ticket to Ride
76 Hey Jude	167 Twist and Shout
78 I Am the Walrus	178 We Can Work It Out
86 I Feel Fine	181 When I'm Sixty-Four
88 I Saw Her Standing There	184 While My Guitar Gently Weeps
90 I Should Have Known Better	187 With a Little Help from My Friends
92 I Want to Hold Your Hand	190 Yellow Submarine
94 I Want to Tell You	192 Yesterday
96 I Will	194 You Like Me Too Much
98 I'll Follow the Sun	196 You Won't See Me
83 I'm Looking Through You	198 You're Going to Lose That Girl
100 I've Just Seen a Face	202 You've Got to Hide Your Love Away
02 If I Fell	200 Your Mother Should Know

All My Loving

Registration 9
Rhythm: Rock

Words and Music by John Lennon
and Paul McCartney

Five Foot Two, Eyes Of Blue

Key of C

D———D#

G E E E G# E

E E A E A E A E

A C A C A G A C

C C C C

B C B E B C B

B A B A

A A B A D A B A

D C B A G F E

D--------D#

G E E E G# E

E E A E A E A E

A C A C A G A C

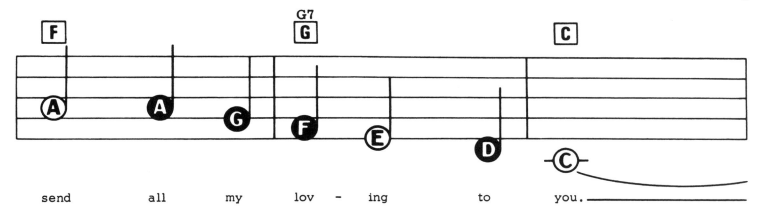

send   all   my   lov - ing   to   you.————————

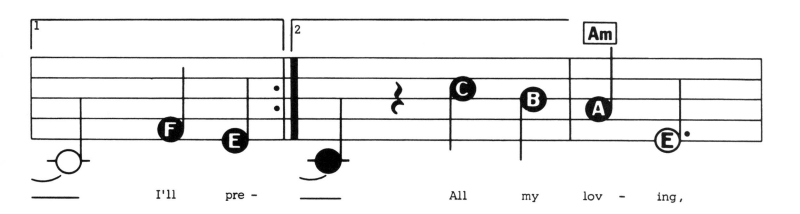

———   I'll   pre - ———   All   my   lov - ing,

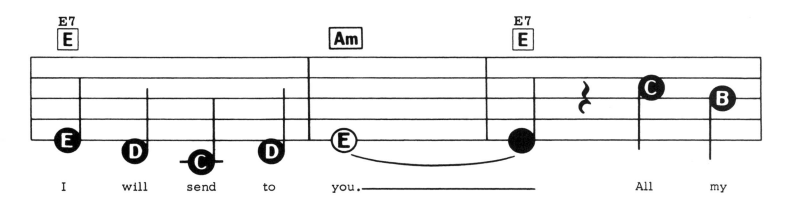

I   will   send   to   you.————————   All   my

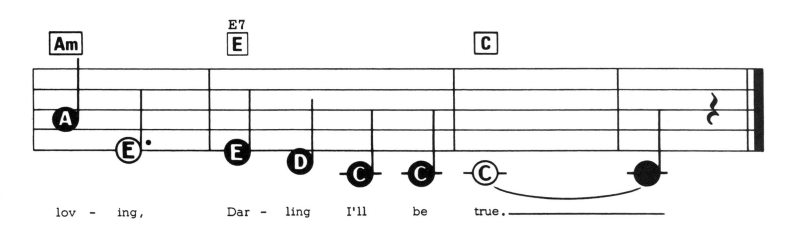

lov - ing,   Dar - ling   I'll   be   true.————————

All You Need Is Love

Registration 5
Rhythm: Shuffle or Swing

Words and Music by John Lennon
and Paul McCartney

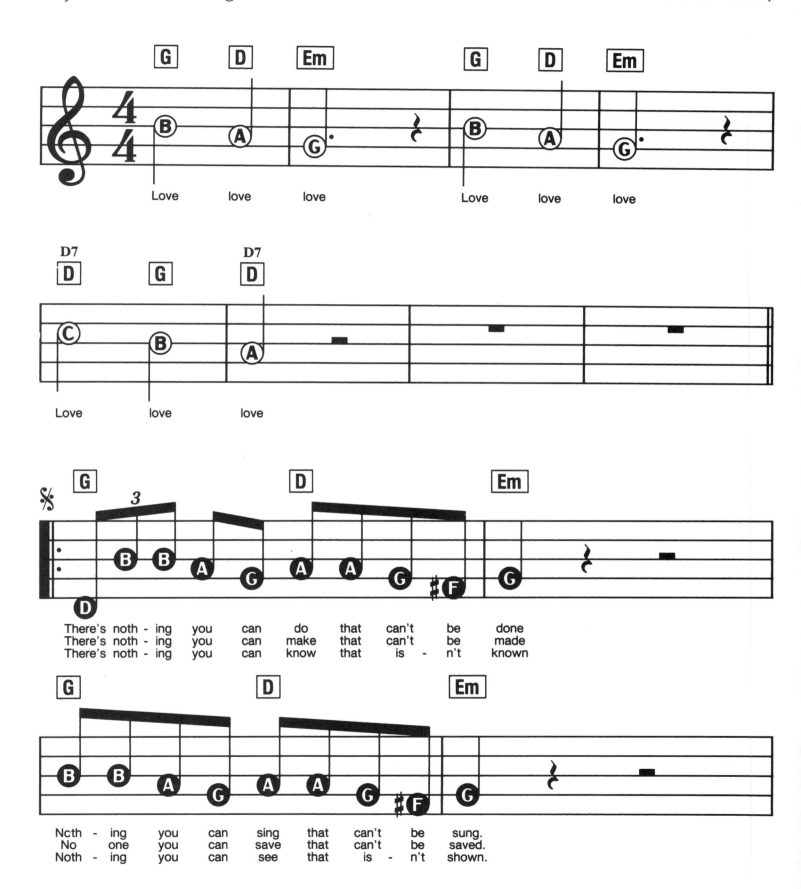

7

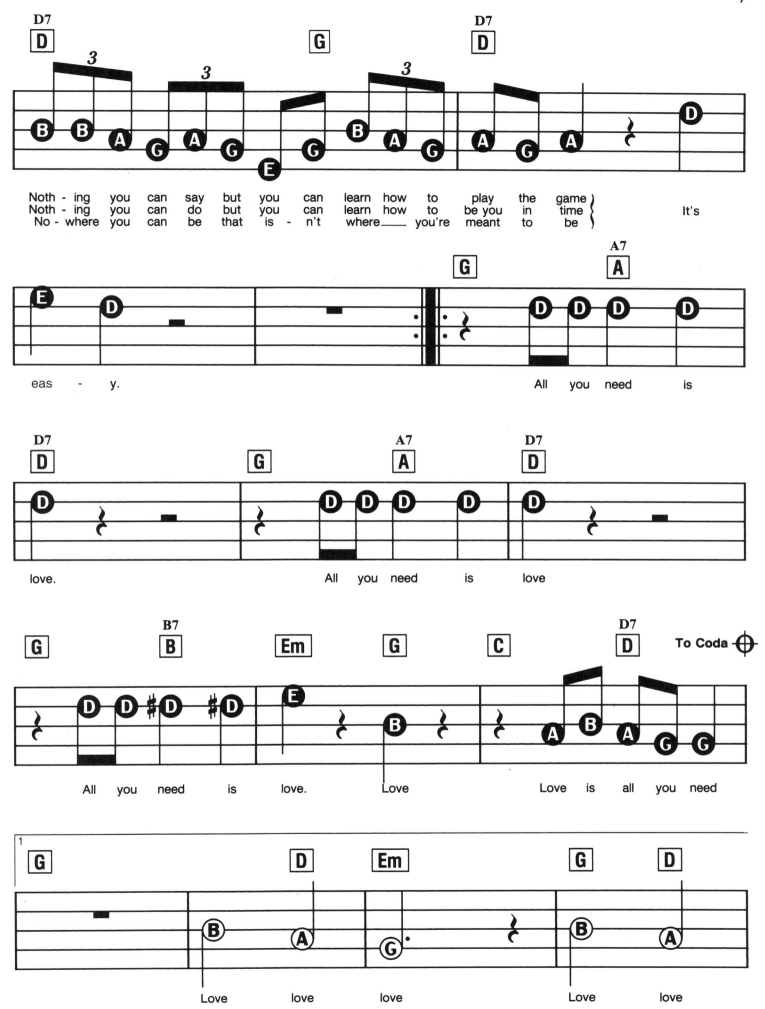

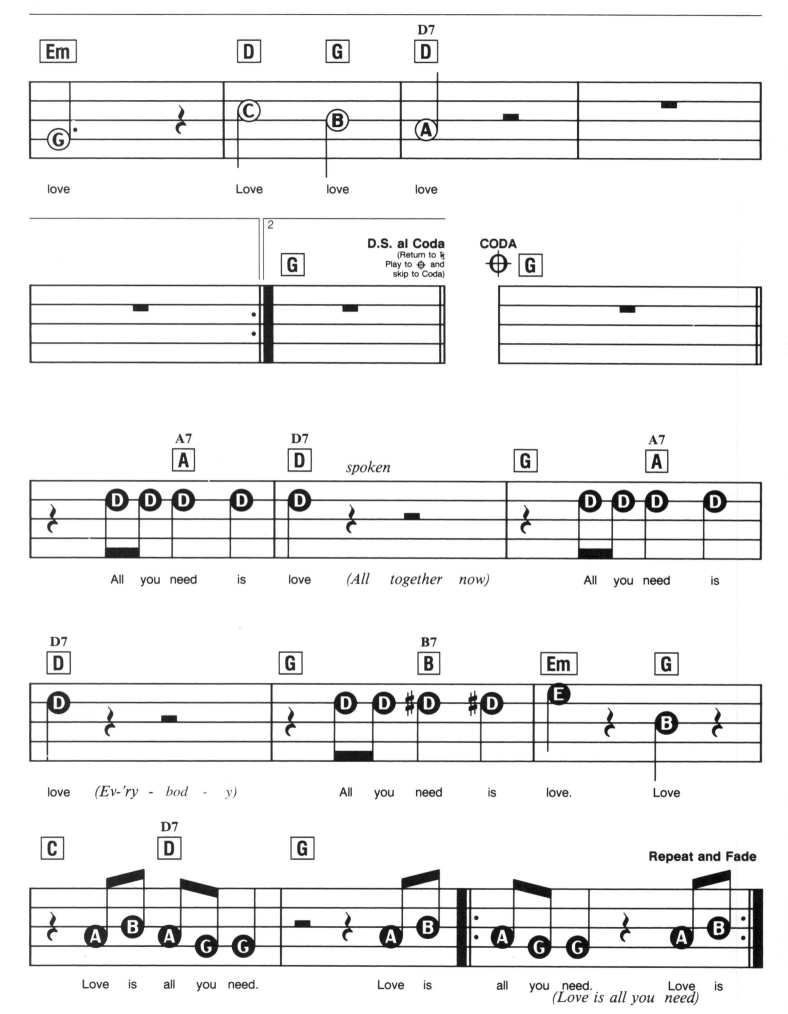

And Your Bird Can Sing

Registration 8
Rhythm: 8 Beat or Rock

Words and Music by John Lennon
and Paul McCartney

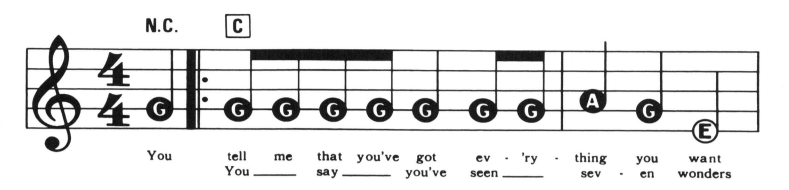

You tell me that you've got ev-'ry-thing you want
You say you've seen sev-en wonders

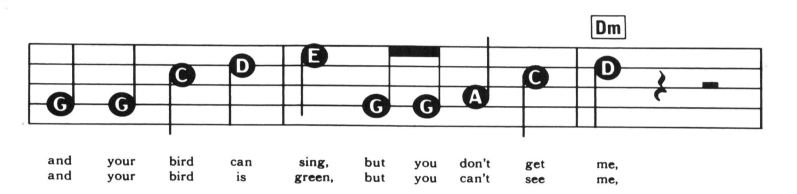

and your bird can sing, but you don't get me,
and your bird is green, but you can't see me,

you don't get me!
you can't see me!

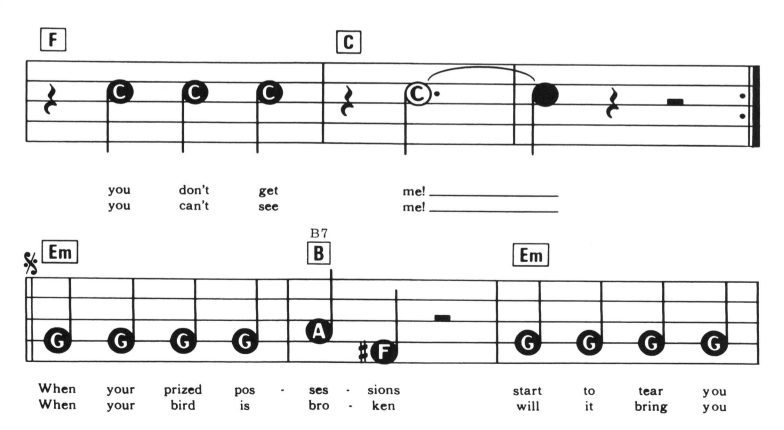

When your prized pos-ses-sions start to tear you
When your bird is bro-ken will it bring you

10

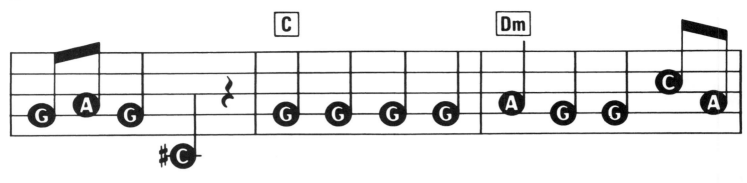

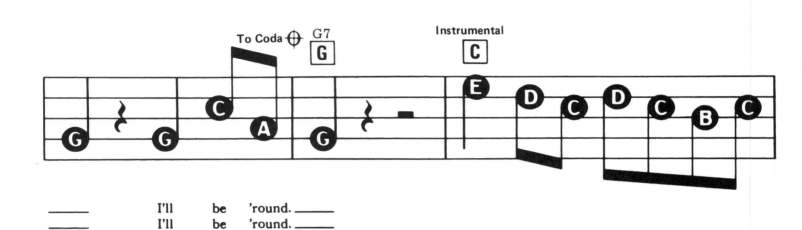

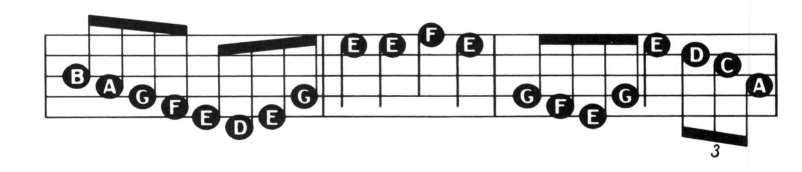

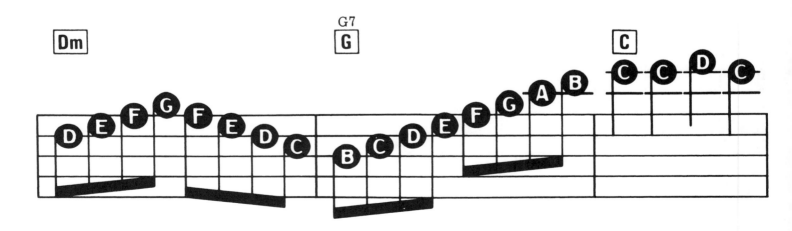

11

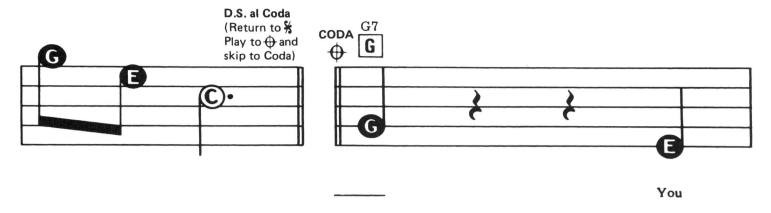

D.S. al Coda
(Return to %
Play to ⊕ and
skip to Coda)

CODA G7

You

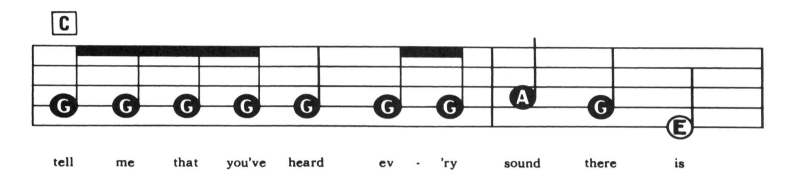

tell me that you've heard ev - 'ry sound there is

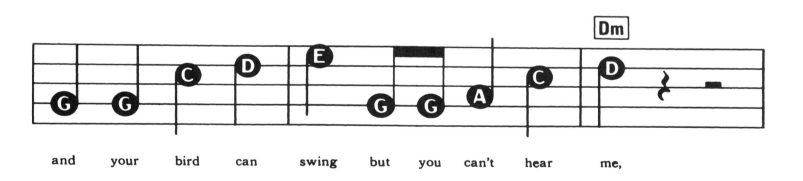

and your bird can swing but you can't hear me,

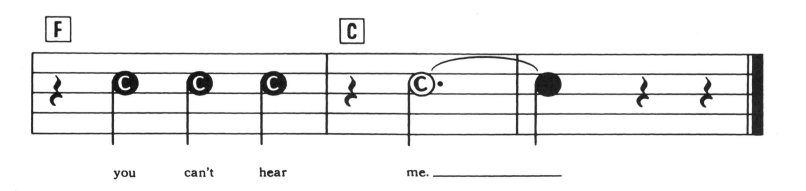

you can't hear me. _____

And I Love Her

Registration 8
Rhythm: Rock or Jazz Rock

Words and Music by John Lennon
and Paul McCartney

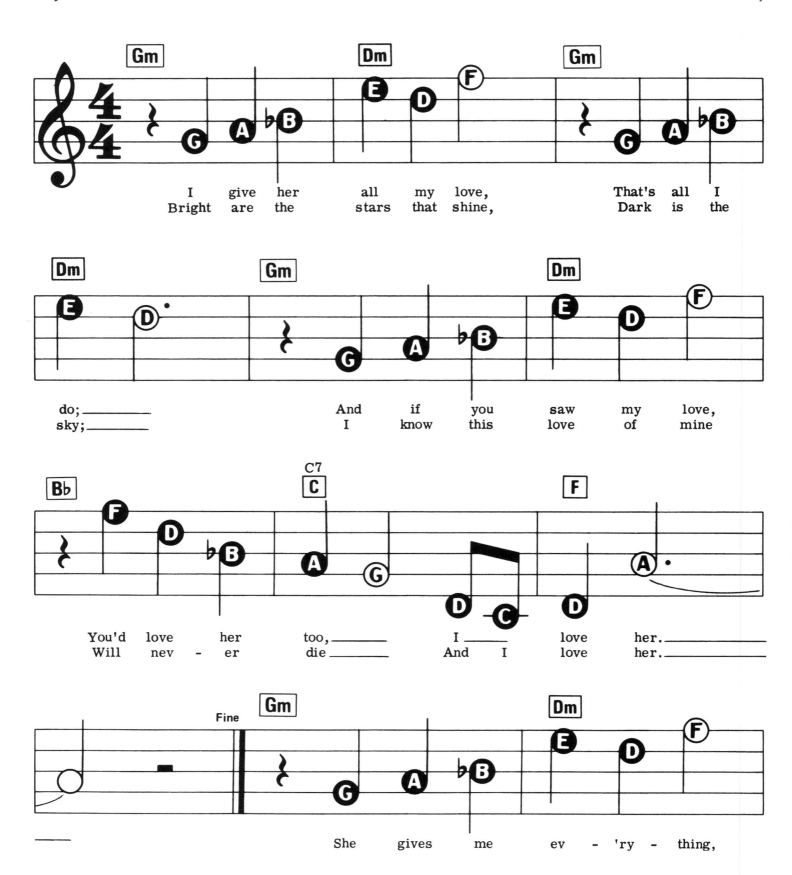

13

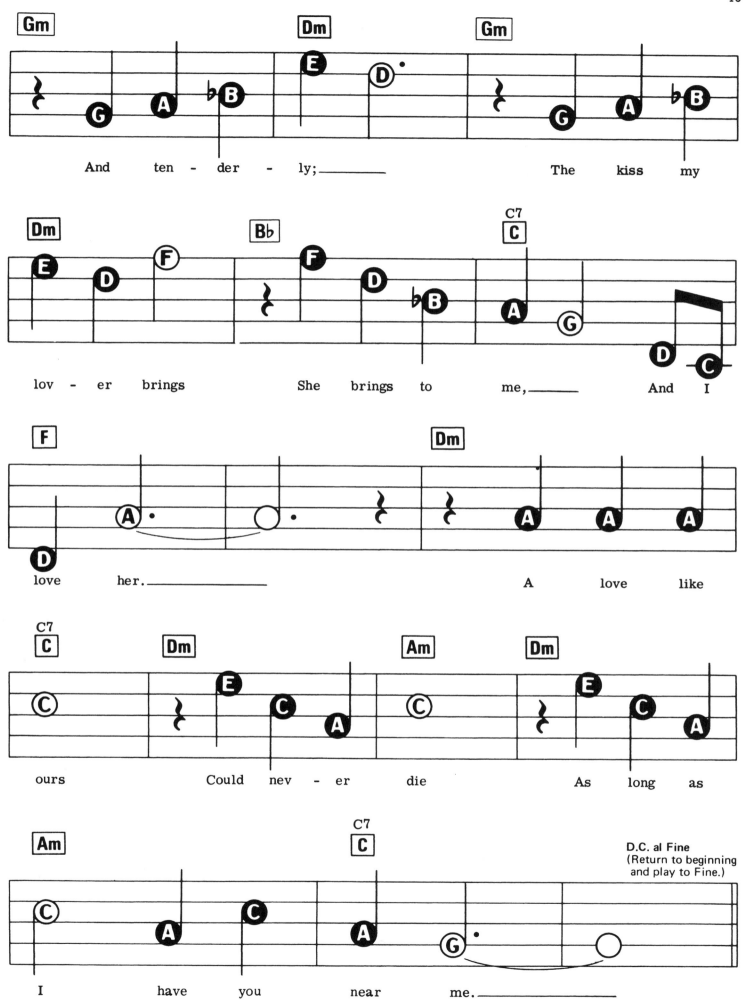

Back in the U.S.S.R.

Registration 4
Rhythm: Rock or Jazz Rock

Words and Music by John Lennon
and Paul McCartney

Flew in from Mi - a - mi Beach, B. O. A. C.
Been a - way so long I hard - ly knew the place
Show me round your snow peaked moun - tains way down south.

Did - n't get to bed last night
Gee it's good to be back home
Take me to your dad - dy's farm

On the way the pa - per bag was
Leave it till to - mor - row to un -
Let me hear your ba - la - lai - kas

on my knee
pack my case
ring - ing out

Man I had a dread - ful fight
Hon - ey dis - con - nect the phone
Come and keep your com - rad warm.

I'm back in the U. S. S.

To Coda ⊕

R. Hey You don't know how luck - y you are

boy.
boy
boys.

Back in the U. S. S.

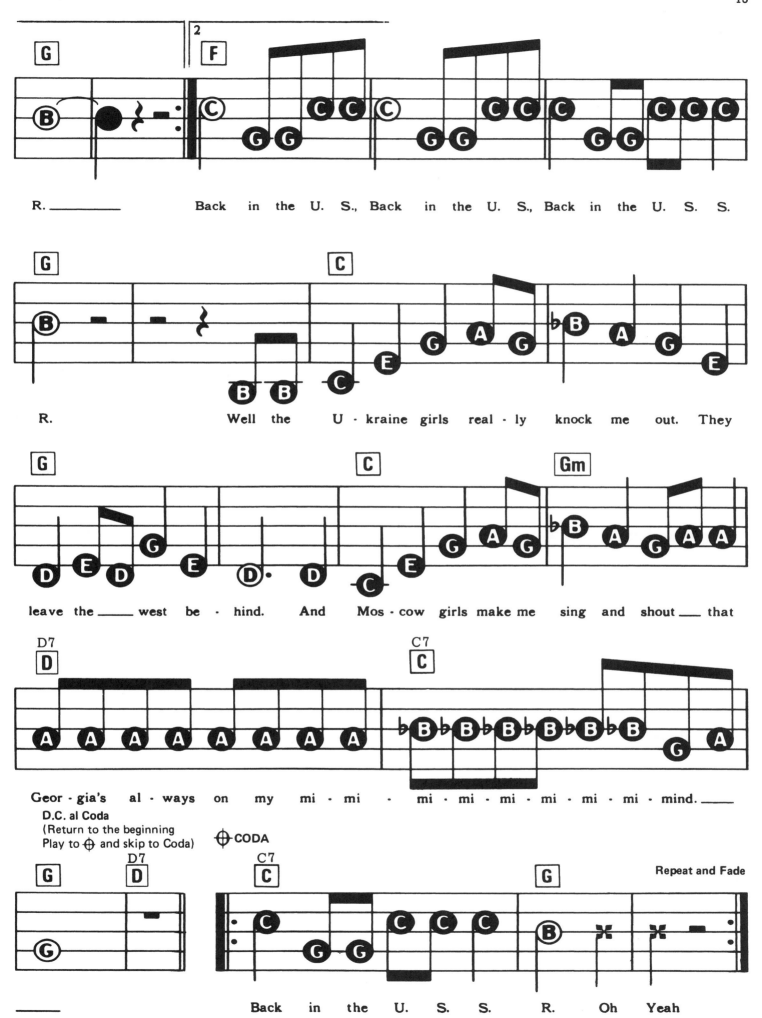

R. _____ Back in the U. S., Back in the U. S., Back in the U. S. S.

R. Well the U - kraine girls real - ly knock me out. They

leave the ____ west be - hind. And Mos - cow girls make me sing and shout ____ that

Geor - gia's al - ways on my mi - mi - mi - mi - mi - mi - mi - mi - mind. _____

D.C. al Coda
(Return to the beginning
Play to ⊕ and skip to Coda) ⊕ CODA

Repeat and Fade

_____ Back in the U. S. S. R. Oh Yeah

Because

Registration 1
Rhythm: Rock or Jazz Rock

Words and Music by John Lennon
and Paul McCartney

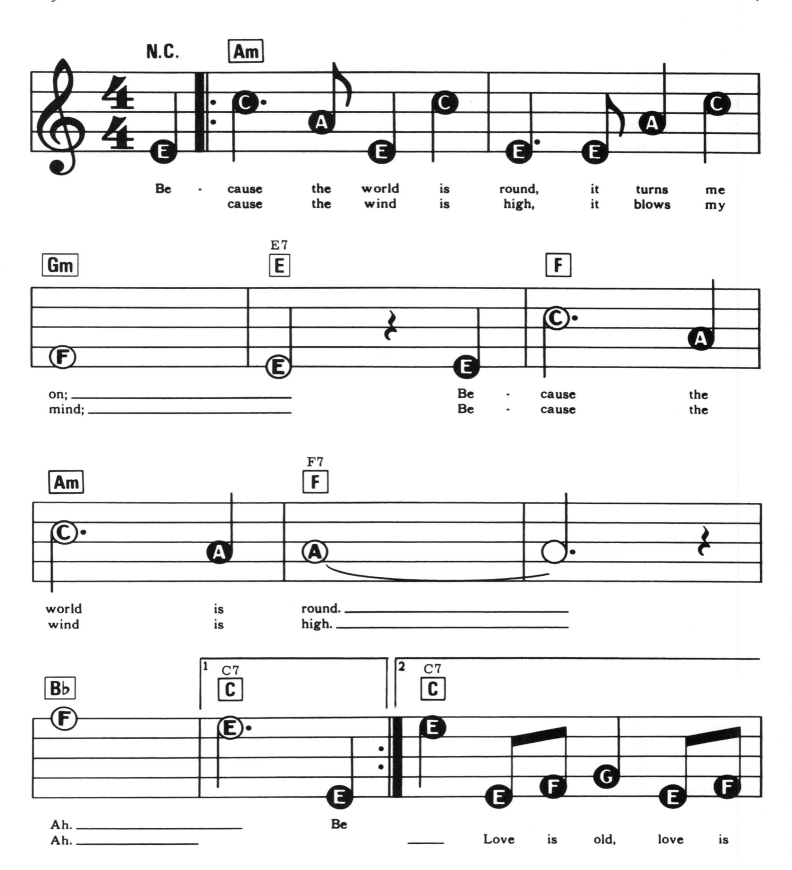

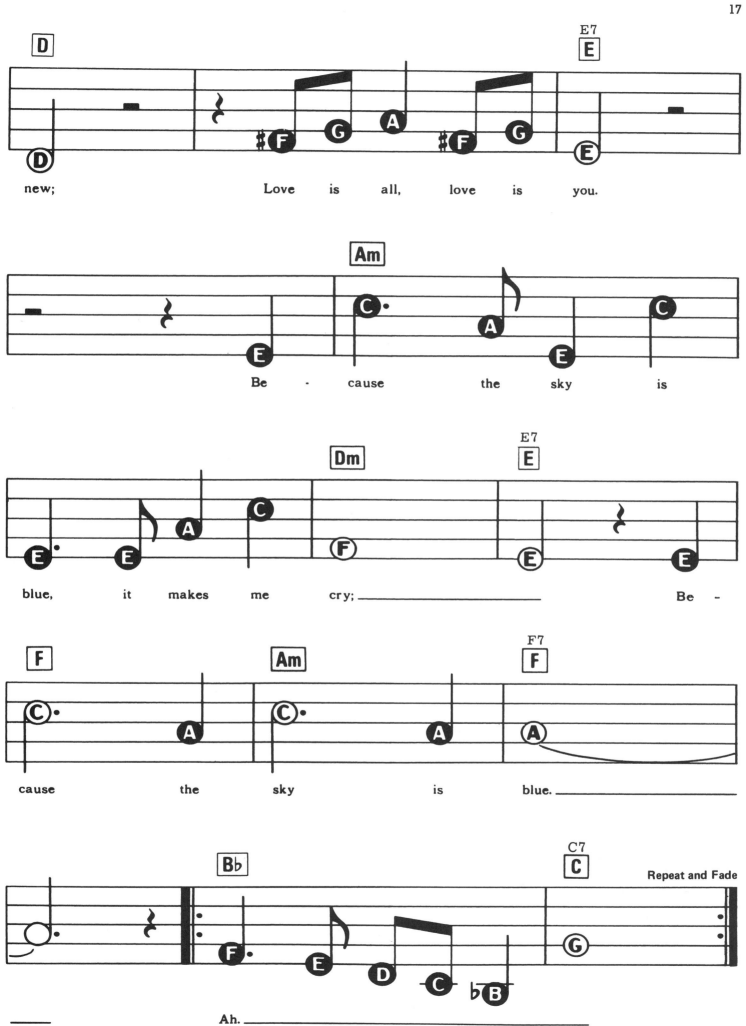

Birthday

18

Registration 2
Rhythm: Rock

Words and Music by John Lennon
and Paul McCartney

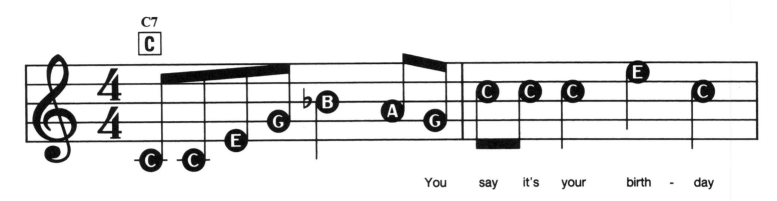

You say it's your birth - day

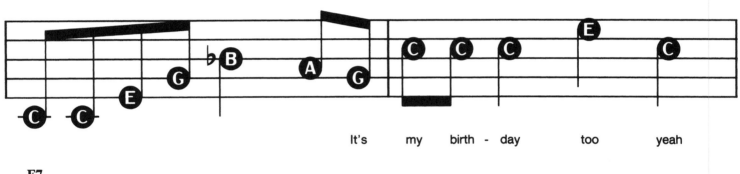

It's my birth - day too yeah

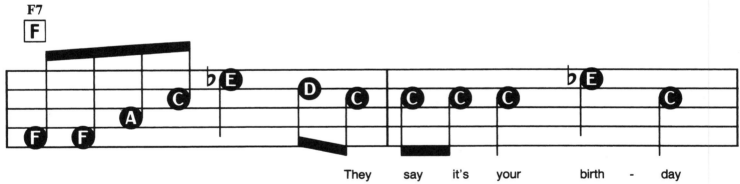

They say it's your birth - day

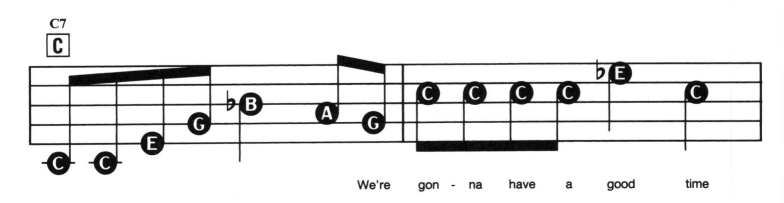

We're gon - na have a good time

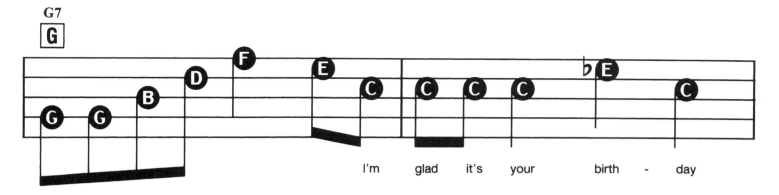

I'm glad it's your birth - day

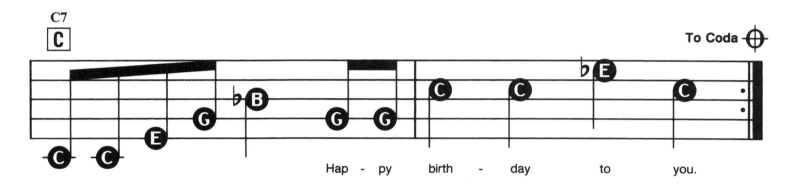

Hap - py birth - day to you.

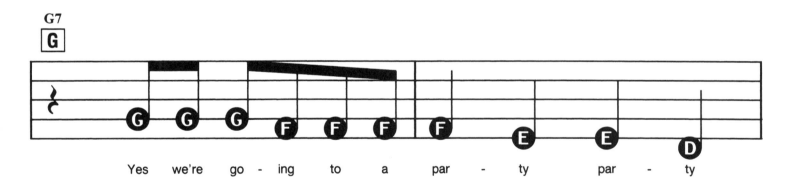

Yes we're go - ing to a par - ty par - ty

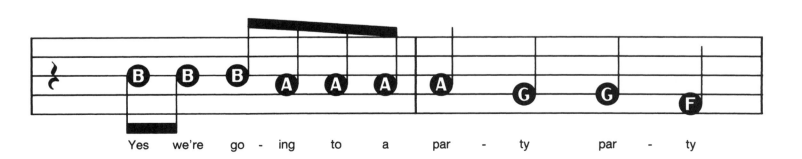

Yes we're go - ing to a par - ty par - ty

20

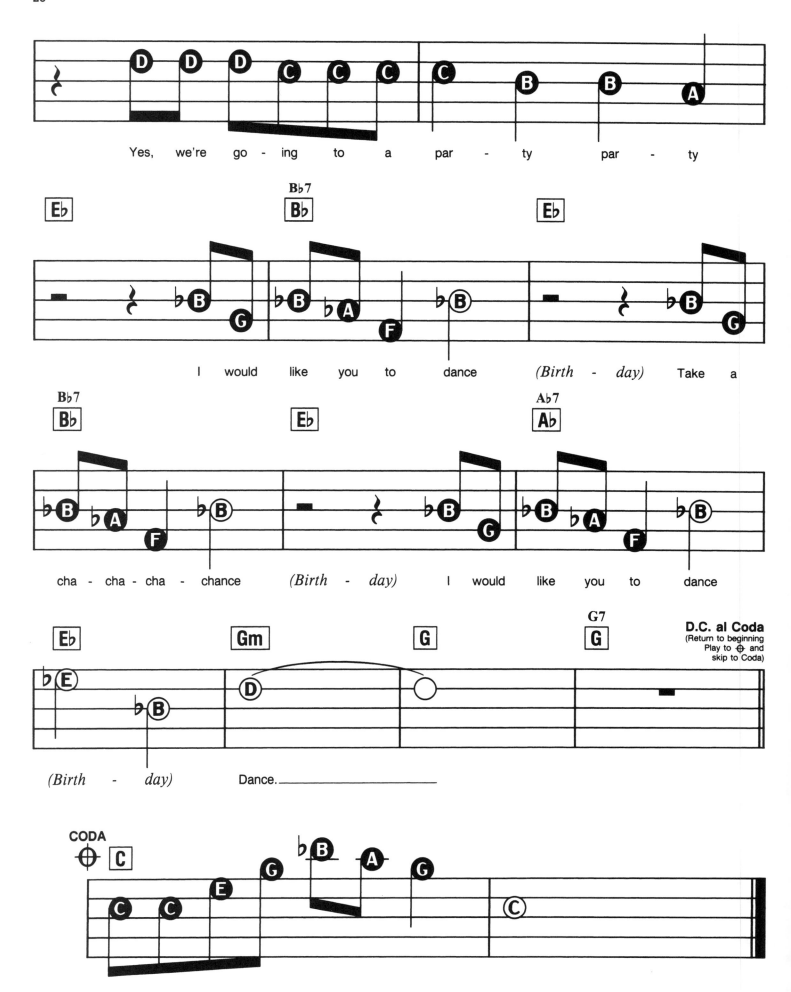

Don't Let Me Down

Registration 2
Rhythm: Rock

Words and Music by John Lennon
and Paul McCartney

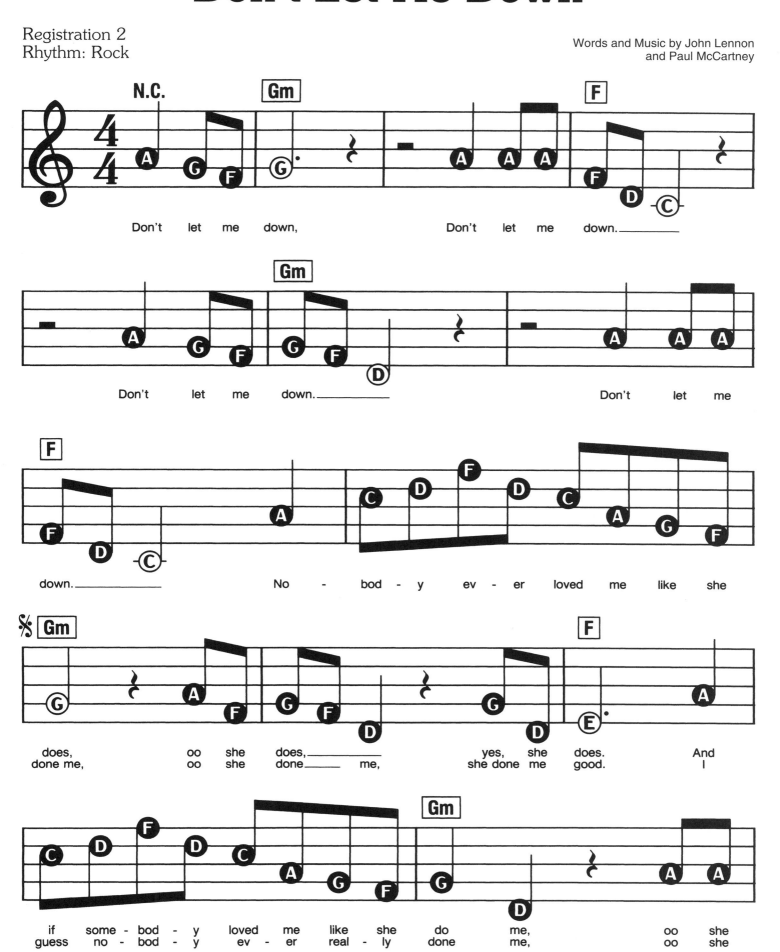

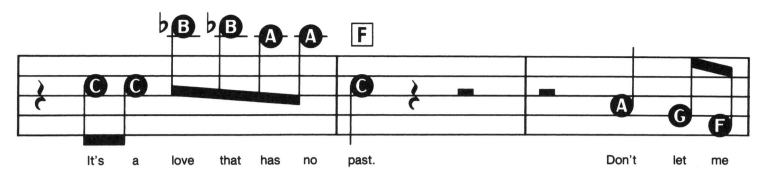

It's a love that has no past. Don't let me

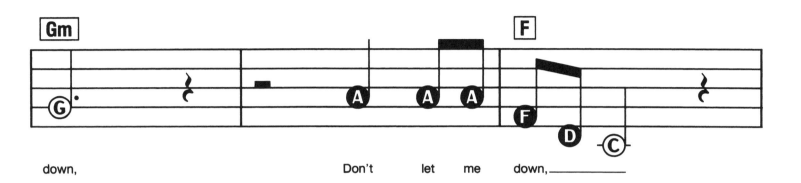

down, Don't let me down,_____

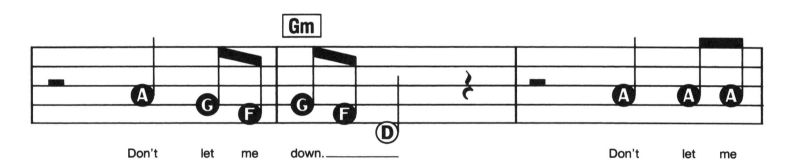

Don't let me down._____ Don't let me

D.S. al Coda
(Return to %
Play to ⊕ and
skip to Coda)

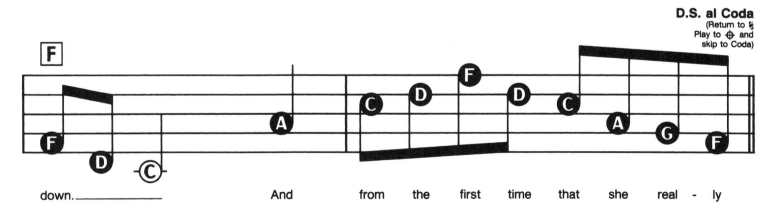

down._____ And from the first time that she real - ly

CODA

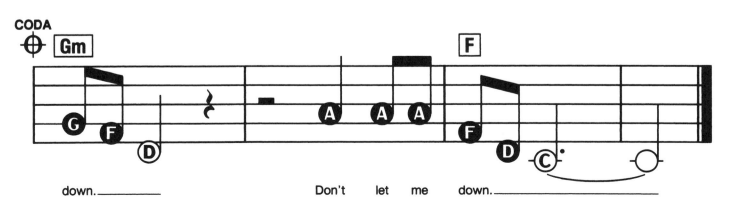

down._____ Don't let me down._____

Blackbird

Registration 8
Rhythm: Rock

Words and Music by John Lennon
and Paul McCartney

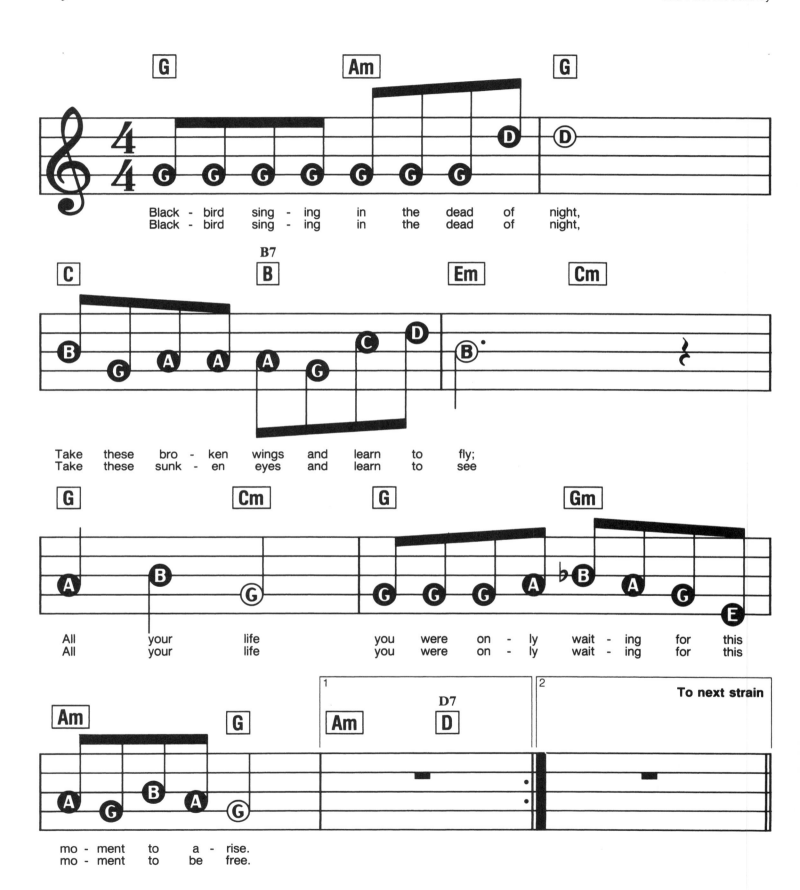

25

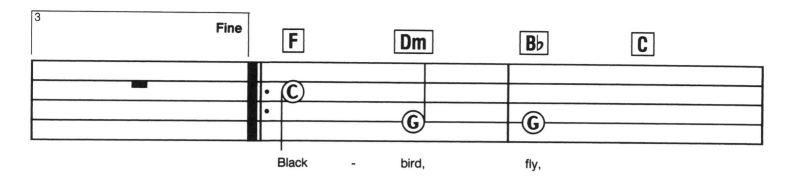

Black - bird, fly,

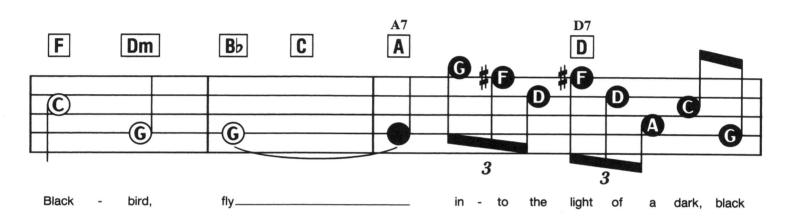

Black - bird, fly_____ in - to the light of a dark, black

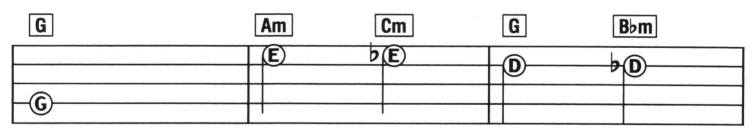

night.   *Instrumental*

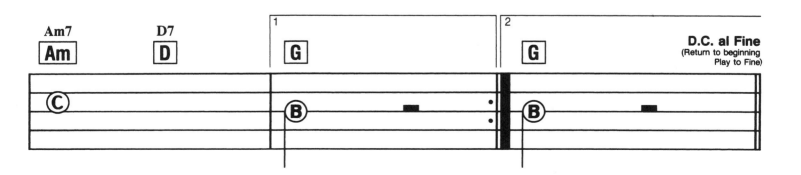

Can't Buy Me Love

Registration 1
Rhythm: Rock

Words and Music by John Lennon
and Paul McCartney

1.2. I'll buy you a dia - mond ring my friend if it
3. Say you don't need no dia - mond ring and _____

makes you feel al - right. I'll get you _____ an - y -
I'll be sat - is - fied. _____ Say you don't want those

thing my friend if it makes you feel al - right. For
kind of things that _____ mon - ey just can't buy. For

To Coda

I don't care too much for mon - ey, mon - ey can't buy me
I don't care too much for mon - ey, mon - ey can't buy me

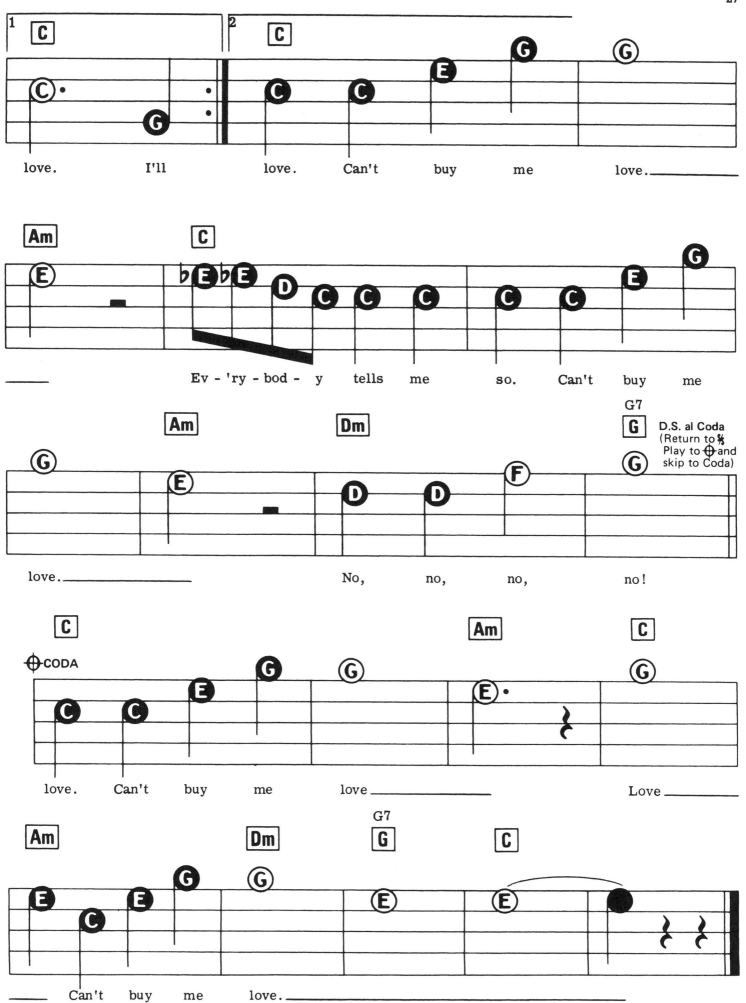

Come Together

Registration 9
Rhythm: Rock

Words and Music by John Lennon
and Paul McCartney

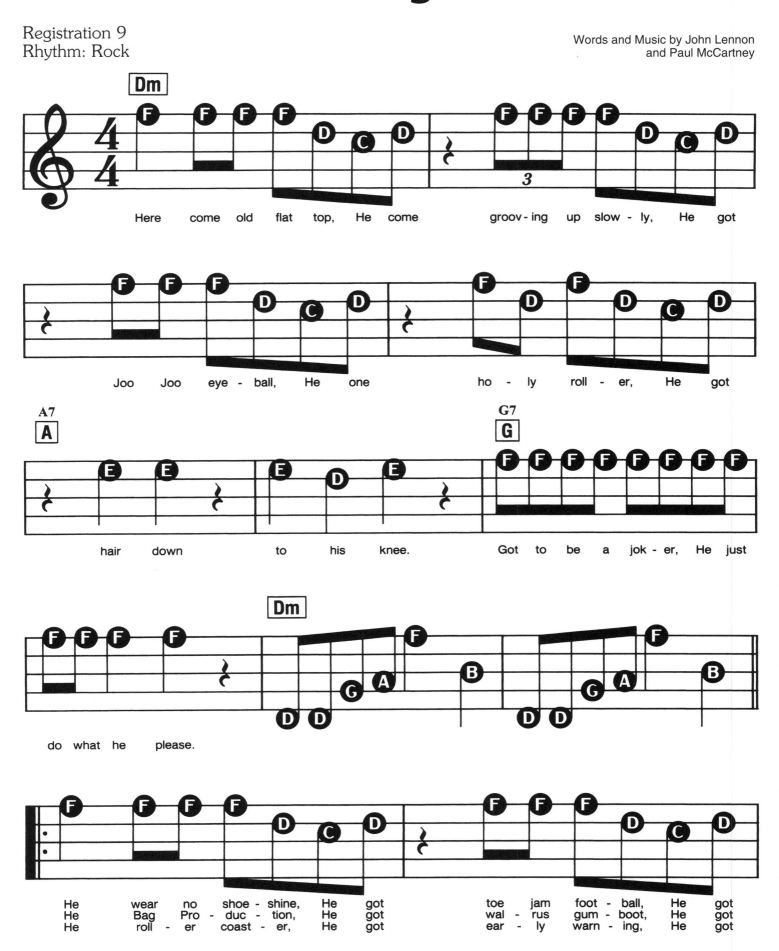

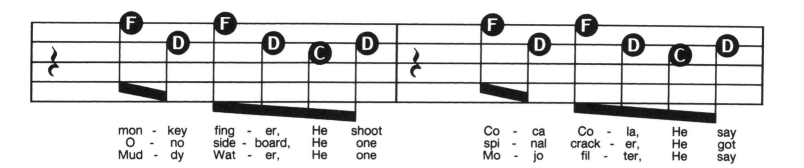

mon - key fing - er, He shoot
O - no side - board, He one
Mud - dy Wat - er, He one

Co - ca Co - la, He say
spi - nal crack - er, He say got
Mo - jo fil - ter, He got say

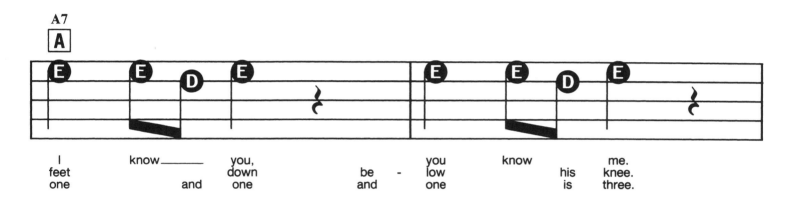

A7

I know＿＿ you, you know me.
feet down be - low his knee.
one and down one and low one is three.

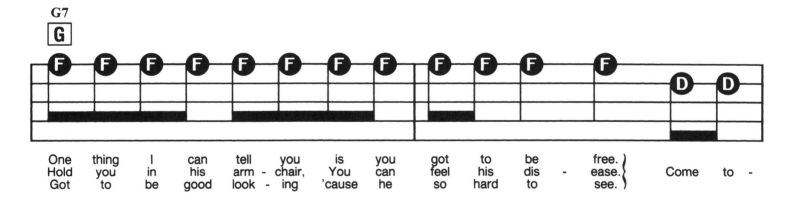

G7

One thing I can tell you is you got to be free.
Hold you in his arm - chair, You can got feel his dis - ease.
Got to be good look - ing 'cause he so hard to see. ｝ Come to -

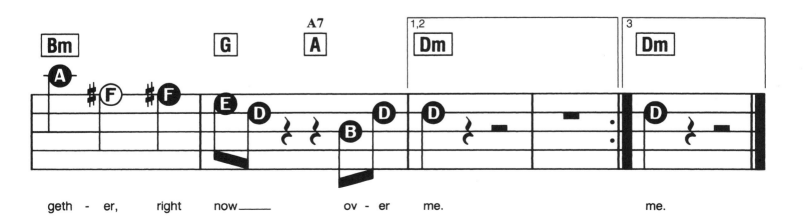

Bm **G** **A7** **A** **1,2** **Dm** **3** **Dm**

geth - er, right now＿＿ ov - er me.   me.

A Day in the Life

Registration 2
Rhythm: Rock

Words and Music by John Lennon
and Paul McCartney

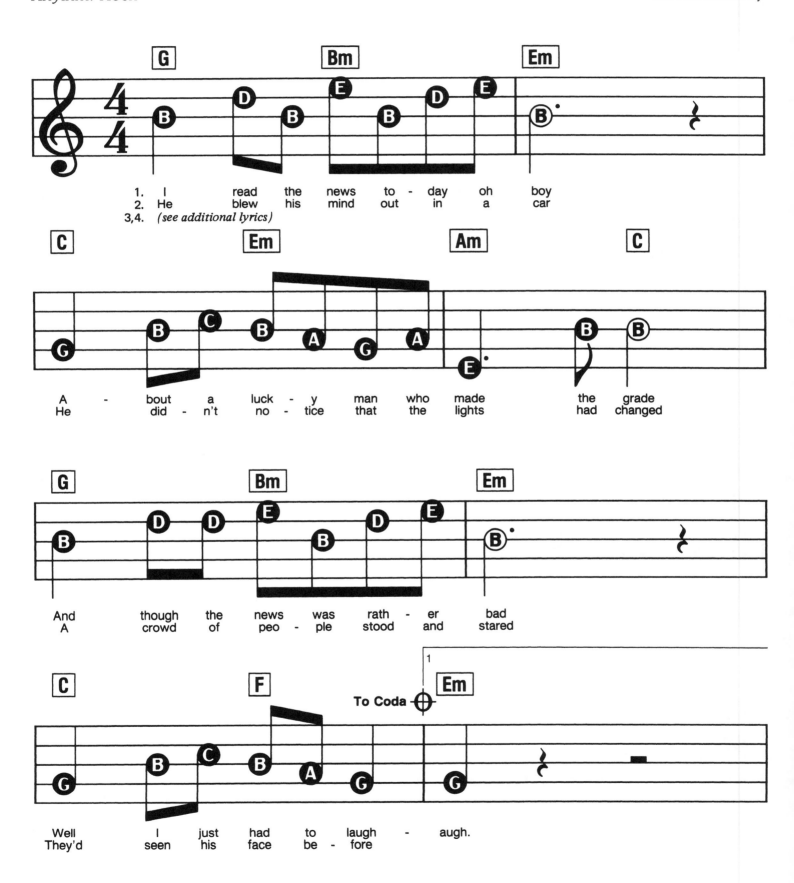

31

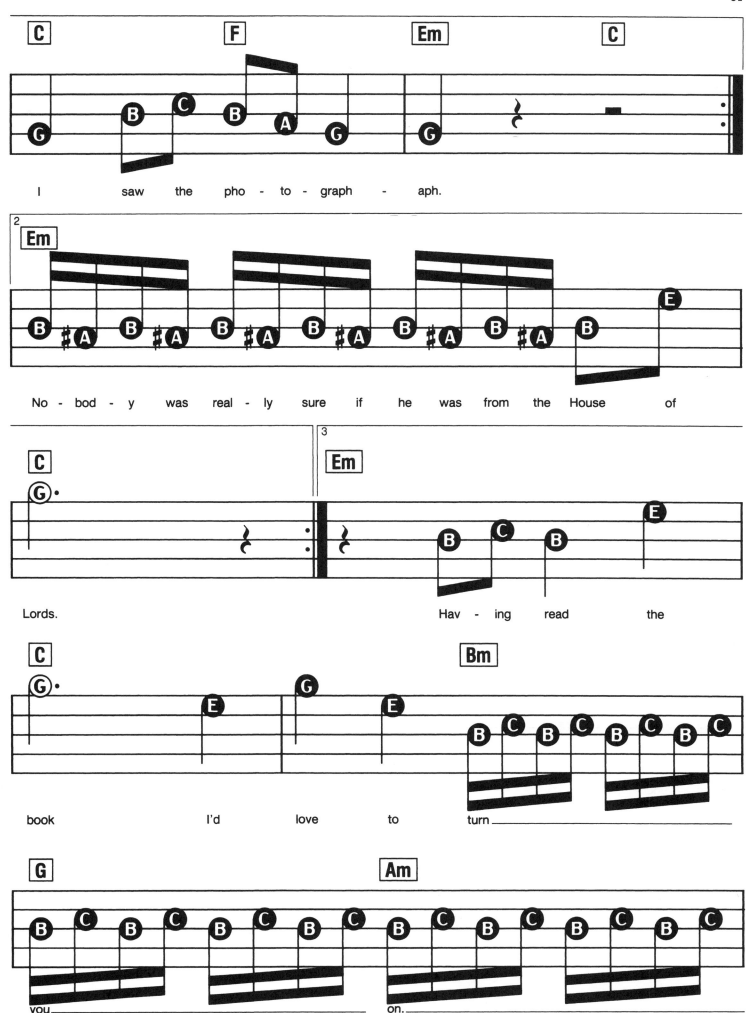

32

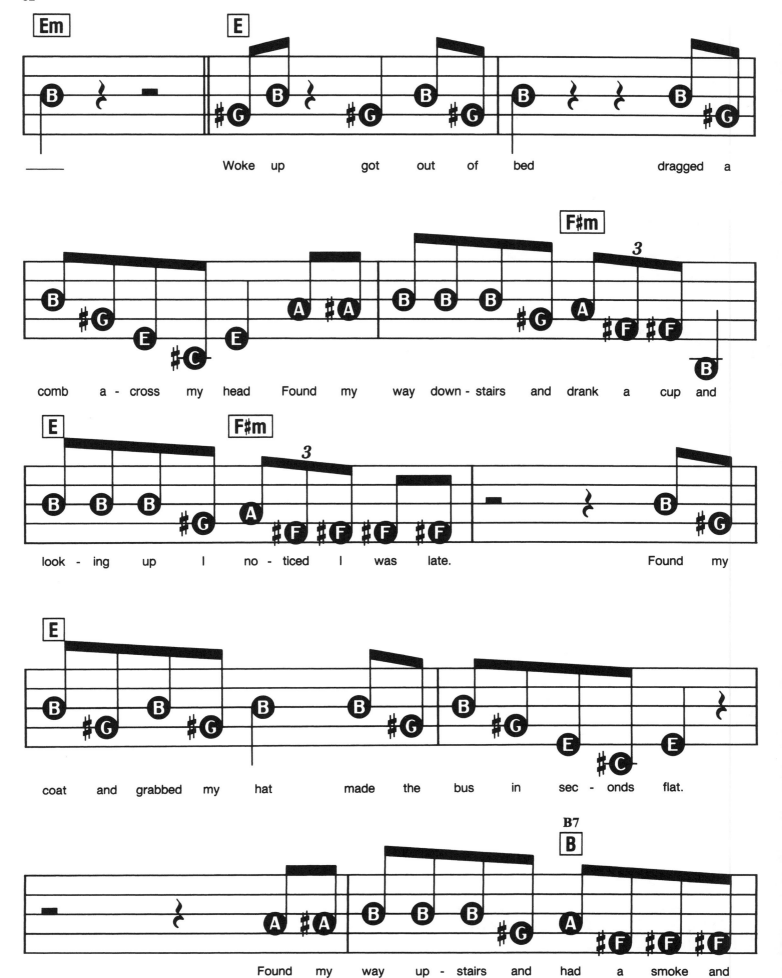

D.S. al Coda
(Return to beginning
Play to ✛ and
skip to Coda)

some - bod - y spoke and I went in - to a dream.

Now they know how man - y holes it takes to fill the Al - bert

Hall. I'd love to turn ____

you _____ on.

3. I saw a film today oh boy
   The English army had just won the war
   A crowd of people turned away
   But I just had to look

4. I heard the news today oh boy
   Four thousand holes in Blackburn Lancashire
   And though the holes were rather small
   They had to count them all

Day Tripper

Registration 2
Rhythm: Rock or Disco

Words and Music by John Lennon
and Paul McCartney

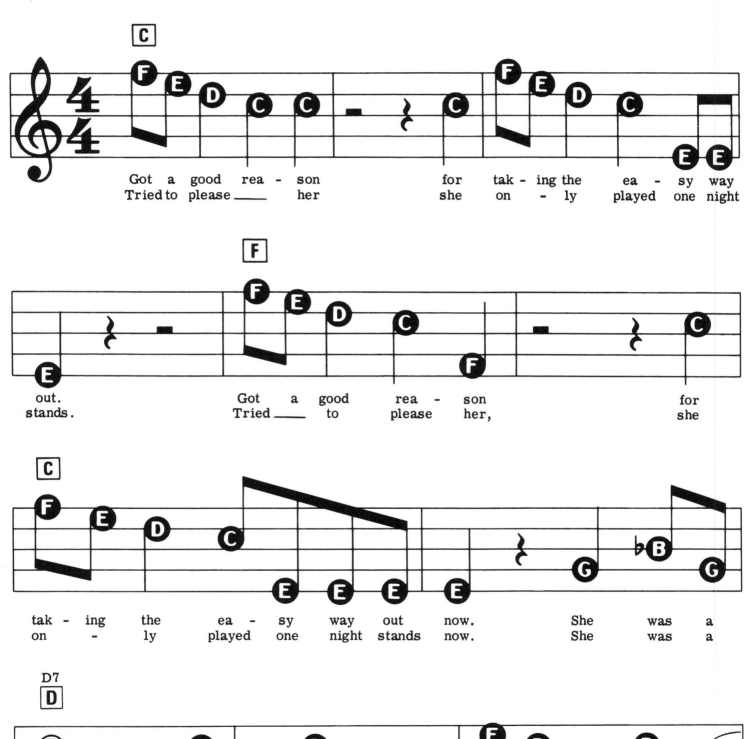

35

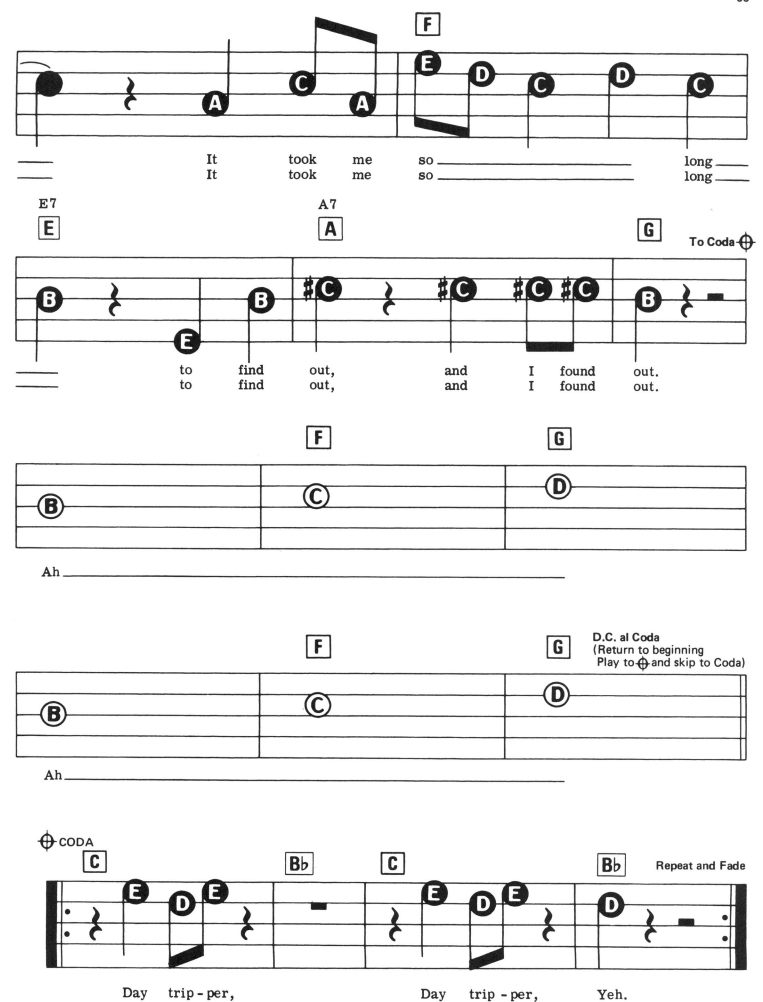

Eight Days a Week

Registration 2
Rhythm: Rock

Words and Music by John Lennon
and Paul McCartney

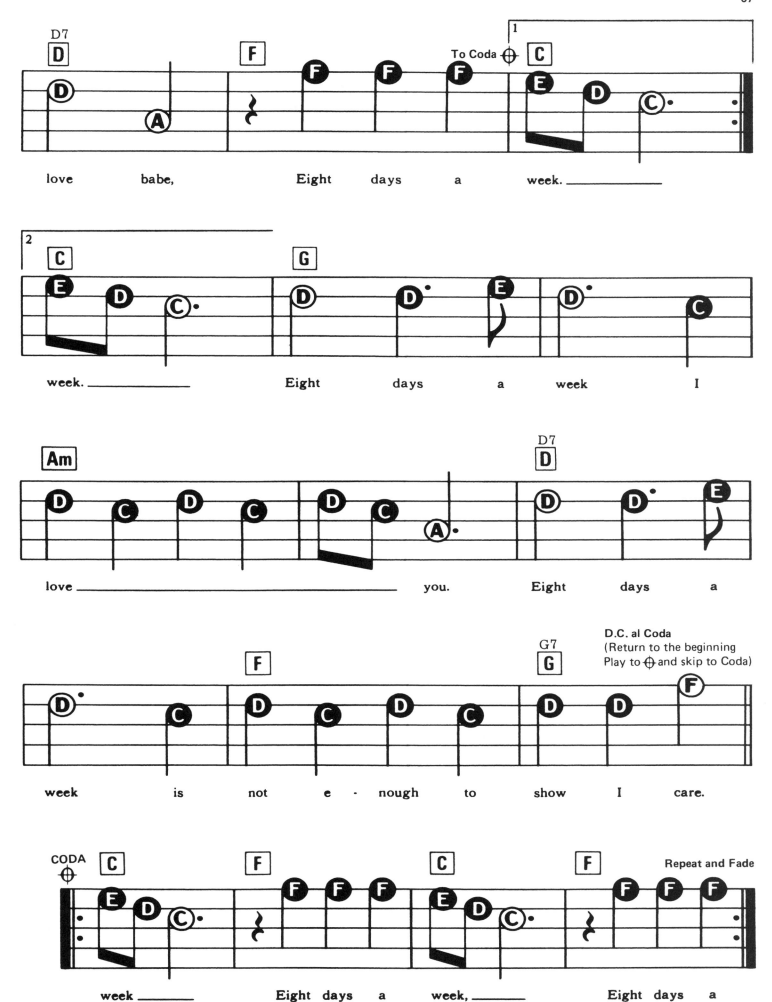

Eleanor Rigby

Registration 9
Rhythm: Rock

Words and Music by John Lennon
and Paul McCartney

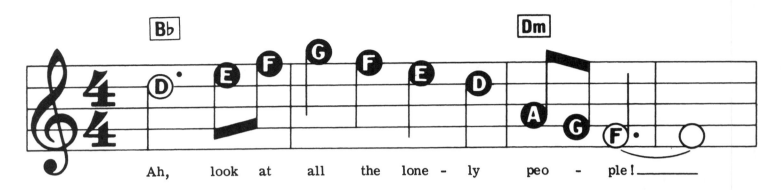

Ah, look at all the lone - ly peo - ple! _____

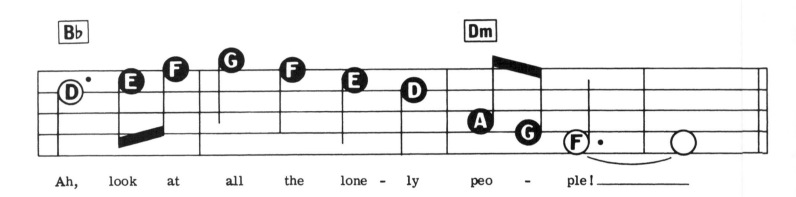

Ah, look at all the lone - ly peo - ple! _____

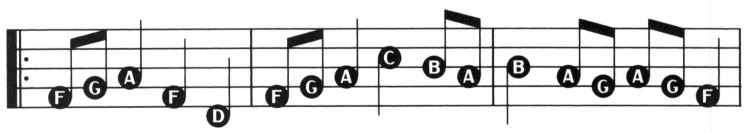

E - lea - nor Rig - by, picks up the rice in the church where a wed - ding has
E - lea - nor Rig - by, died in the church and was bur - ied a - long with her

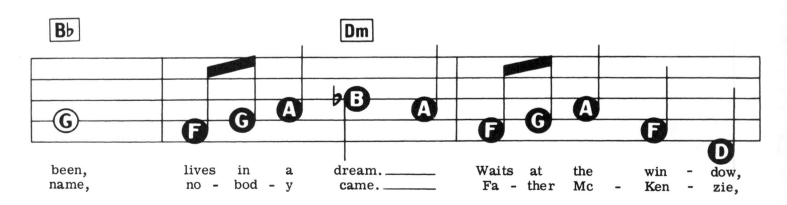

been, lives in a dream. _____ Waits at the win - dow,
name, no - bod - y came. _____ Fa - ther Mc - Ken - zie,

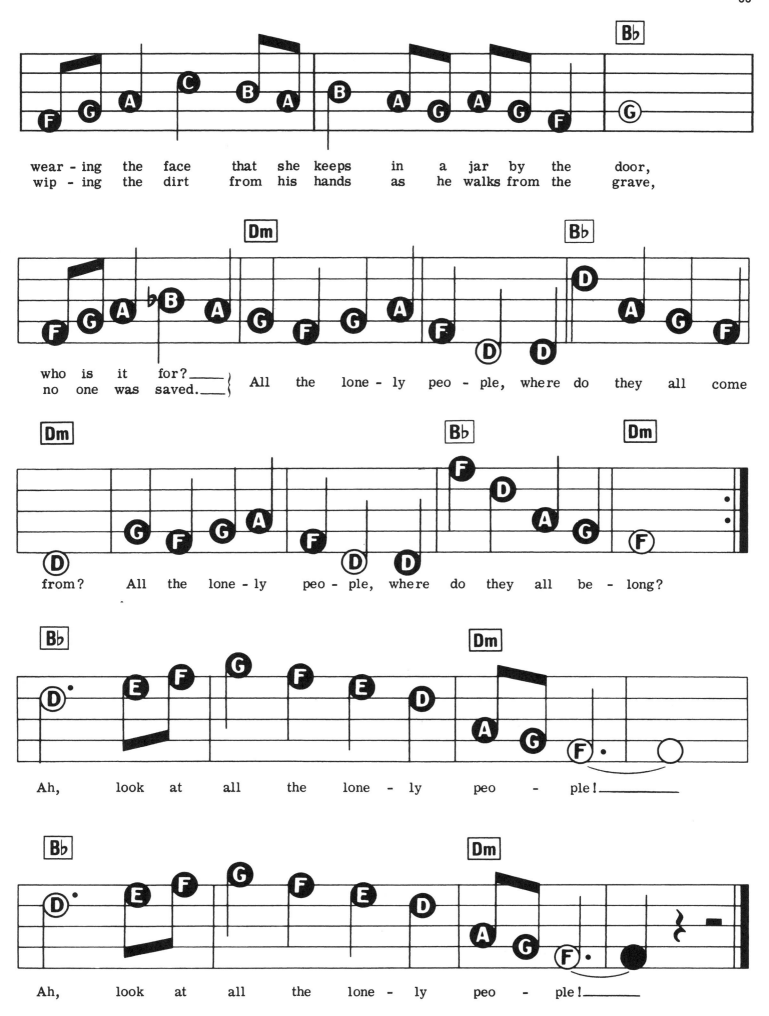

Fixing a Hole

Registration 2
Rhythm: Rock or Jazz Rock

Words and Music by John Lennon
and Paul McCartney

wrong, I'm right where I be · long I'm right where I be · long _____

See the peo · ple stand · ing there who dis · a · gree and nev · er win and
Sil · ly peo · ple run a · round they wor · ry me and nev · er ask me

won · der why they don't get in my door I'm
why they don't get past in my door _____ I'm

paint · ing the room in a col · our · ful way, and
tak · ing my time for a num · ber of things that

when my mind is wan · der · ing there I will go _____
weren't im · por · tant yes · ter · day and I

42

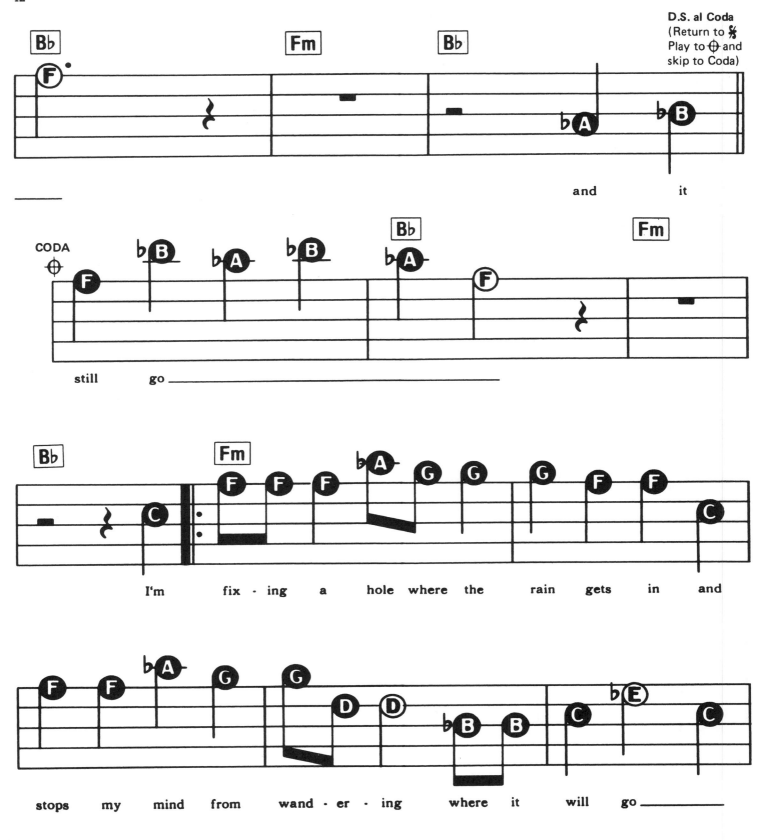

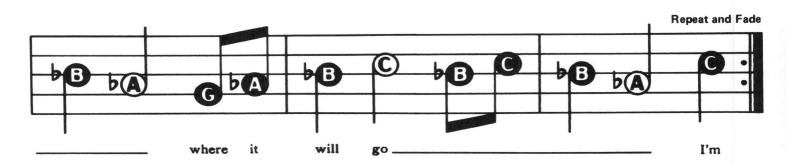

Good Day Sunshine

Registration 5
Rhythm: Shuffle or Swing

Words and Music by John Lennon
and Paul McCartney

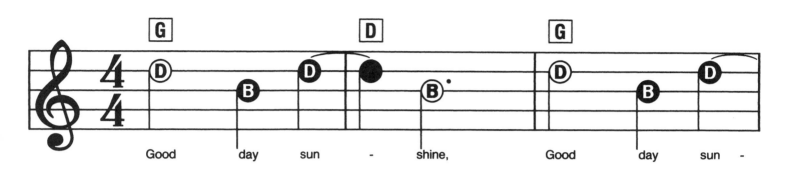

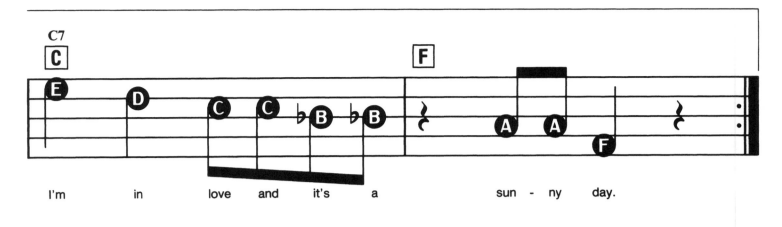

I'm   in   love   and   it's   a   sun - ny   day.

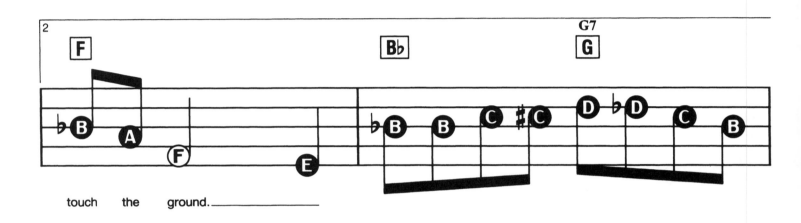

touch   the   ground._____

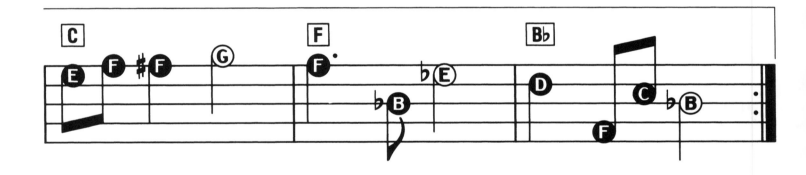

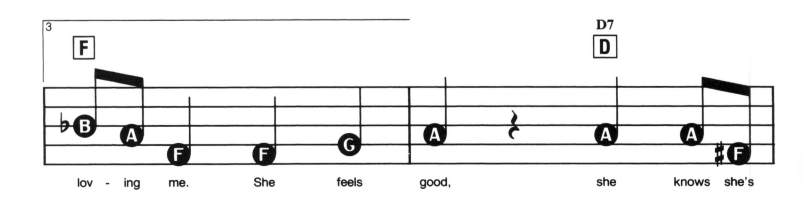

lov - ing   me.   She   feels   good,   she   knows   she's

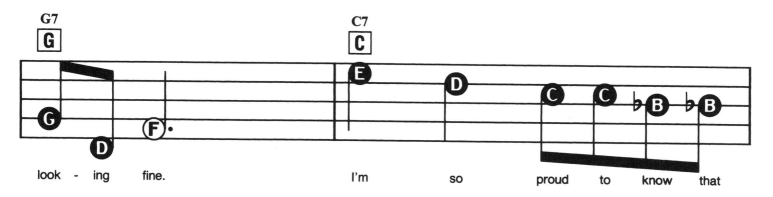

look - ing fine.   I'm   so   proud   to   know   that

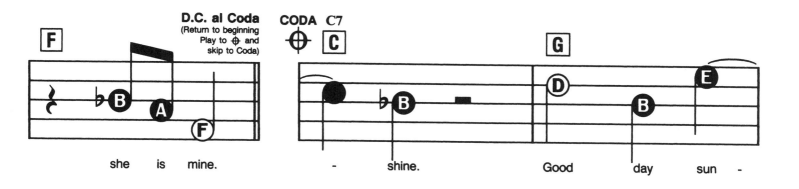

she is mine.   - shine.   Good   day   sun -

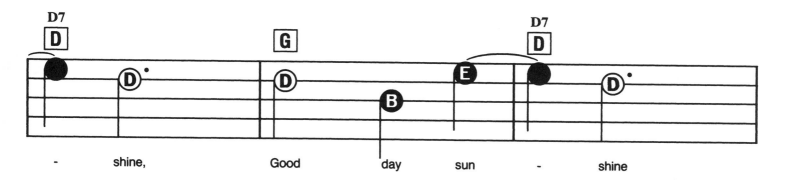

- shine,   Good   day   sun -   shine

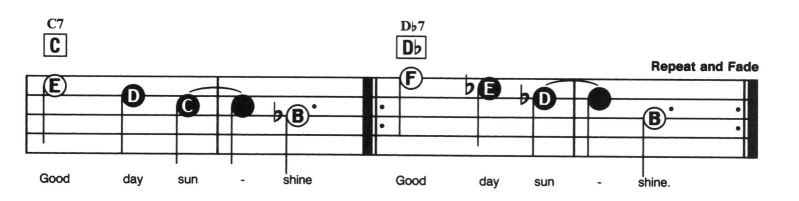

Good   day   sun -   shine   Good   day   sun -   shine.

The Fool on the Hill

Registration 1
Rhythm: Rock or Bossa Nova

Words and Music by John Lennon
and Paul McCartney

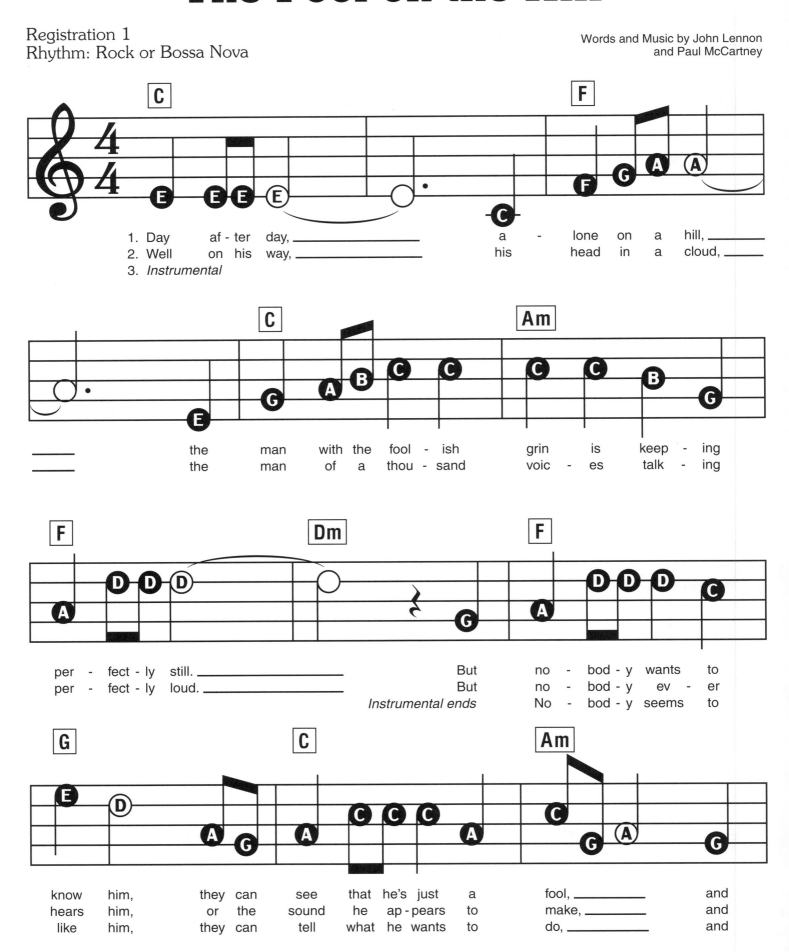

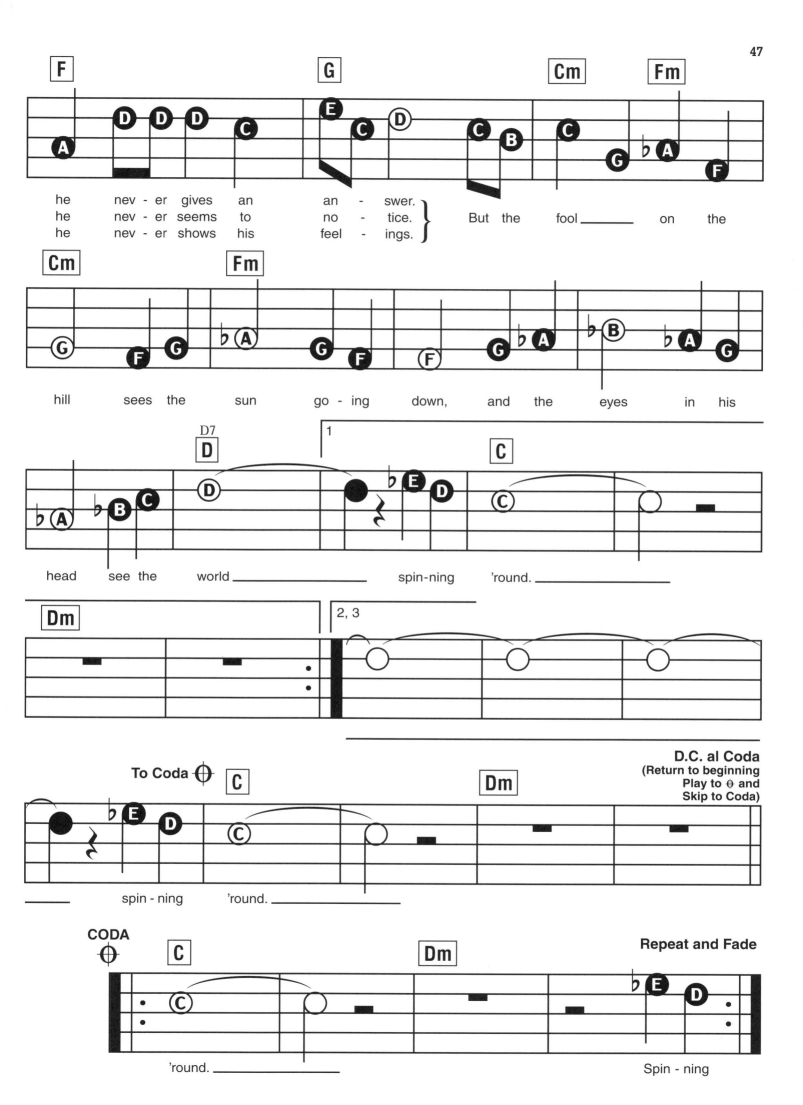

Get Back

Registration 8
Rhythm: Rock

Words and Music by John Lennon
and Paul McCartney

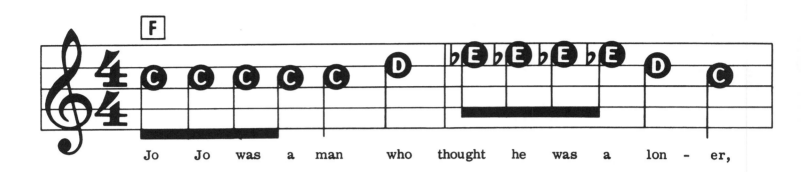

Jo Jo was a man who thought he was a lon - er,

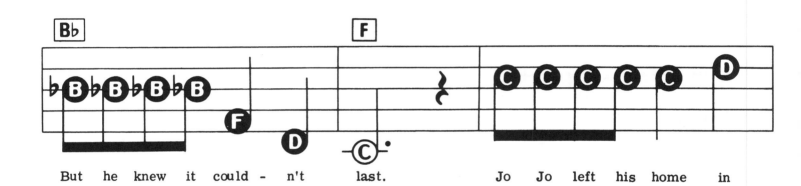

But he knew it could - n't last. Jo Jo left his home in

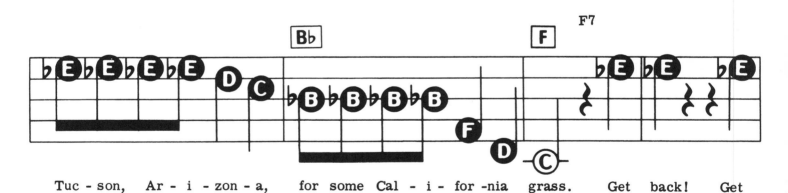

Tuc - son, Ar - i - zon - a, for some Cal - i - for -nia grass. Get back! Get

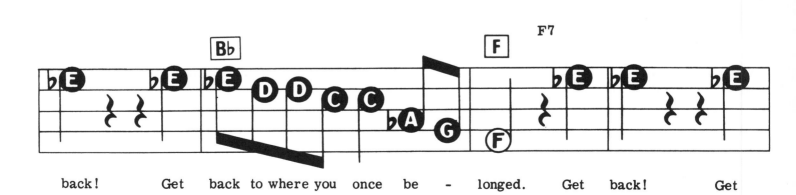

back! Get back to where you once be - longed. Get back! Get

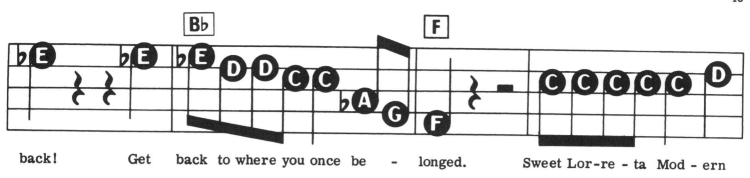

back! Get back to where you once be - longed. Sweet Lor-re - ta Mod - ern

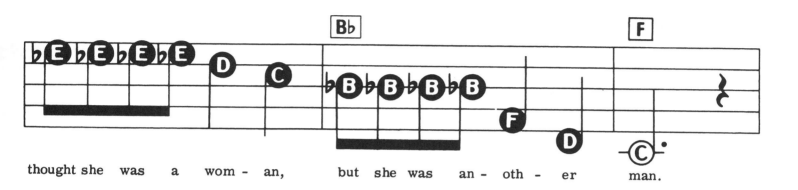

thought she was a wom - an, but she was an - oth - er man.

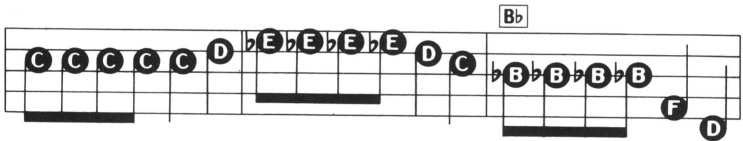

All the girls a -round her say she's got it com - ing, But, she gets it while she

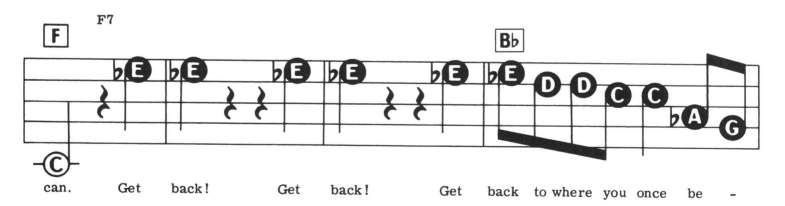

can. Get back! Get back! Get back to where you once be -

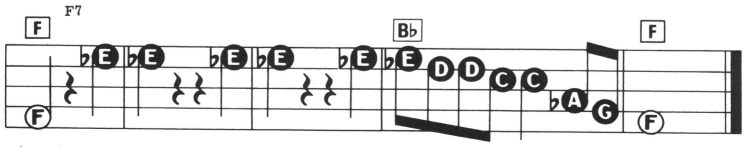

longed. Get back! Get back! Get back to where you once be - longed.

Good Night

Registration 3
Rhythm: Ballad

Words and Music by John Lennon
and Paul McCartney

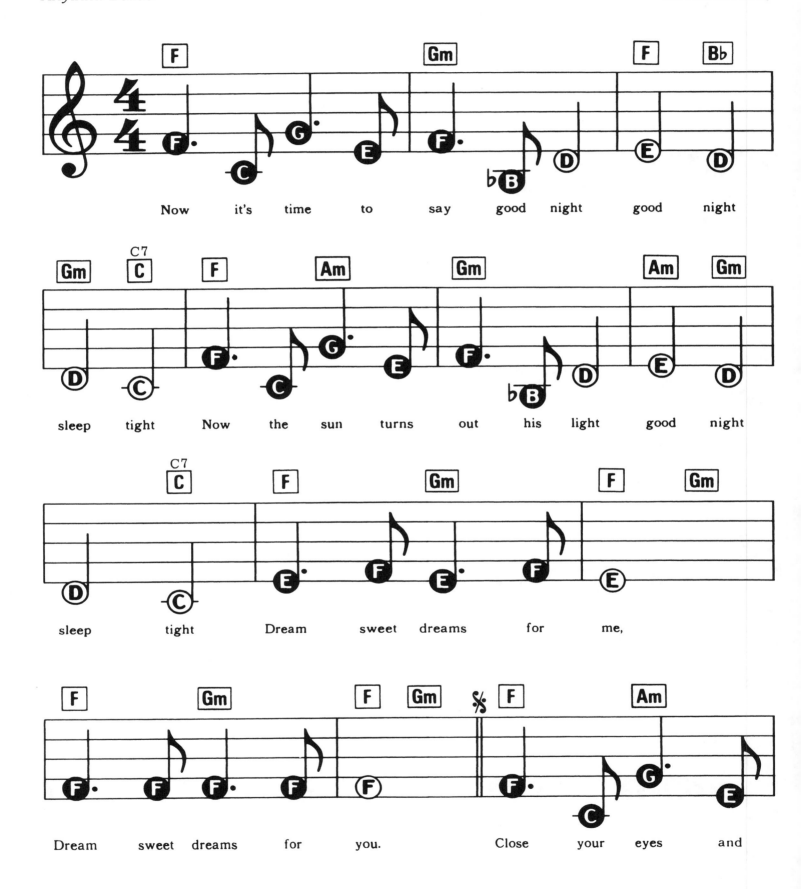

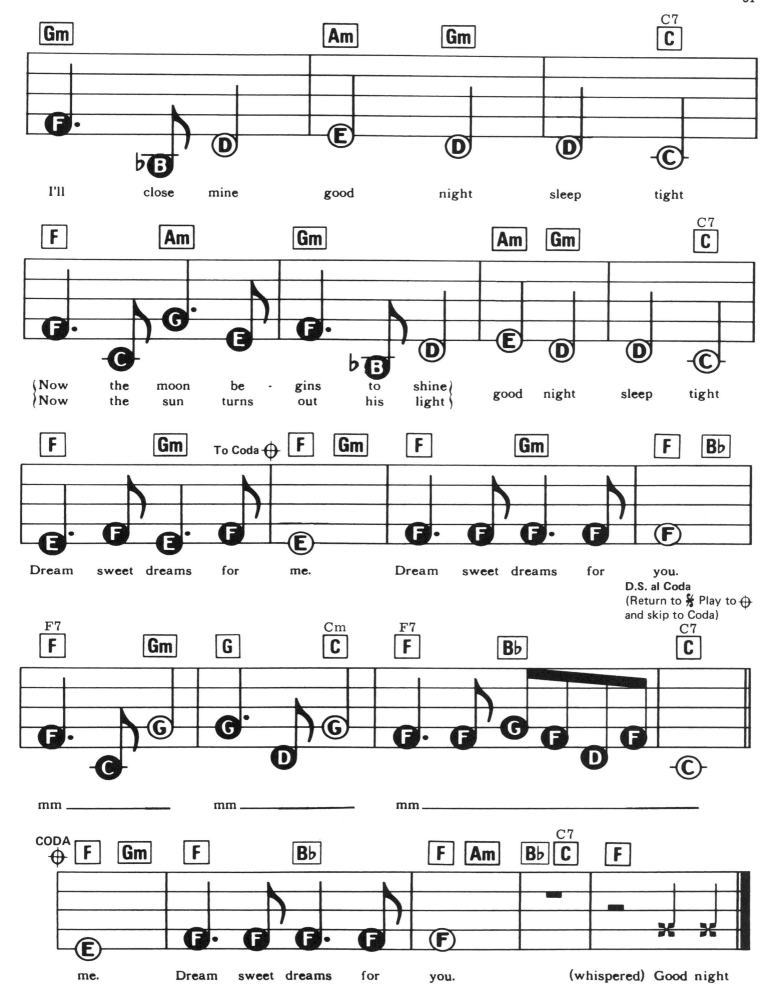

Got to Get You Into My Life

Registration 9
Rhythm: Rock or Jazz Rock

Words and Music by John Lennon
and Paul McCartney

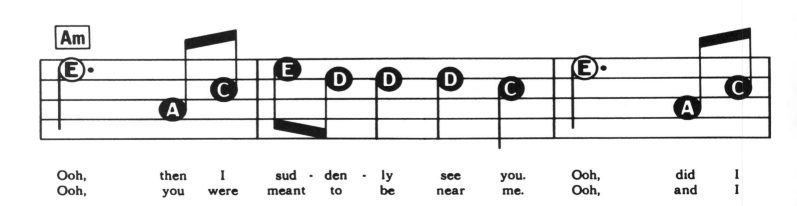

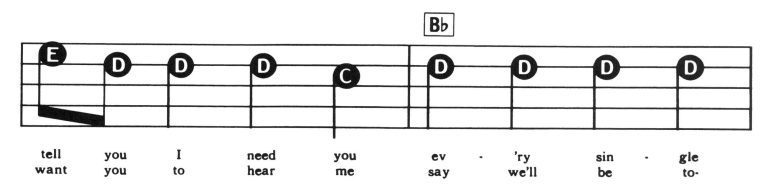

tell   you   I   need   you   ev - 'ry   sin - gle
want   you   to   hear   me   say   we'll   be   to-

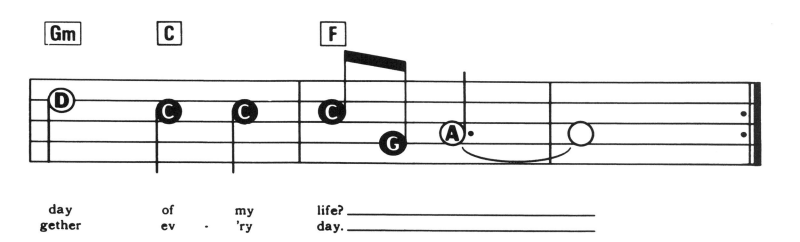

day   of   my   life?
gether   ev - 'ry   day.

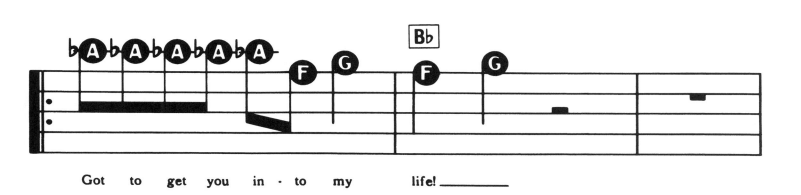

Got   to   get   you   in - to   my   life!

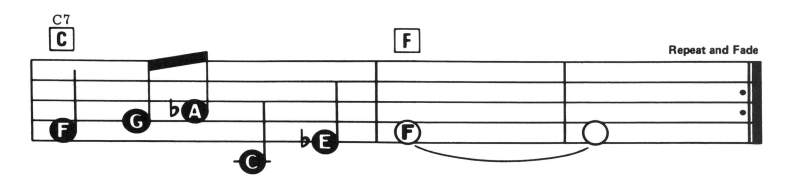

A Hard Day's Night

Registration 7
Rhythm: Rock or Jazz Rock

Words and Music by John Lennon
and Paul McCartney

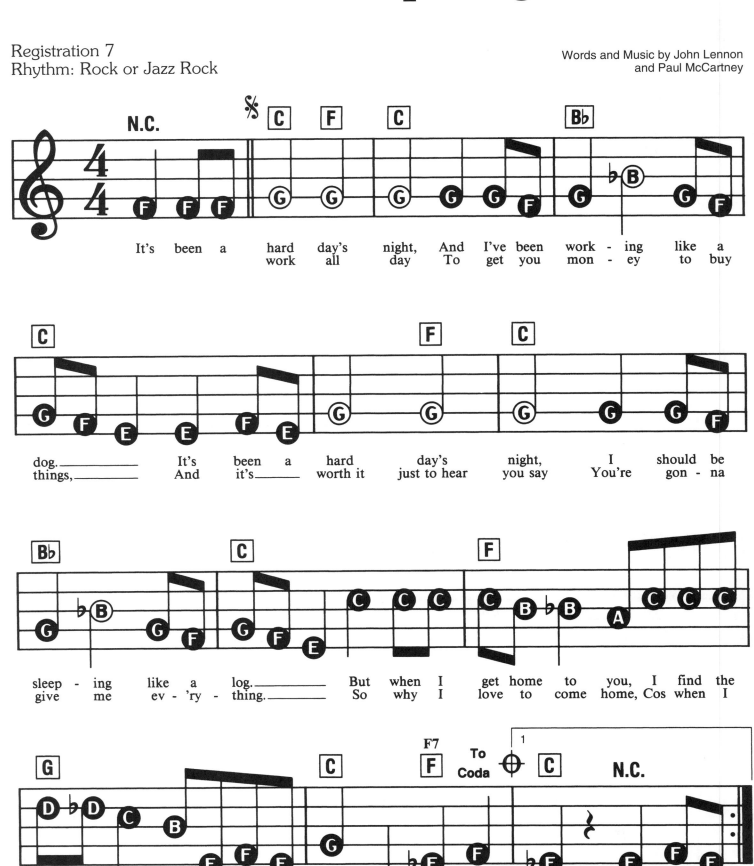

Hello, Goodbye

Registration 3
Rhythm: Rock or Latin Rock

Words and Music by John Lennon
and Paul McCartney

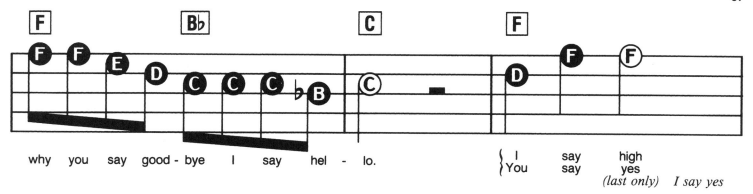

why you say good-bye I say hel-lo.

{ I say high
You say say yes
(last only) I say yes

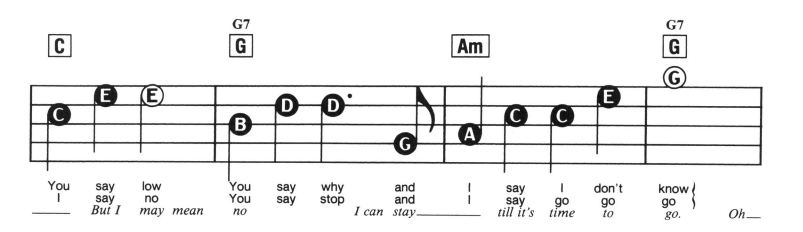

You say low You say why and I say I don't know
I say no You say stop and I say go go
But I may mean no *You say why stop* *I can stay* *till it's time to go.* *Oh*

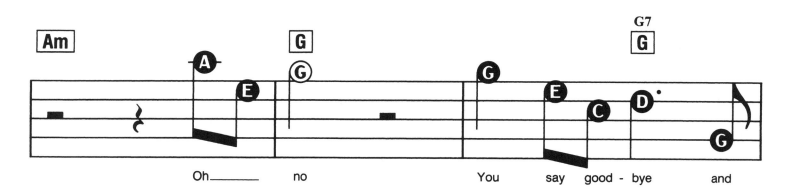

Oh no You say good-bye and

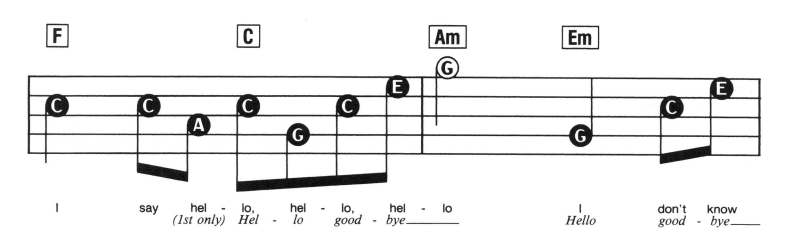

I say hel-lo, hel-lo, hel-lo I don't know
(1st only) Hel-lo good-bye *Hello good-bye*

58

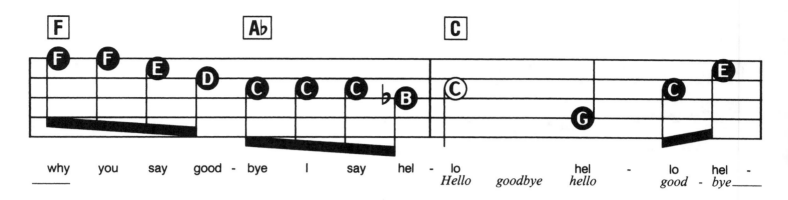

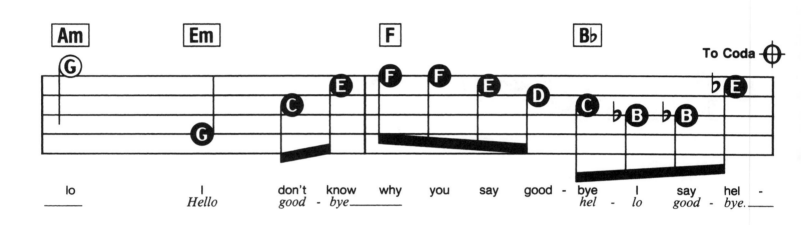

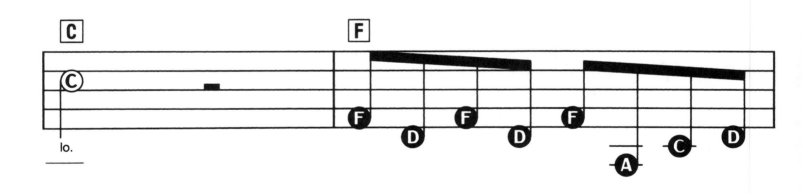

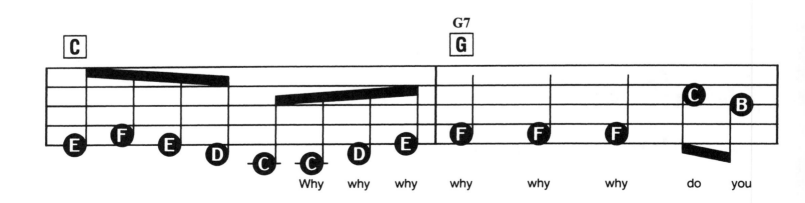

59

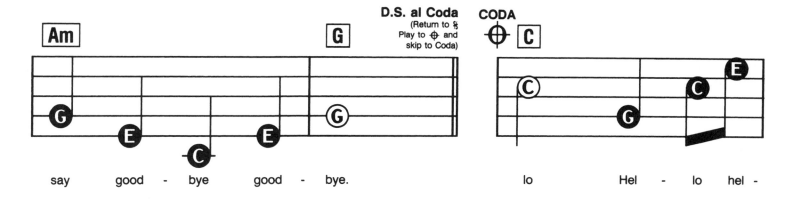

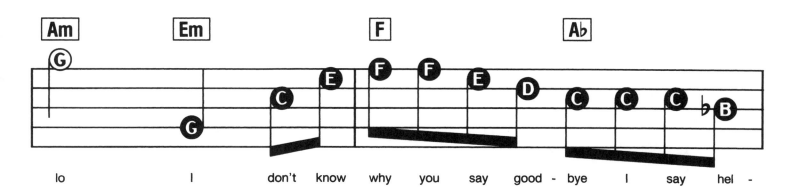

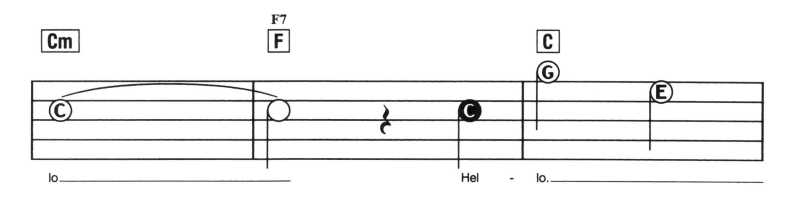

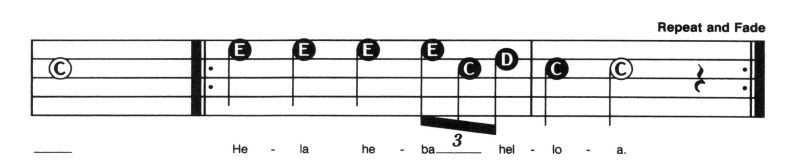

Help!

Registration 3
Rhythm: Rock or Jazz Rock

Words and Music by John Lennon
and Paul McCartney

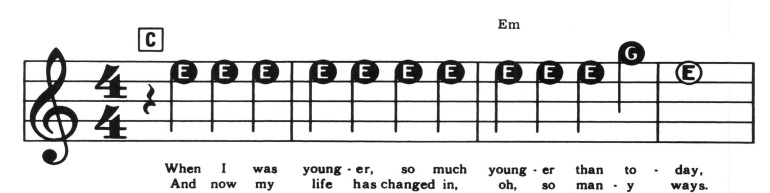

When I was young-er, so much young-er than to-day,
And now my life has changed in, oh, so man-y ways.

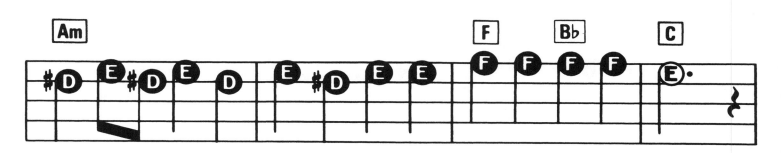

I nev-er need-ed an-y-bod-y's help in an-y way.
My _____ in-de-pen-dence seems to van-ish in the haze.

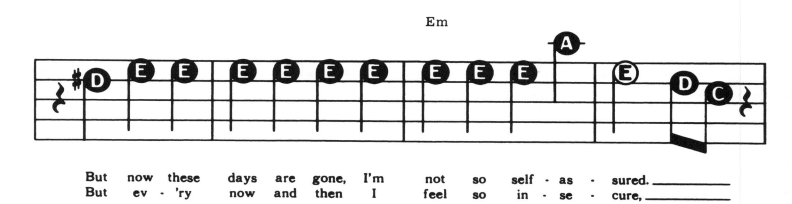

But now these days are gone, I'm not so self-as-sured. _____
But ev-'ry now and then I feel so in-se-cure, _____

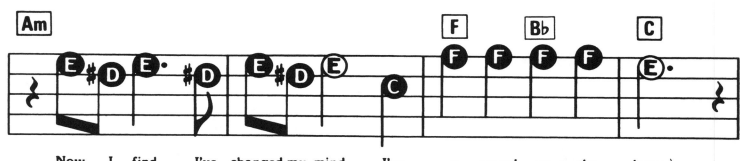

Now I find I've changed my mind, I've o-pened up the doors.
I know that I just need you like I've nev-er done be-fore.

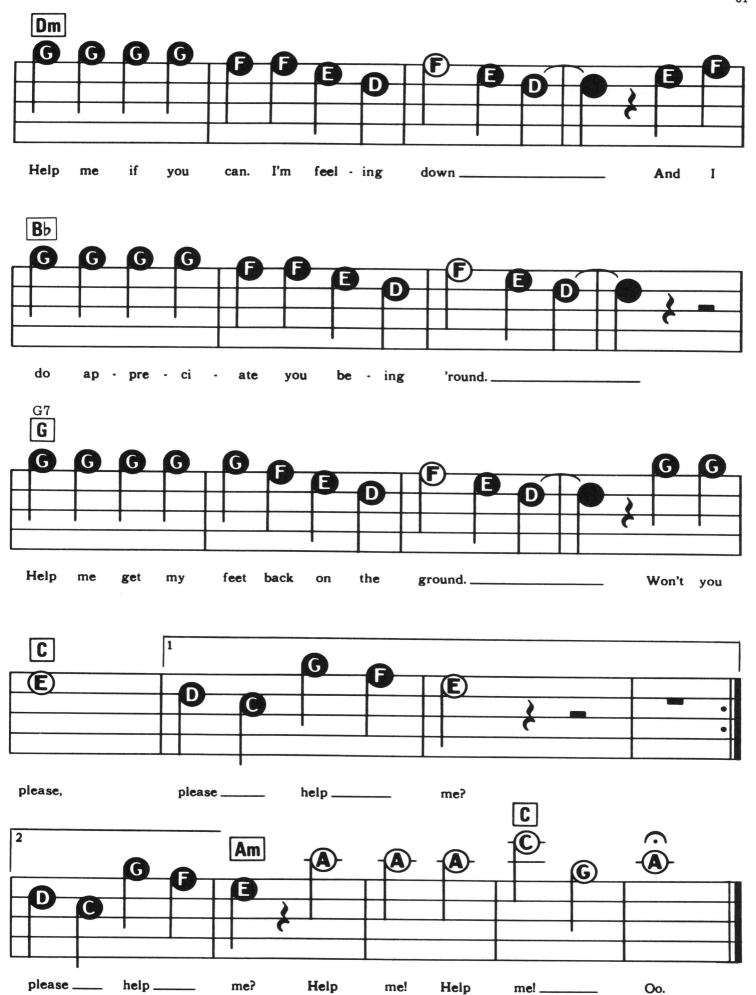

61

Help me if you can. I'm feel-ing down _____ And I

do ap · pre · ci · ate you be · ing 'round. _____

Help me get my feet back on the ground. _____ Won't you

please, please _____ help _____ me?

please _____ help _____ me? Help me! Help me! _____ Oo.

Helter Skelter

Registration 4
Rhythm: Rock

Words and Music by John Lennon
and Paul McCartney

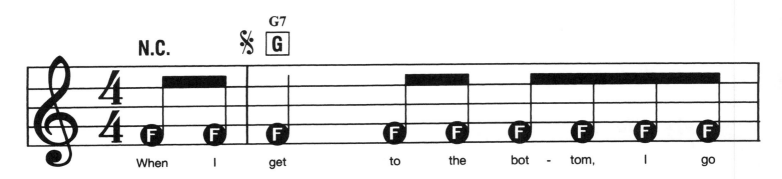

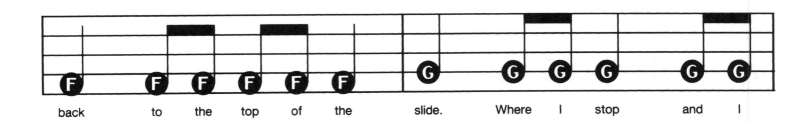

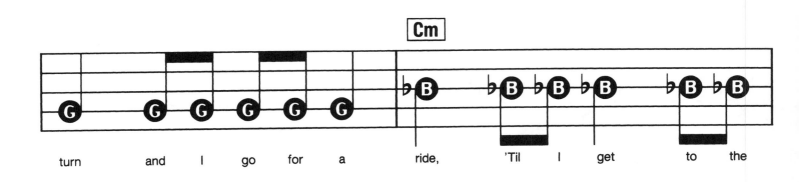

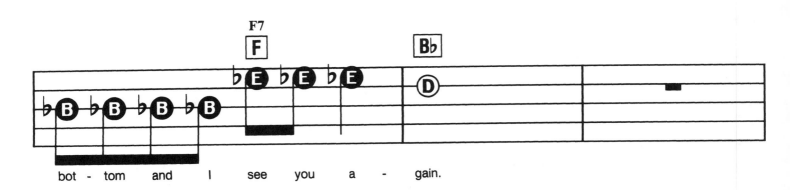

shout

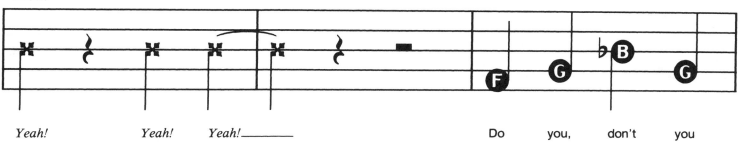

Yeah!   Yeah!   Yeah!_____   Do   you,   don't   you

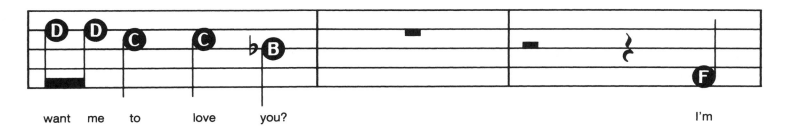

want   me   to   love   you?   I'm

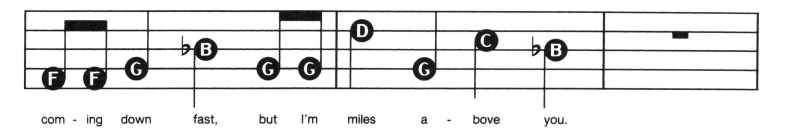

com - ing   down   fast,   but   I'm   miles   a - bove   you.

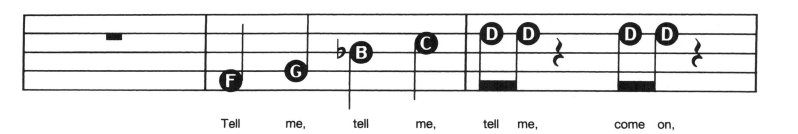

Tell   me,   tell   me,   tell   me,   come   on,

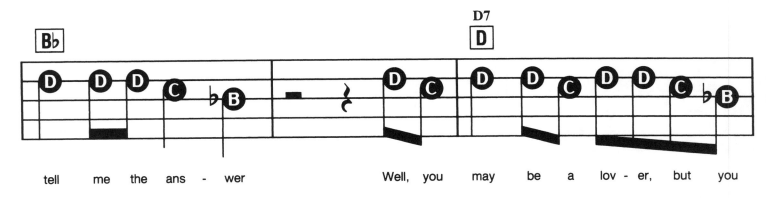

tell me the ans - wer   Well, you may be a lov - er, but you

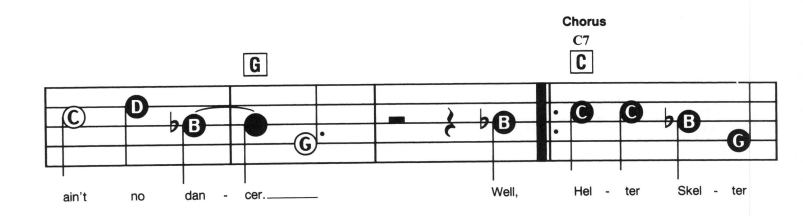

ain't no dan - cer._____   Well, Hel - ter Skel - ter

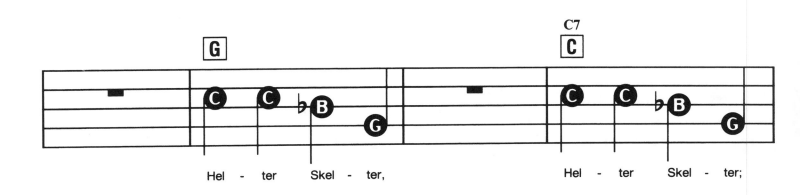

Hel - ter Skel - ter,   Hel - ter Skel - ter;

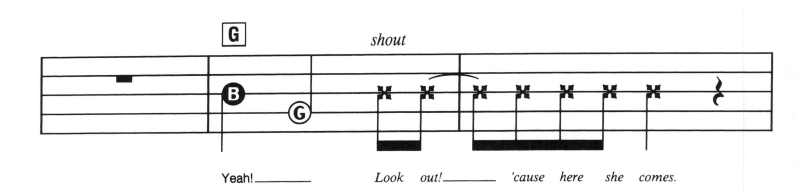

Yeah!_____   *Look out!*_____ *'cause here she comes.*

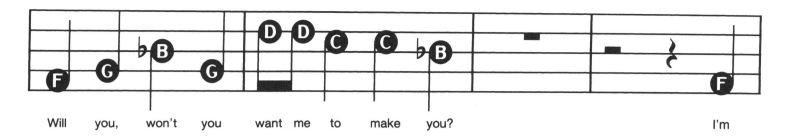

Will you, won't you want me to make you? I'm

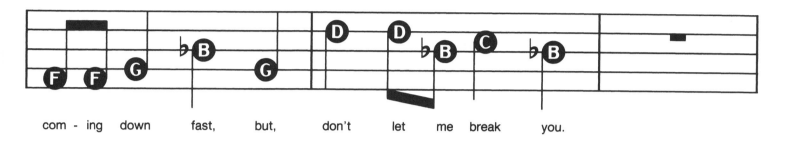

com - ing down fast, but, don't let me break you.

Bb

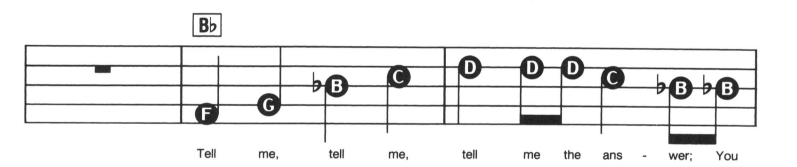

Tell me, tell me, tell me the ans - wer; You

D7

D

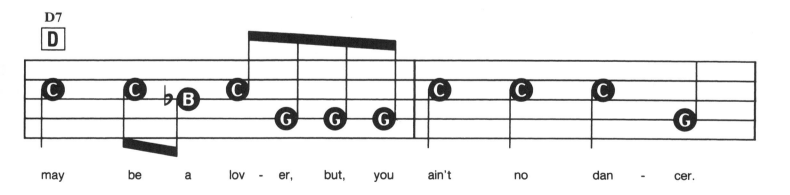

may be a lov - er, but, you ain't no dan - cer.

G

shout

D.S.
(Return to 𝄋 and
Fade on Chorus)

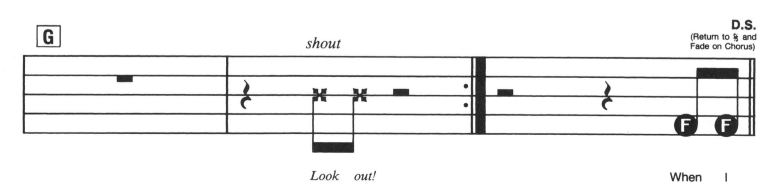

Look out! When I

Here Comes the Sun

Registration 7
Rhythm: Rock

Words and Music by
George Harrison

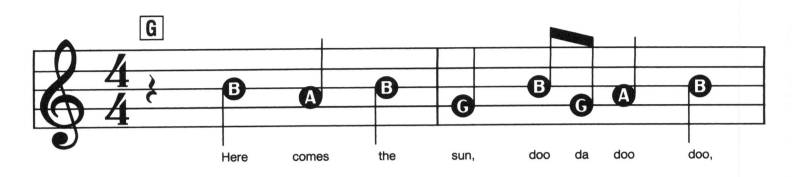

Here comes the sun, doo da doo doo,

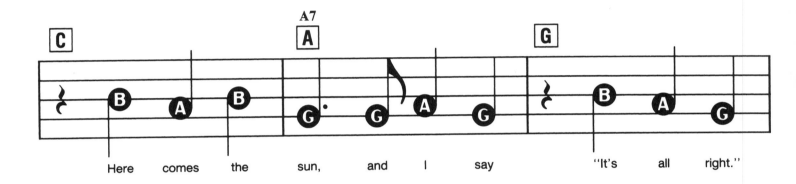

Here comes the sun, and I say "It's all right."

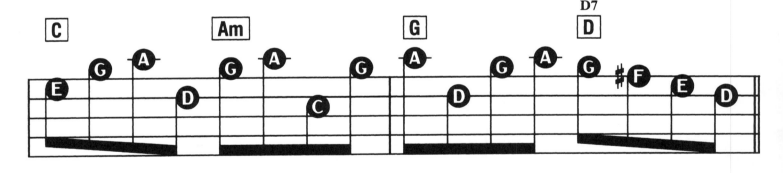

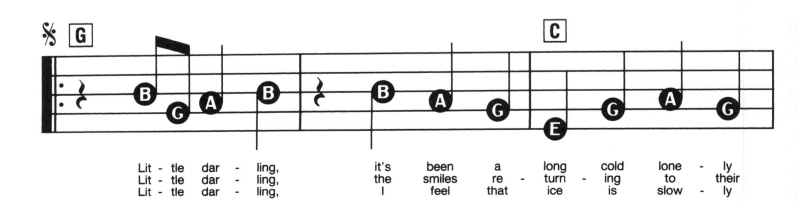

Lit - tle dar - ling, it's been a long cold lone - ly
Lit - tle dar - ling, the smiles re - turn - ing to their
Lit - tle dar - ling, I feel that ice is slow - ly

67

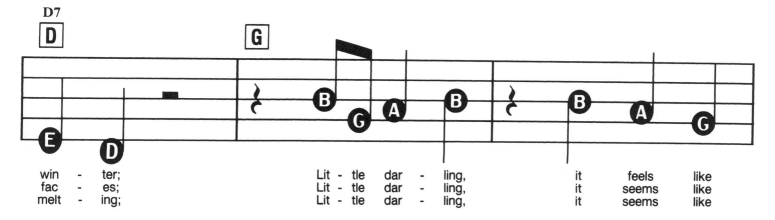

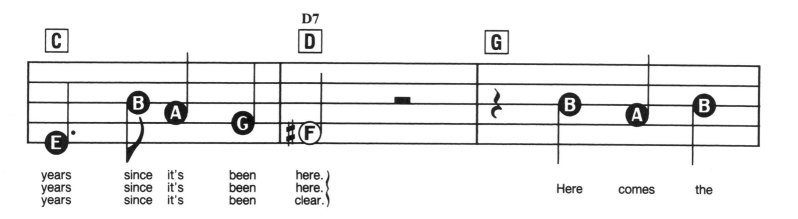

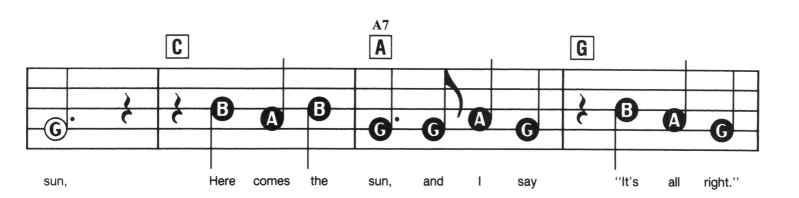

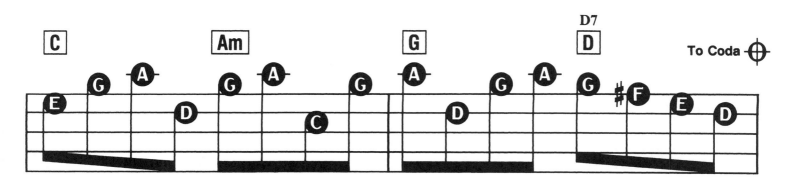

68

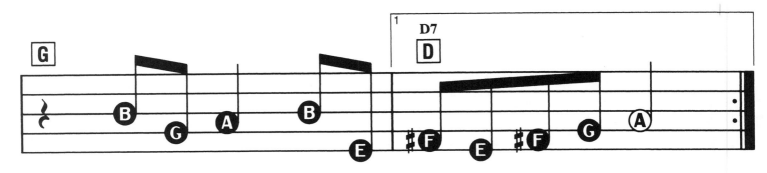

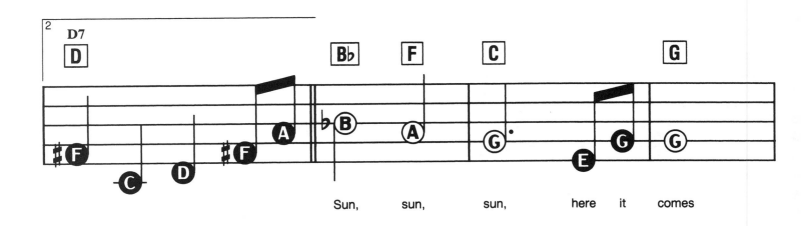

Sun, sun, sun, here it comes

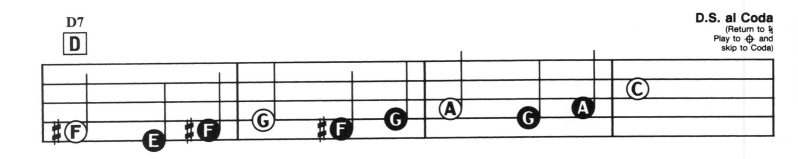

D.S. al Coda
(Return to %
Play to ⊕ and
skip to Coda)

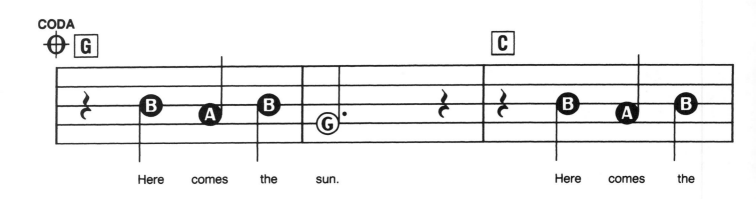

Here comes the sun.   Here comes the

69

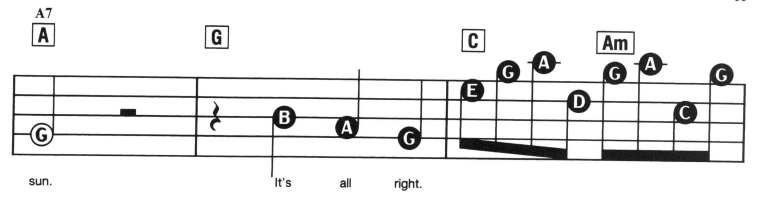

sun.   It's   all   right.

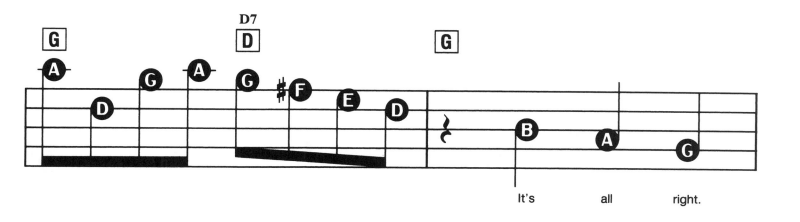

It's   all   right.

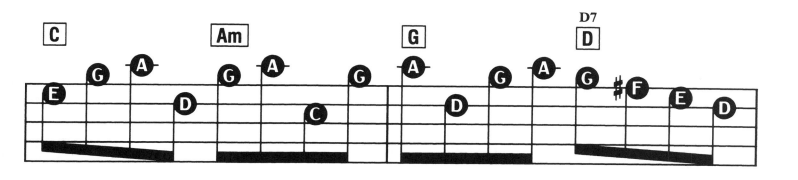

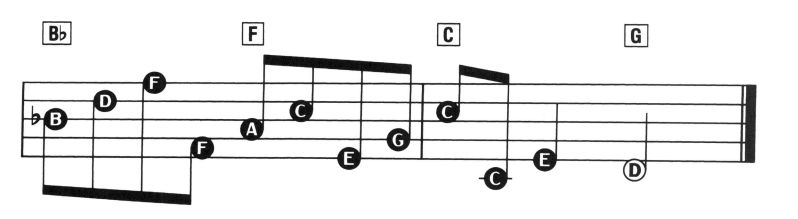

Here, There and Everywhere

Registration 2
Rhythm: 8 Beat or Rock

Words and Music by John Lennon
and Paul McCartney

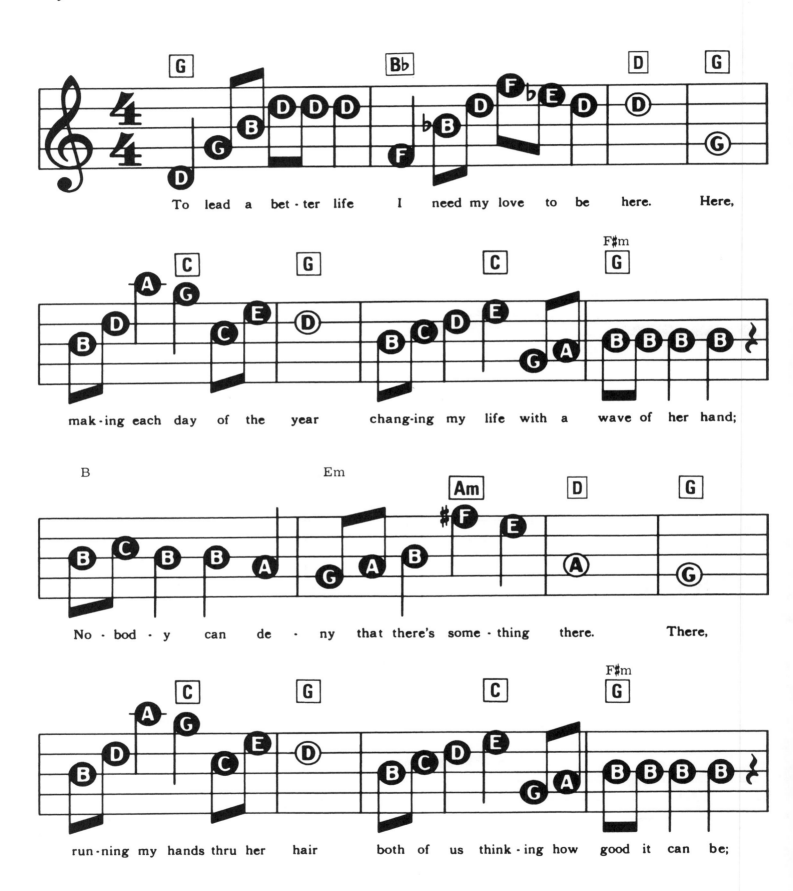

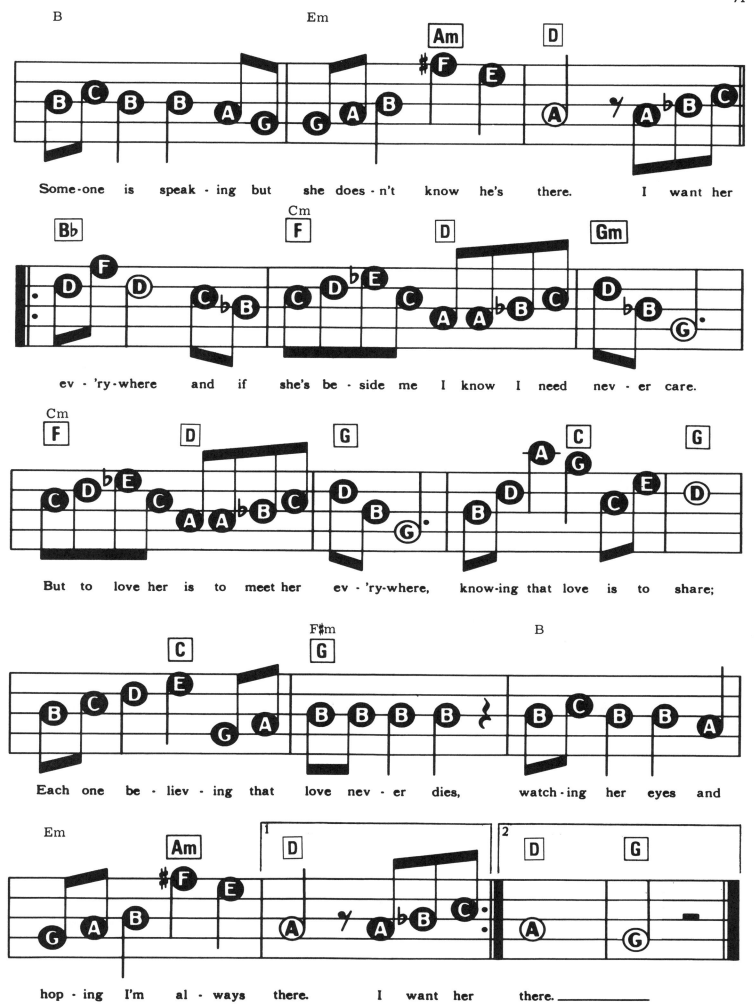

71

Hey Bulldog

Registration 8
Rhythm: 8 Beat or Rock

Words and Music by John Lennon
and Paul McCartney

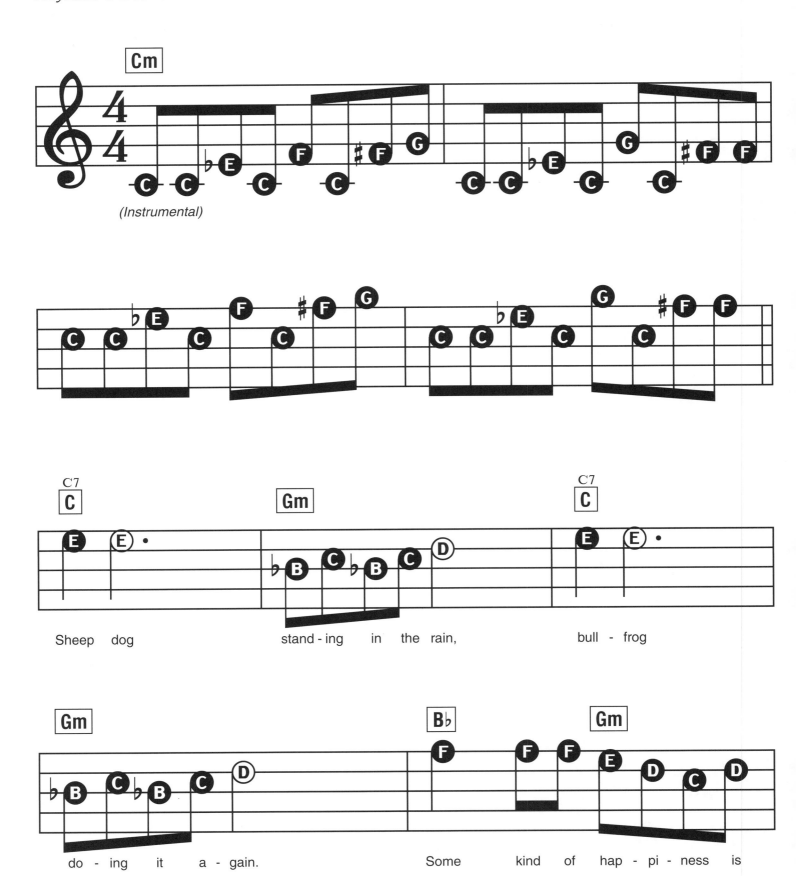

(Instrumental)

Sheep dog   stand - ing in the rain,   bull - frog

do - ing it a - gain.   Some kind of hap - pi - ness is

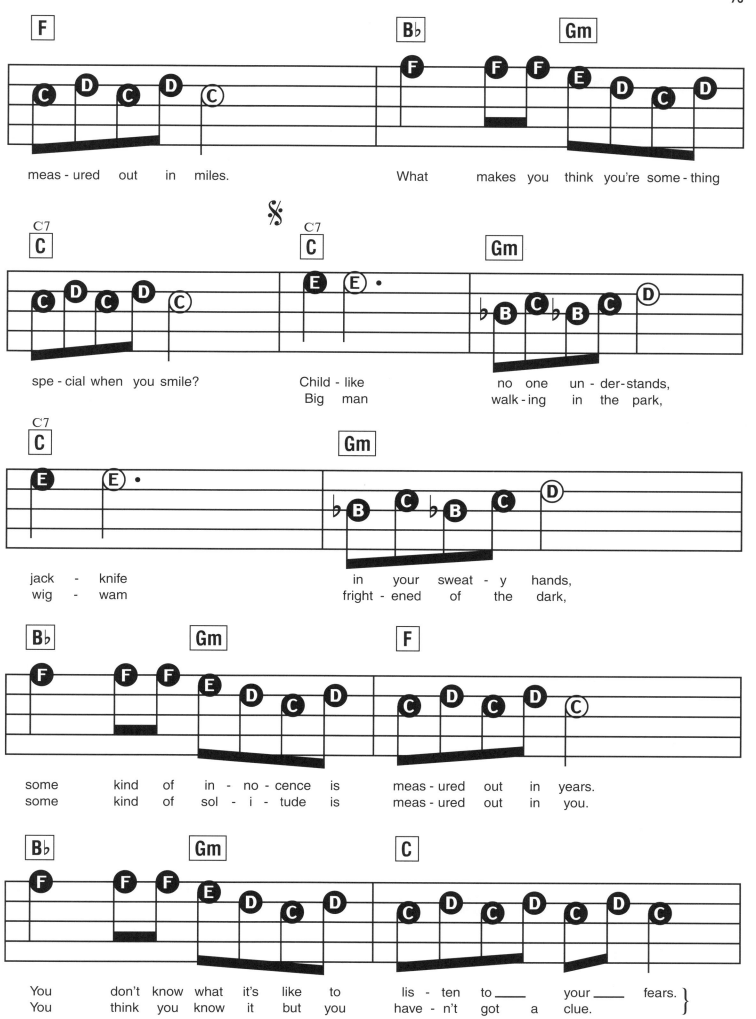

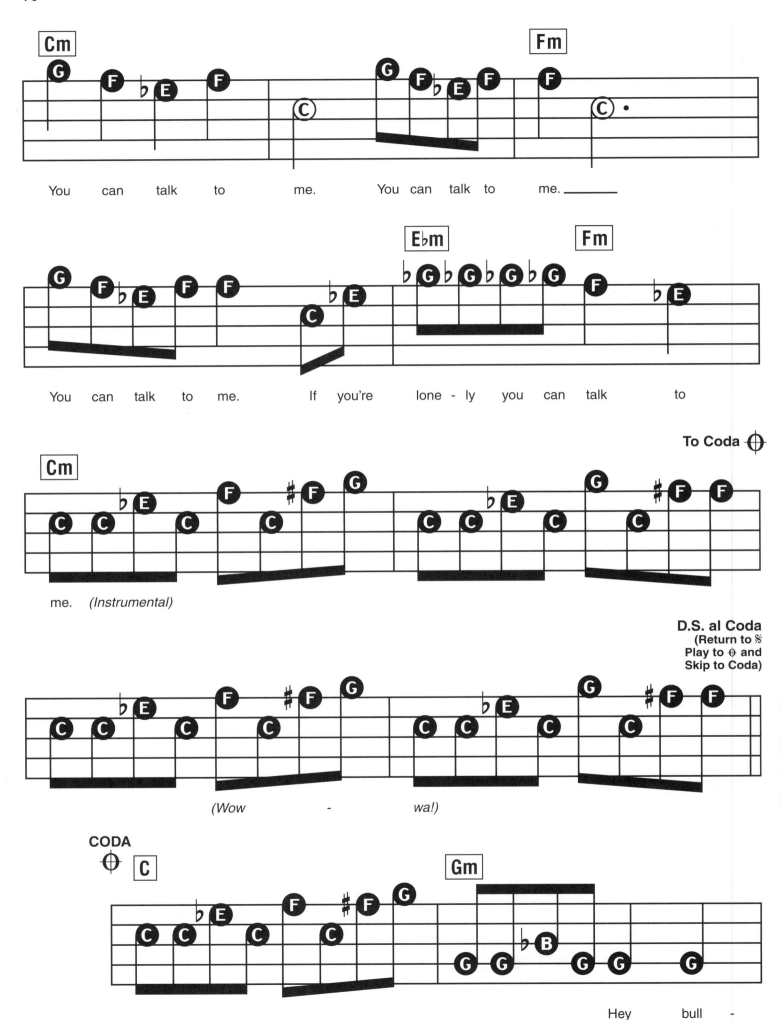

You can talk to me. You can talk to me. _____

You can talk to me. If you're lone - ly you can talk to

To Coda ⊕

me. *(Instrumental)*

D.S. al Coda
(Return to 𝄋
Play to ⊕ and
Skip to Coda)

(Wow - wa!)

CODA
⊕

Hey bull -

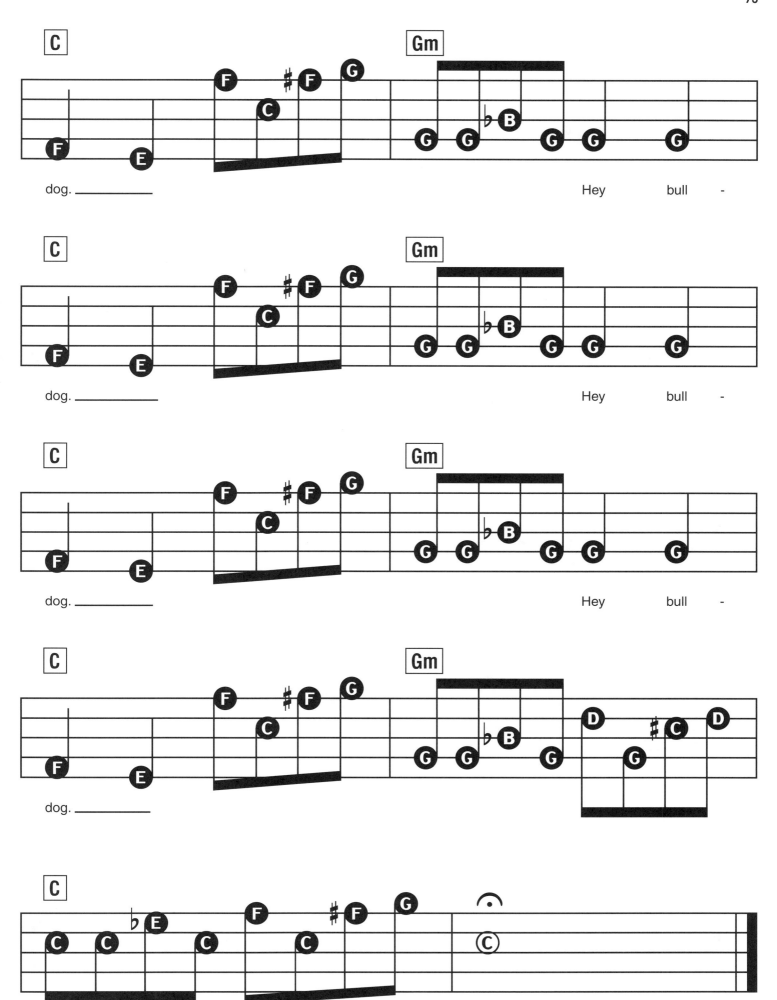

Hey Jude

Registration 2
Rhythm: Pops or 8 Beat

Words and Music by John Lennon
and Paul McCartney

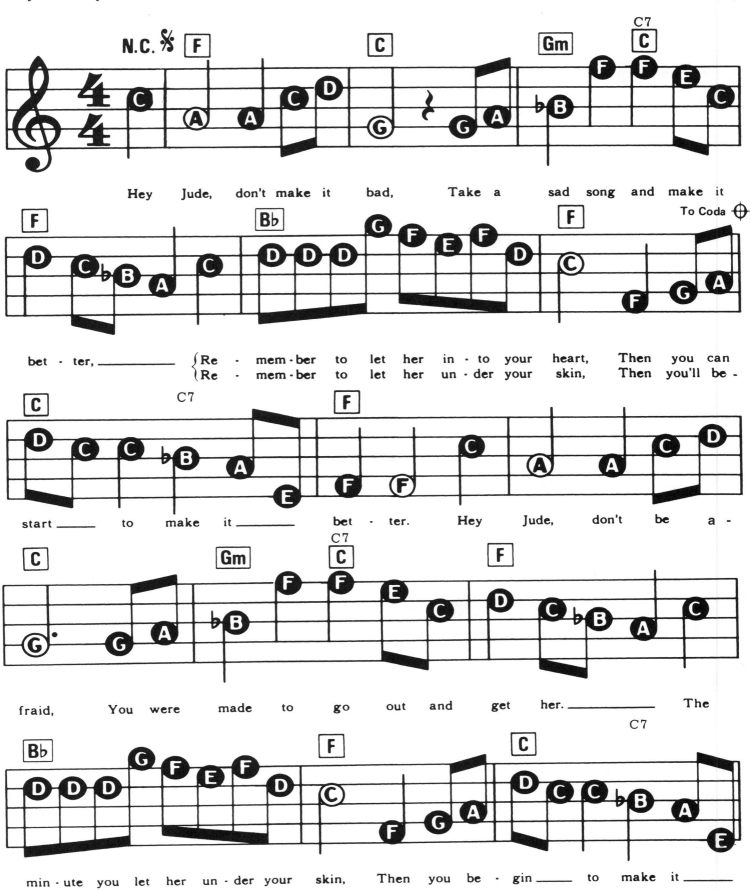

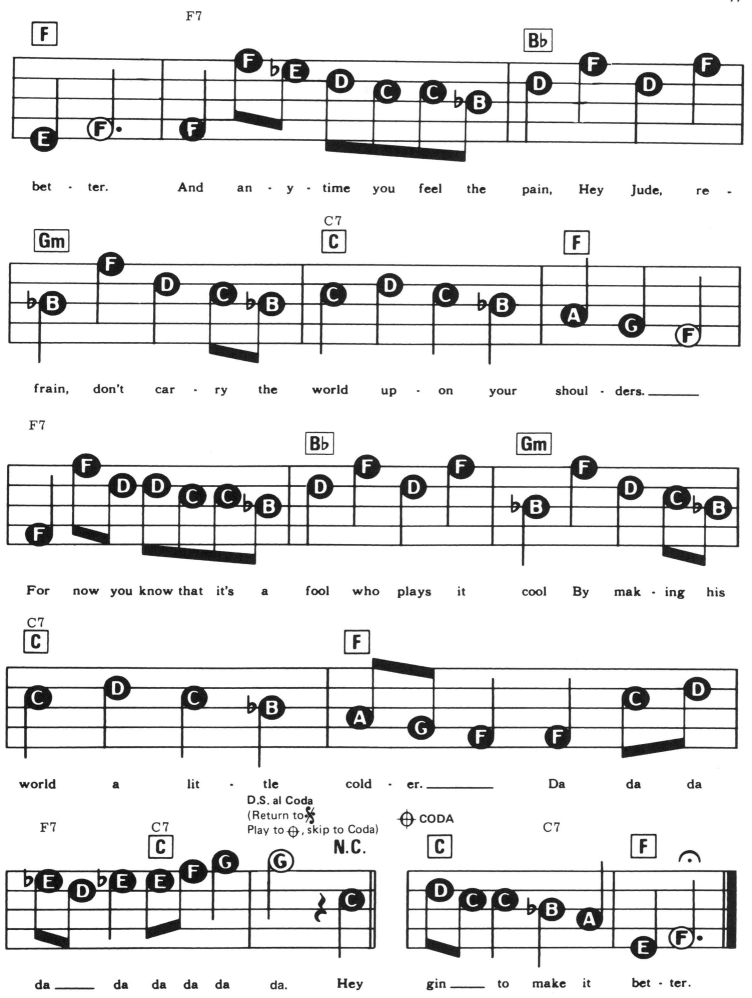

I Am the Walrus

Registration 5
Rhythm: Rock

Words and Music by John Lennon
and Paul McCartney

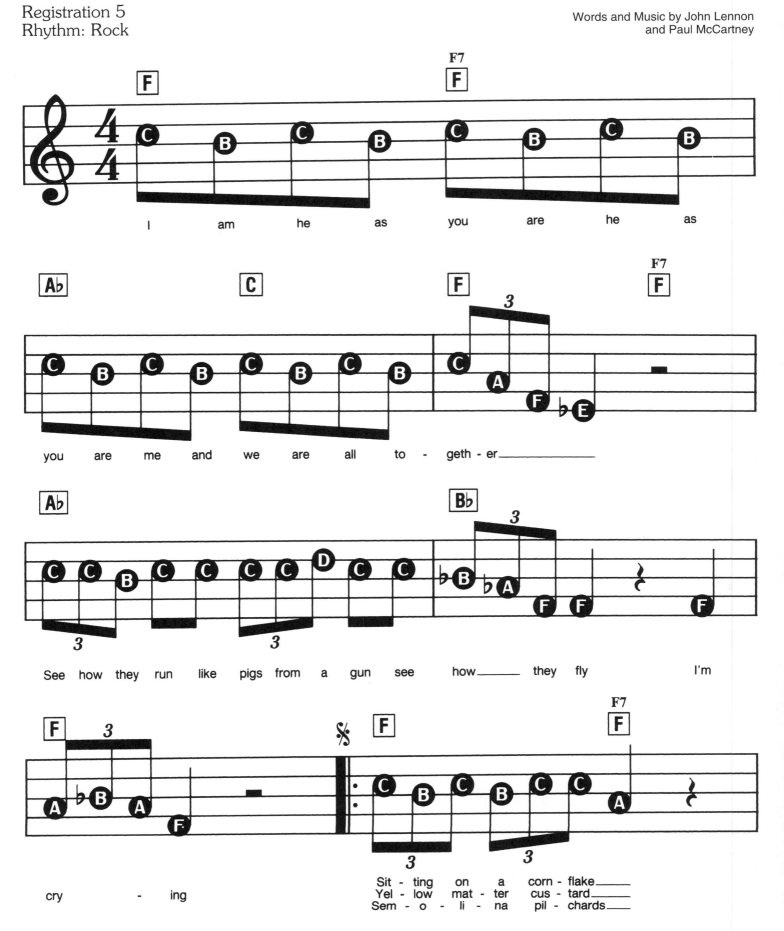

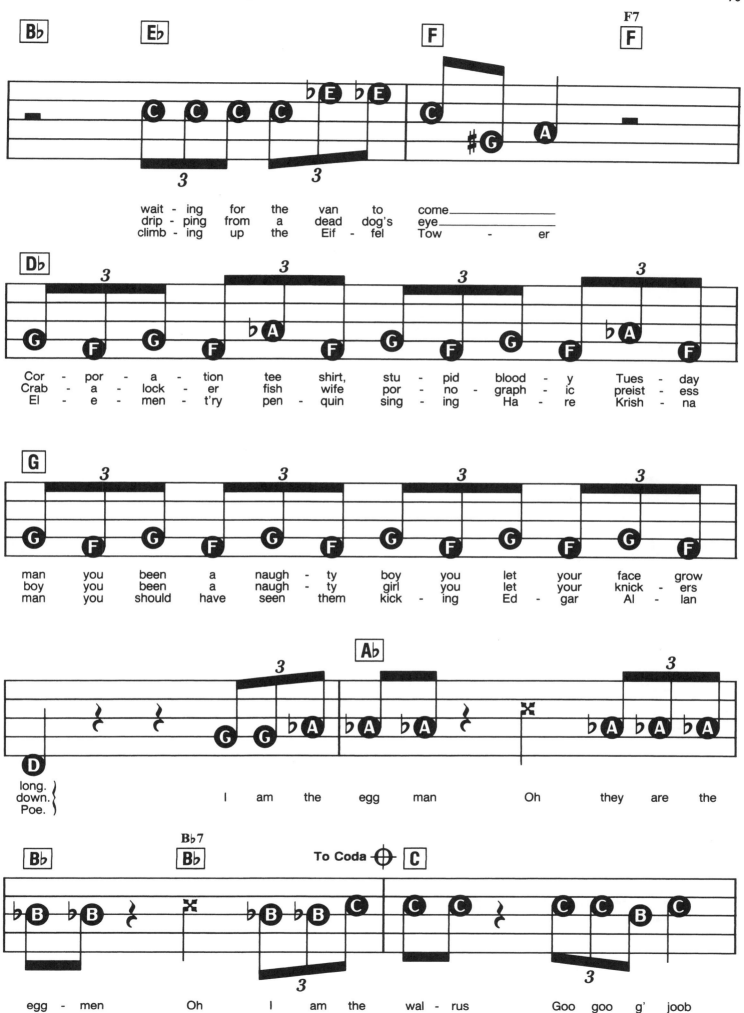

80

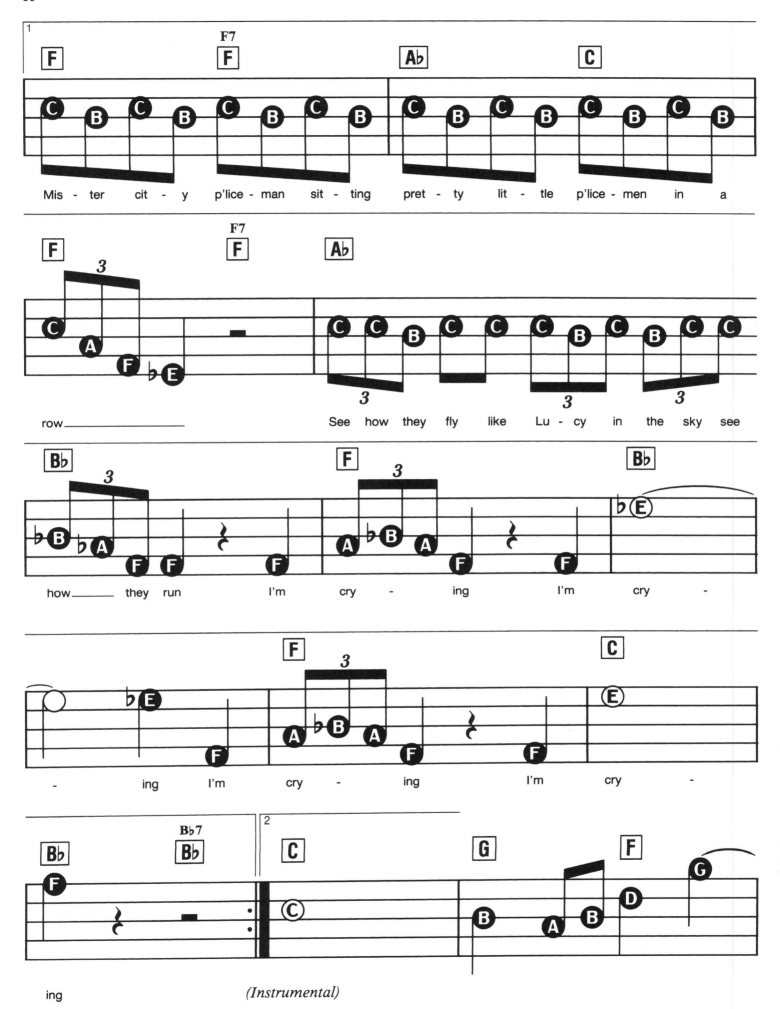

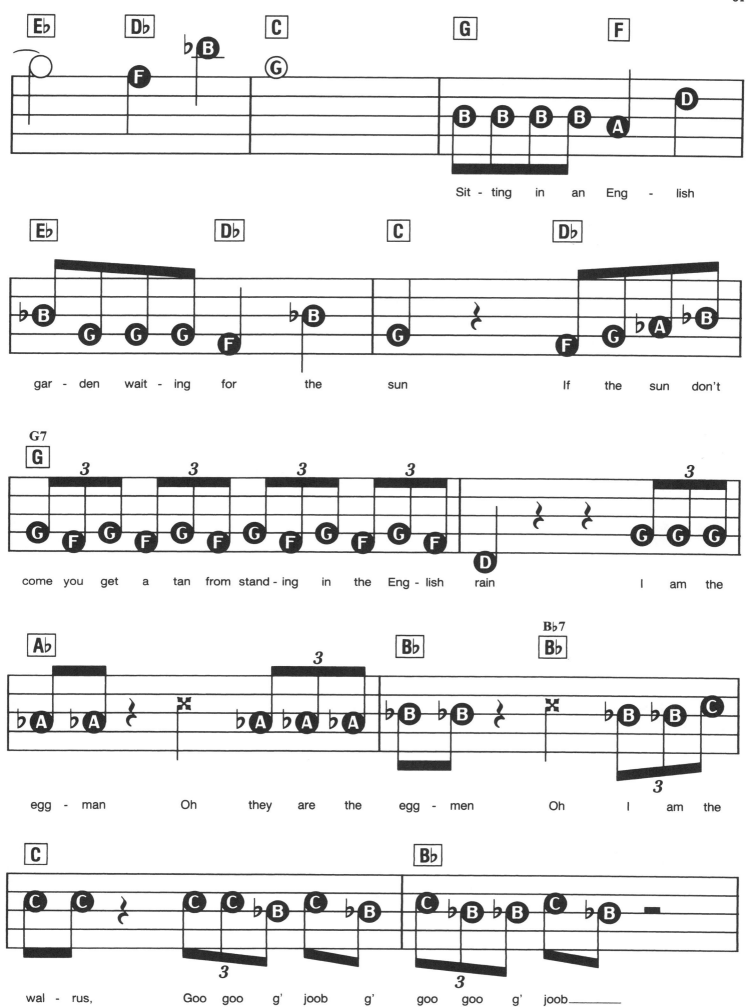

I'm Looking Through You

Registration 2
Rhythm: Rock

Words and Music by John Lennon
and Paul McCartney

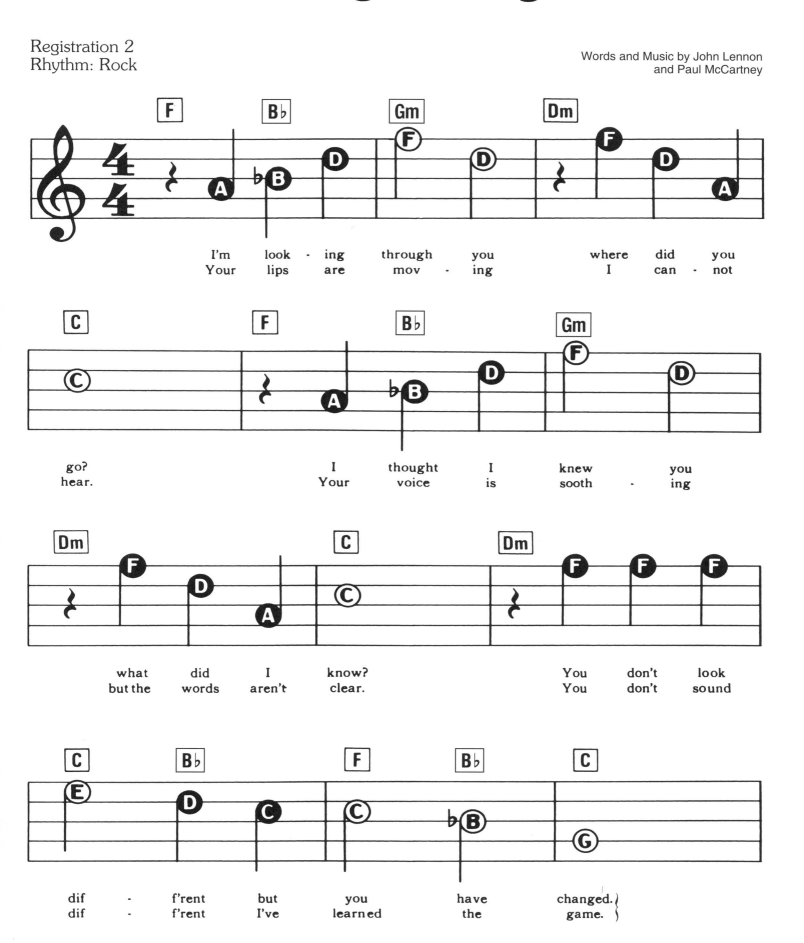

84

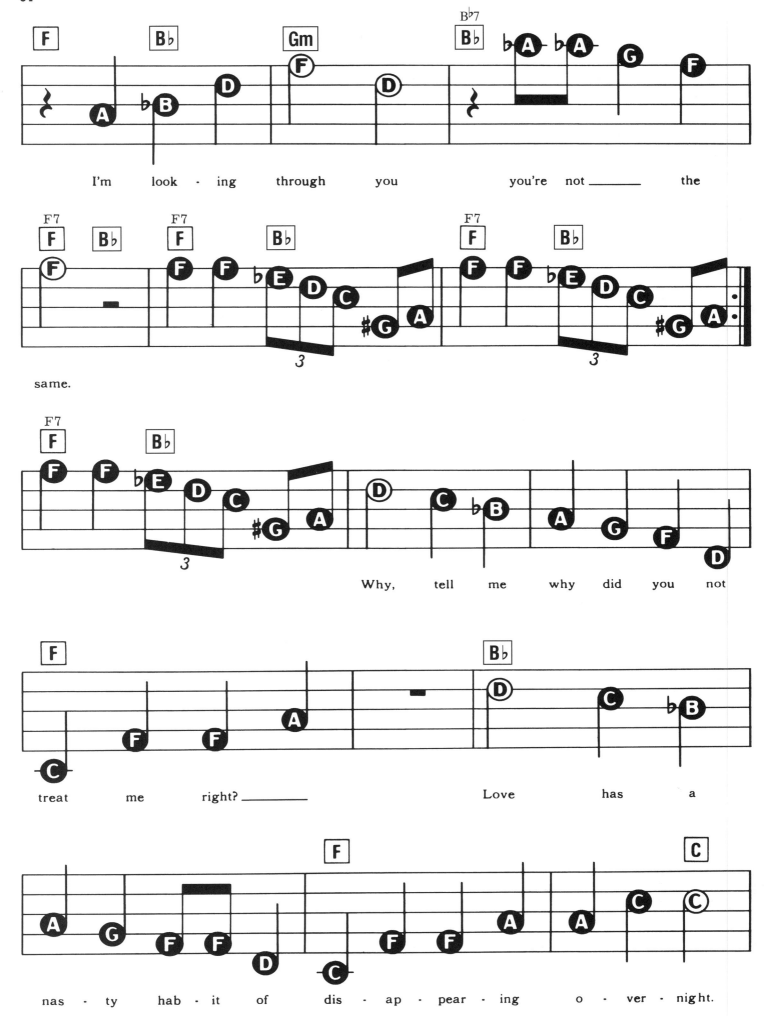

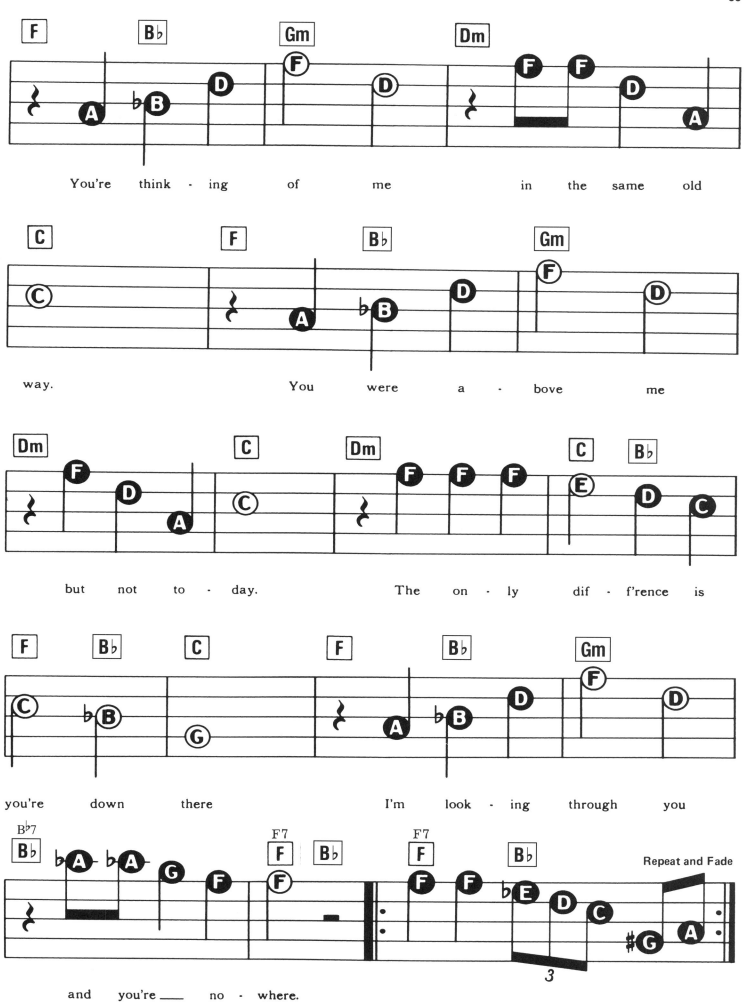

You're think-ing of me in the same old

way. You were a-bove me

but not to-day. The on-ly dif-f'rence is

you're down there I'm look-ing through you

and you're ___ no-where.

I Feel Fine

Registration 9
Rhythm: Rock or Jazz Rock

Words and Music by John Lennon
and Paul McCartney

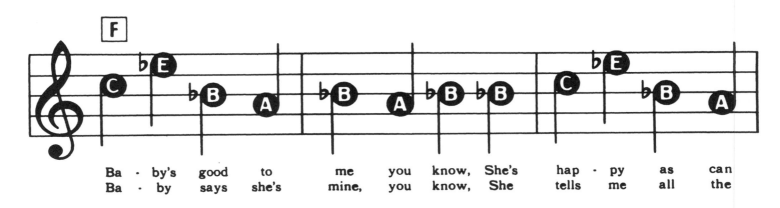

Ba - by's good to me you know, She's hap - py as can
Ba - by says she's mine, you know, She tells me all the

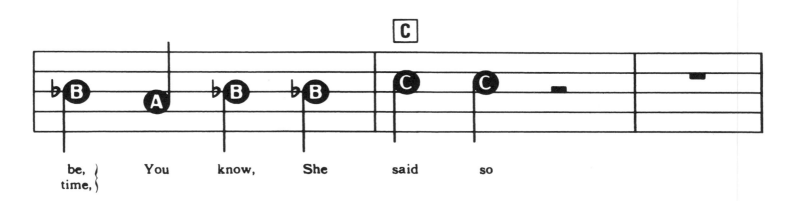

be, } You know, She said so
time, }

I'm in love with her and I feel _____ fine. _____

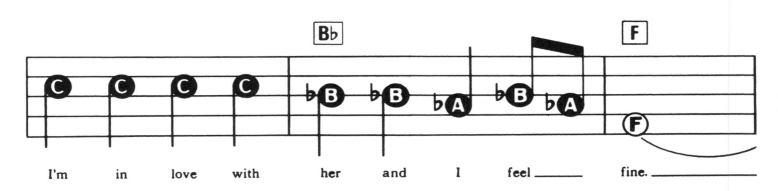

_____ I'm so glad that

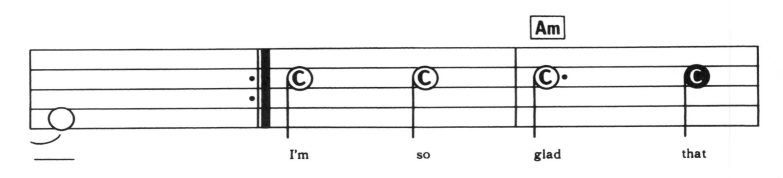

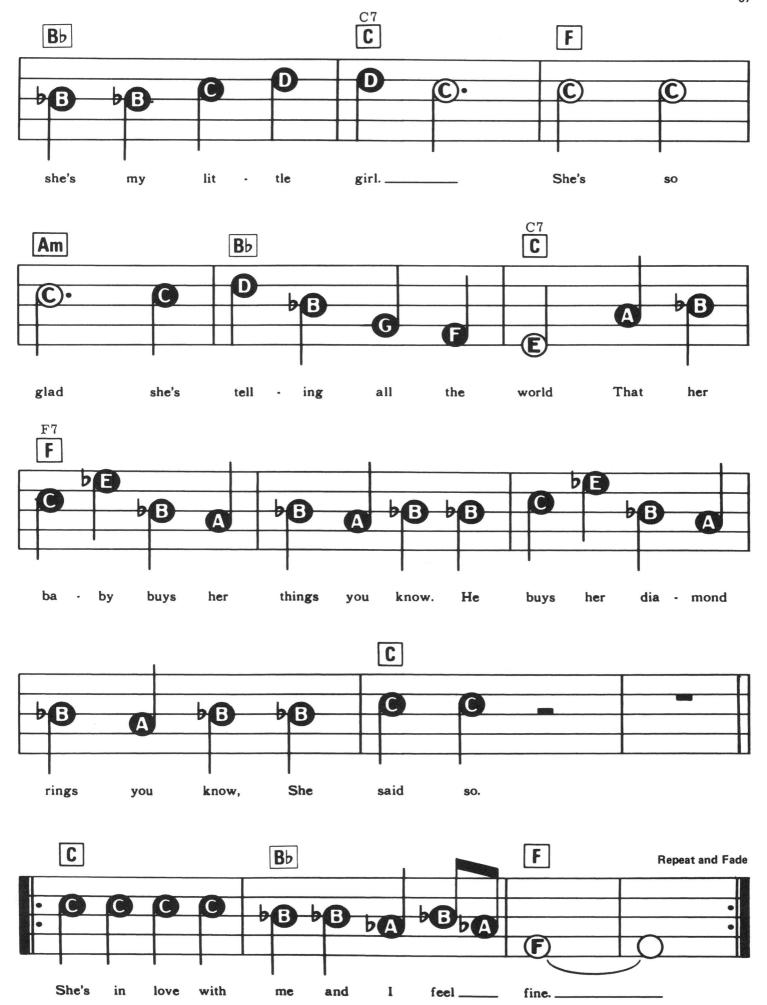

I Saw Her Standing There

Registration 2
Rhythm: Rock

Words and Music by John Lennon
and Paul McCartney

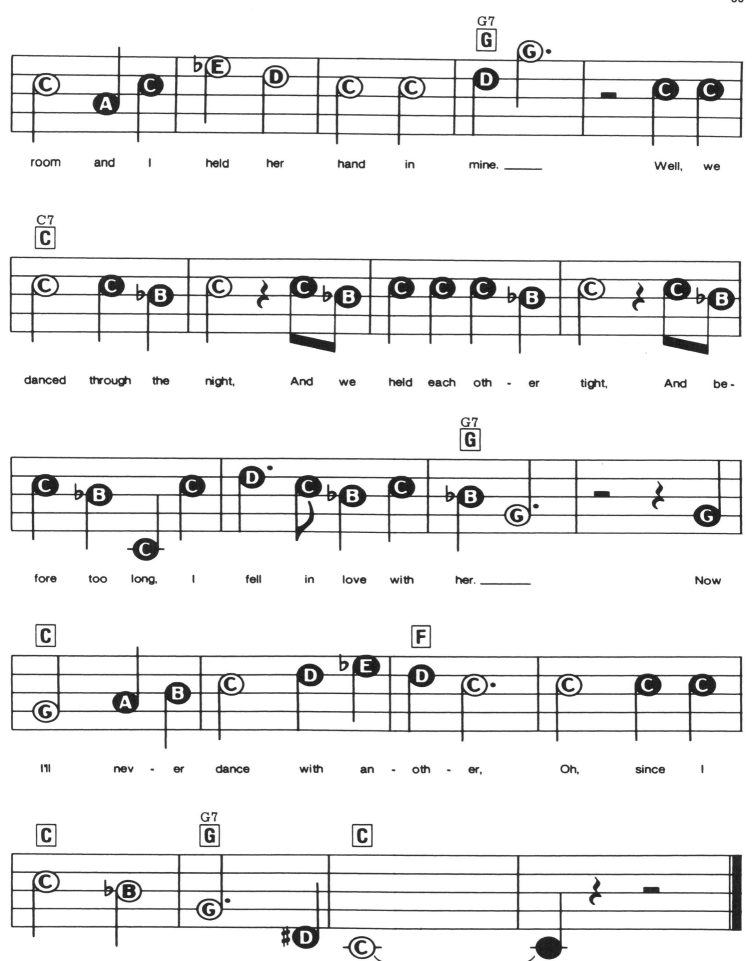

room and I held her hand in mine. _____ Well, we

danced through the night, And we held each oth - er tight, And be -

fore too long, I fell in love with her. _____ Now

I'll nev - er dance with an - oth - er, Oh, since I

saw her stand - ing there. _____

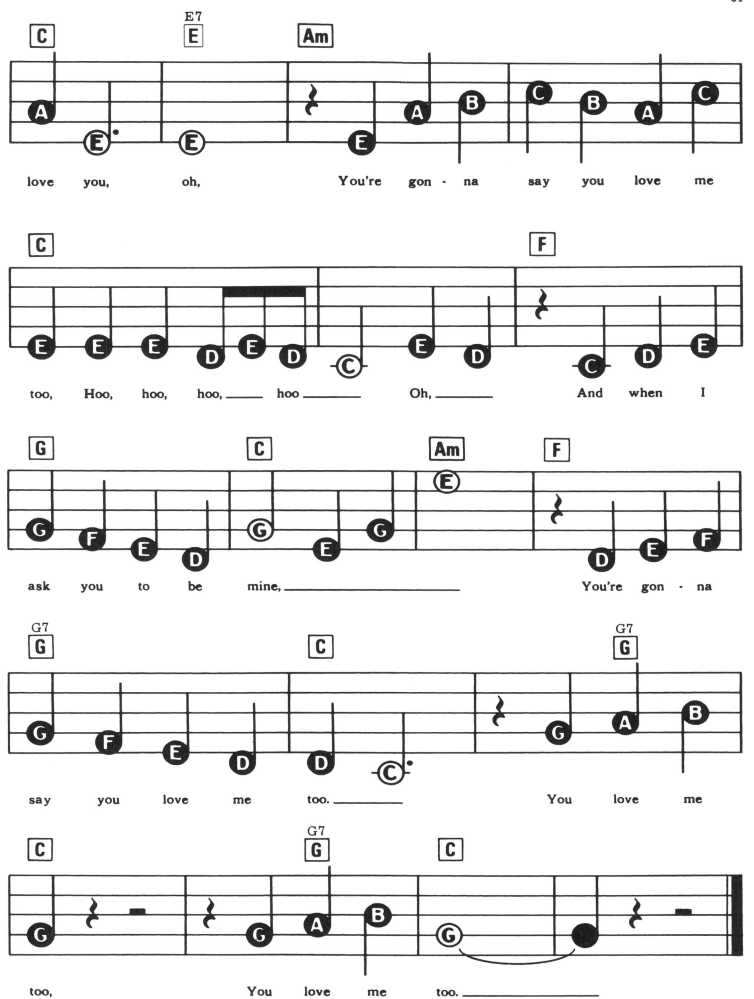

I Want to Hold Your Hand

Registration 3
Rhythm: Rock

Words and Music by John Lennon
and Paul McCartney

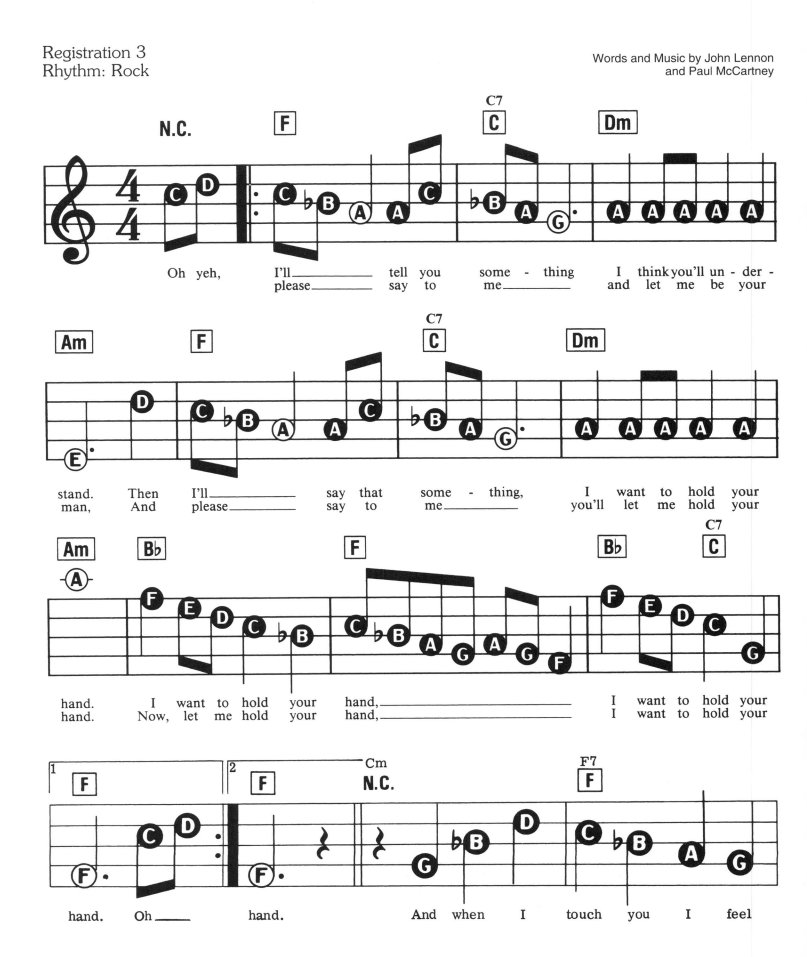

93

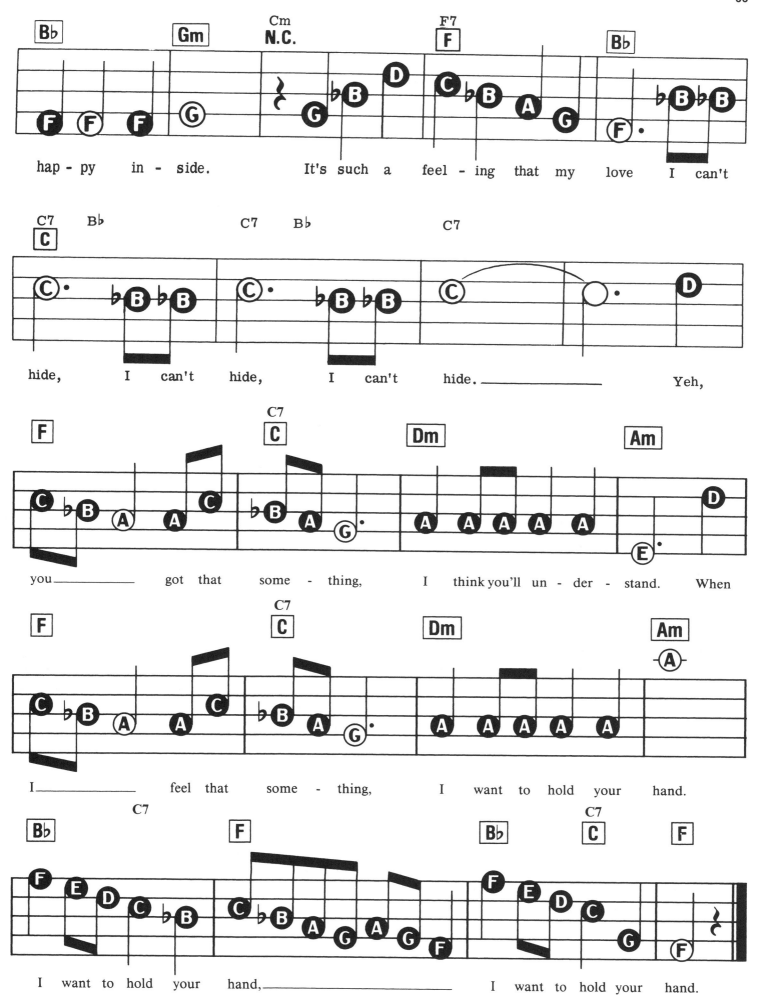

I Want to Tell You

Registration 4
Rhythm: Rock

Words and Music by
George Harrison

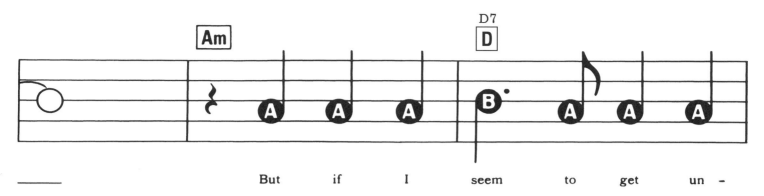

But if I seem to get un -

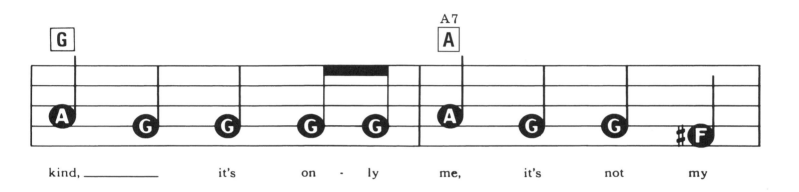

kind, _____ it's on - ly me, it's not my

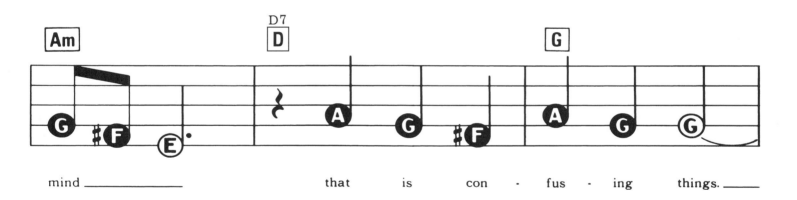

mind _____ that is con - fus - ing things. _____

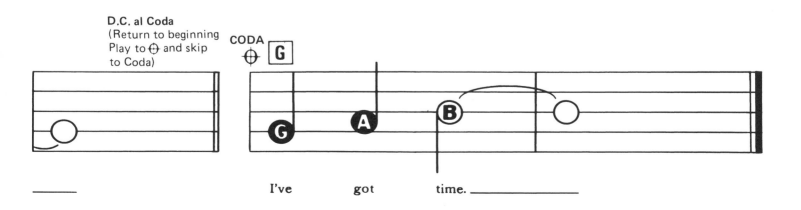

D.C. al Coda
(Return to beginning
Play to ⊕ and skip
to Coda)

CODA

_____   I've got time. _____

I Will

Registration 4
Rhythm: Rock or Slow Rock

Words and Music by John Lennon
and Paul McCartney

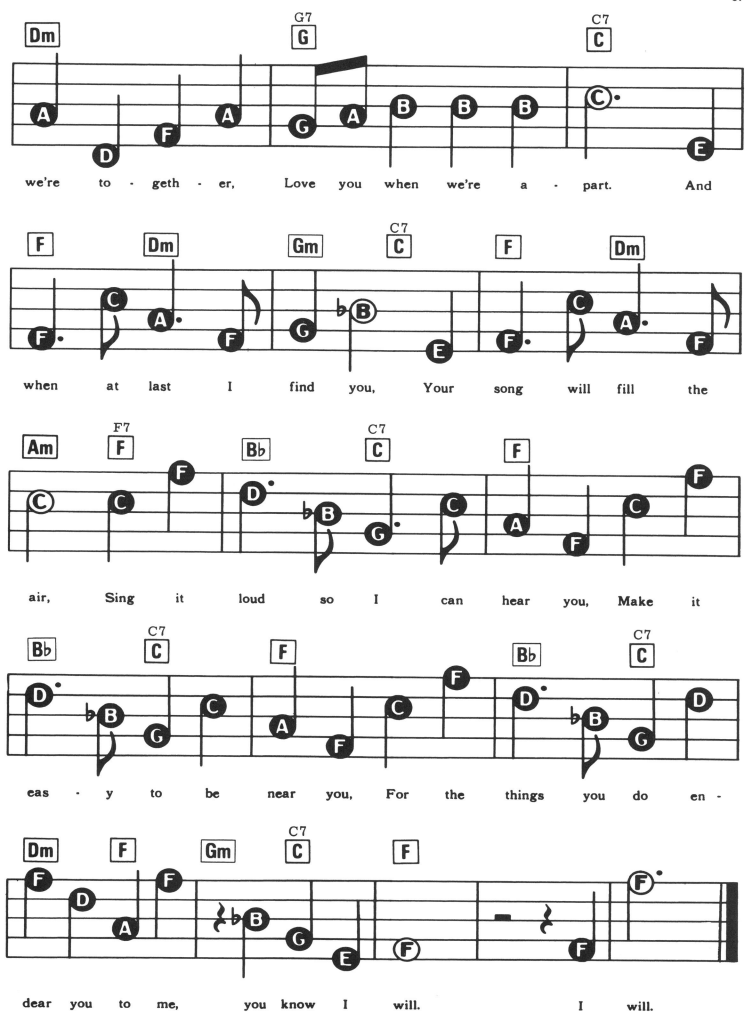

I'll Follow the Sun

Registration 9
Rhythm: Rock or Latin

Words and Music by John Lennon
and Paul McCartney

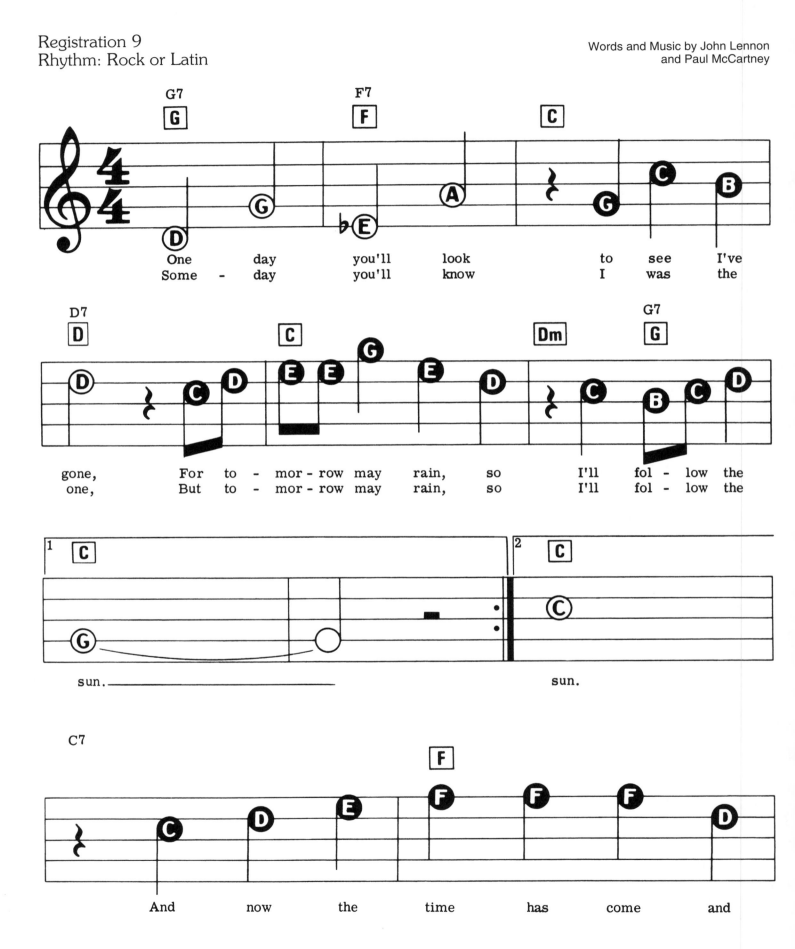

One   day   you'll   look   to   see   I've
Some - day   you'll   know   I   was   the

gone,   For   to - mor - row   may   rain,   so   I'll   fol - low   the
one,   But   to - mor - row   may   rain,   so   I'll   fol - low   the

sun. _____   sun.

And   now   the   time   has   come   and

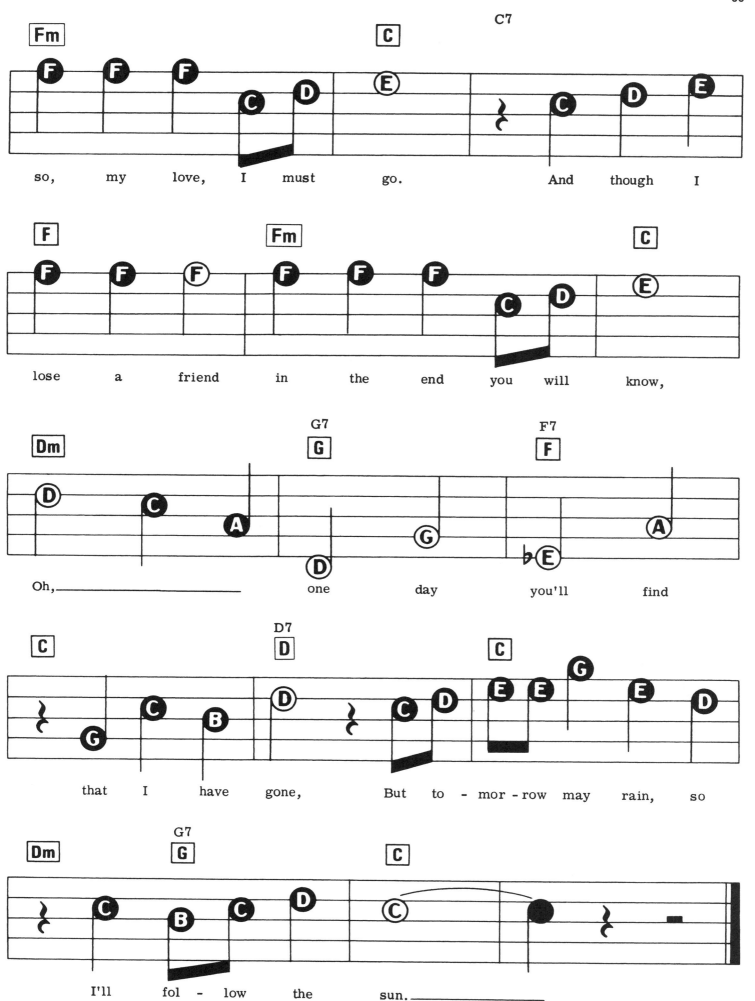

I've Just Seen a Face

Registration 4
Rhythm: Rock

Words and Music by John Lennon
and Paul McCartney

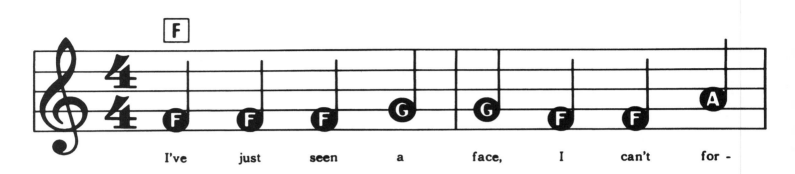

I've just seen a face, I can't for-

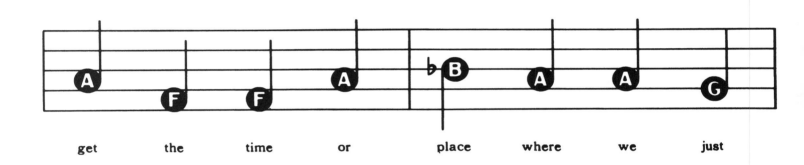

get the time or place where we just

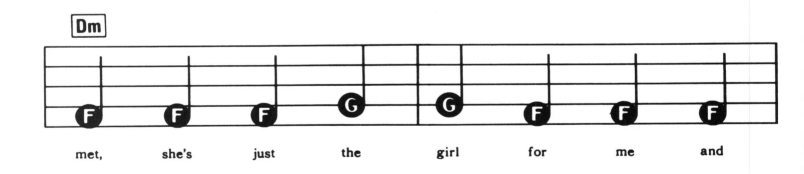

met, she's just the girl for me and

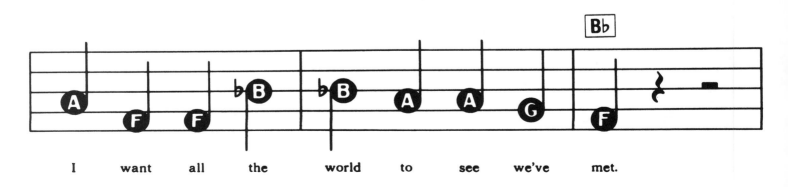

I want all the world to see we've met.

101

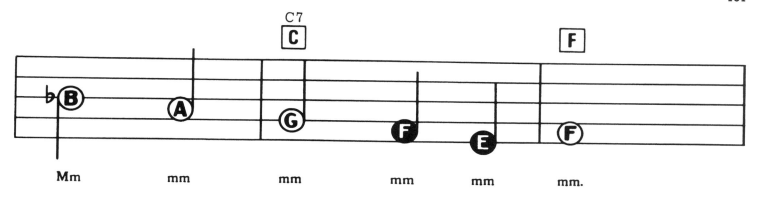

Mm   mm   mm   mm   mm   mm.

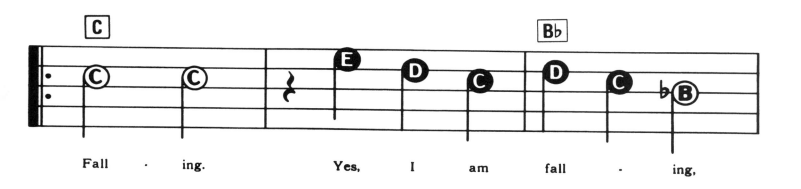

Fall · ing.   Yes, I am fall · ing,

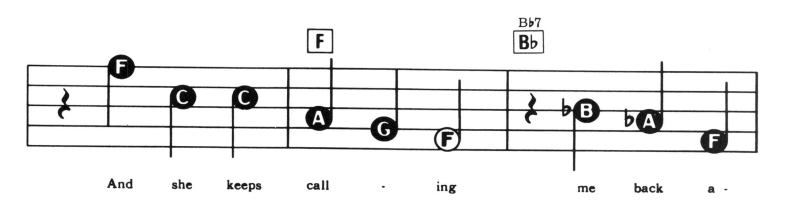

And she keeps call · ing   me back a -

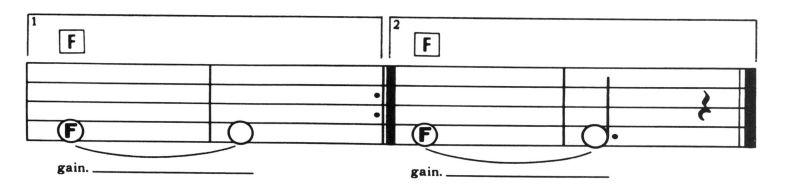

gain. _____   gain. _____

If I Fell

102

Registration 9
Rhythm: Rock or Latin

Words and Music by John Lennon
and Paul McCartney

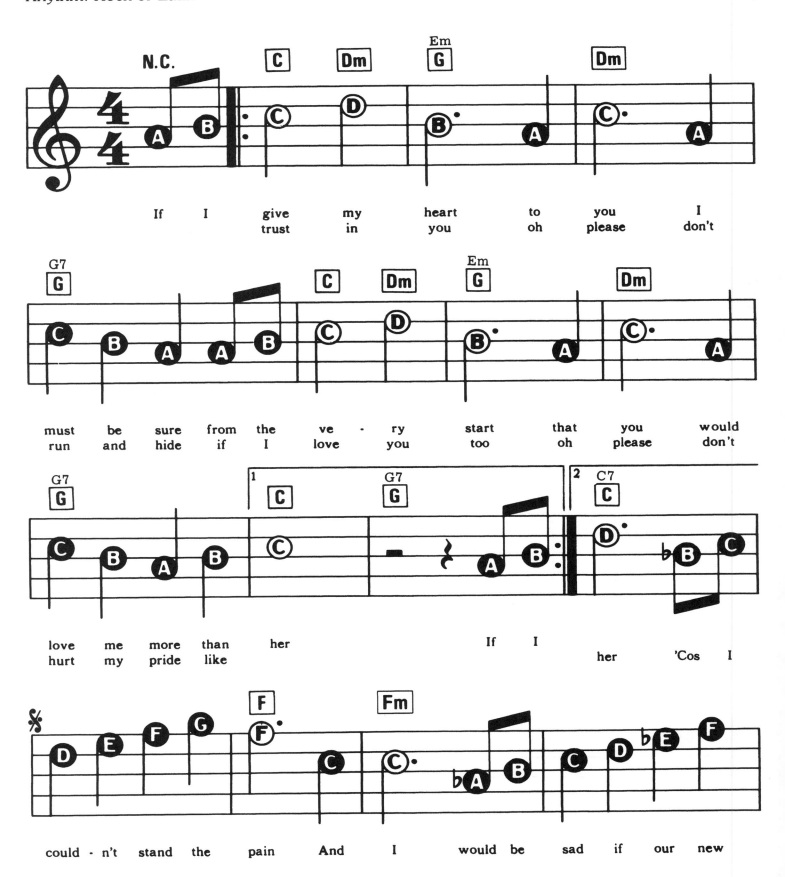

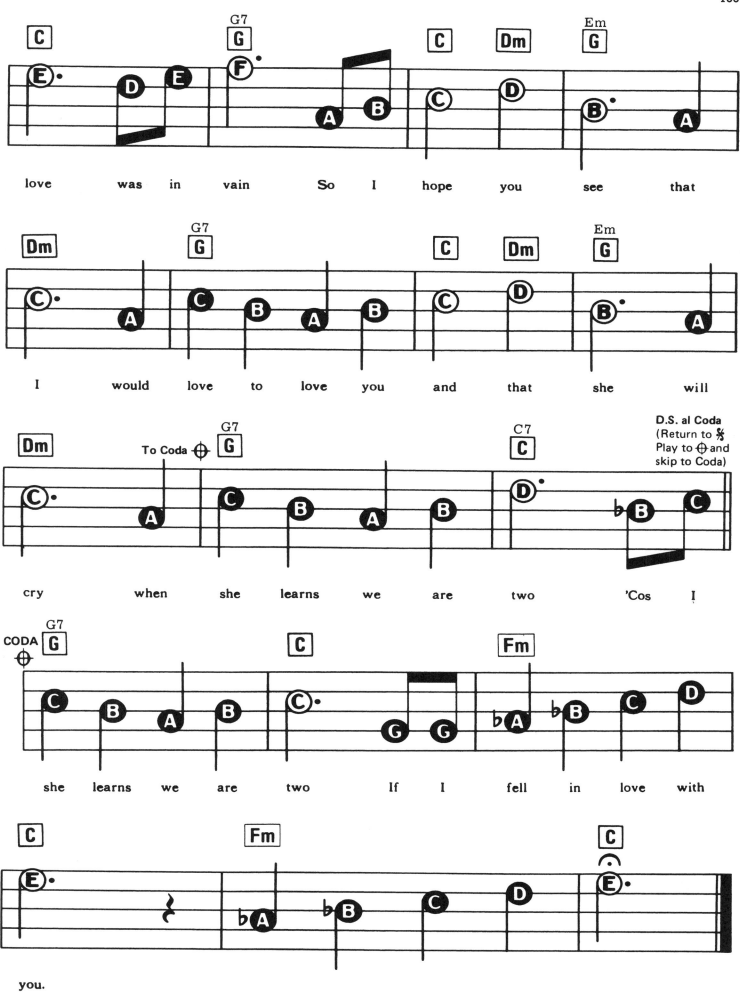

If I Needed Someone

Registration 8
Rhythm: 8 Beat

Words and Music by
George Harrison

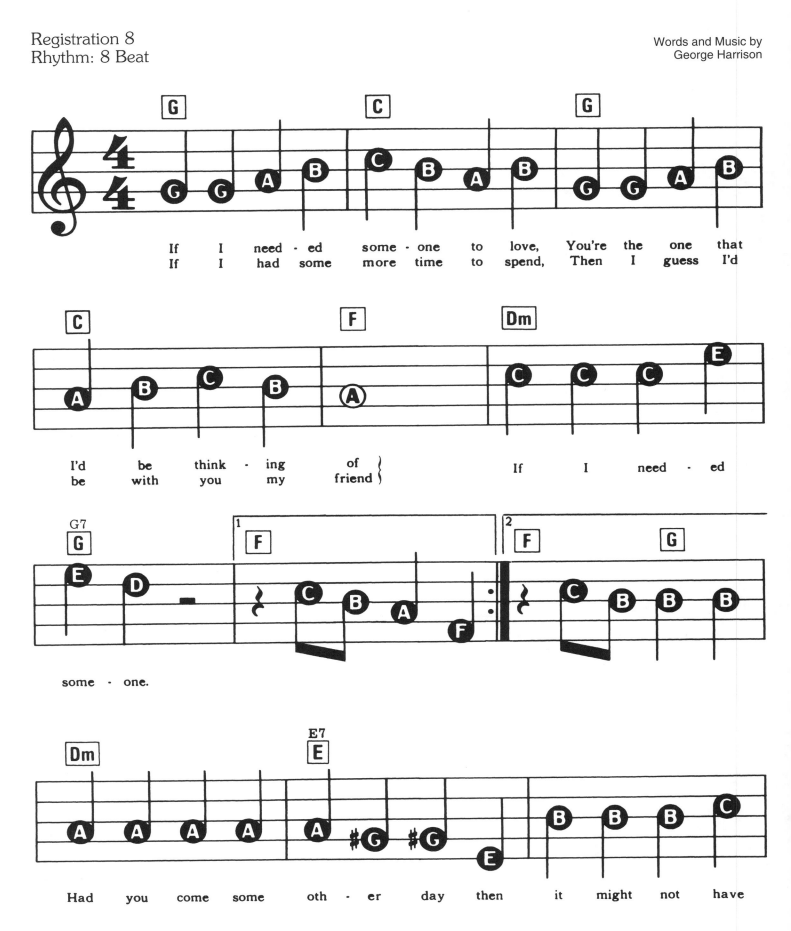

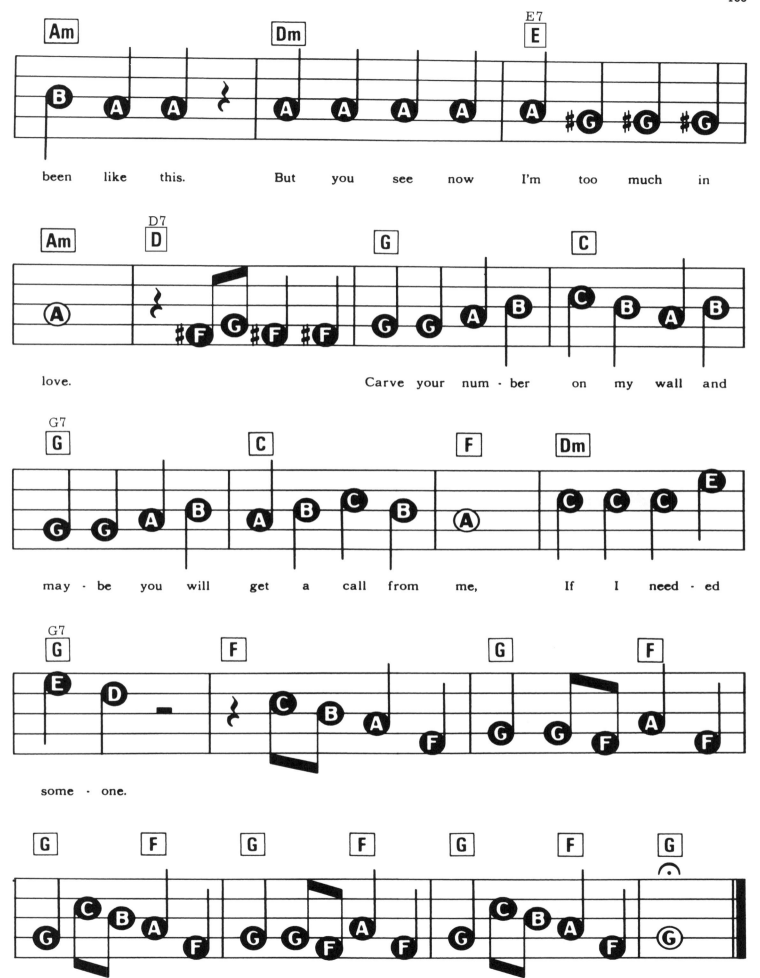

In My Life

Registration 2
Rhythm: Rock or Jazz Rock

Words and Music by John Lennon
and Paul McCartney

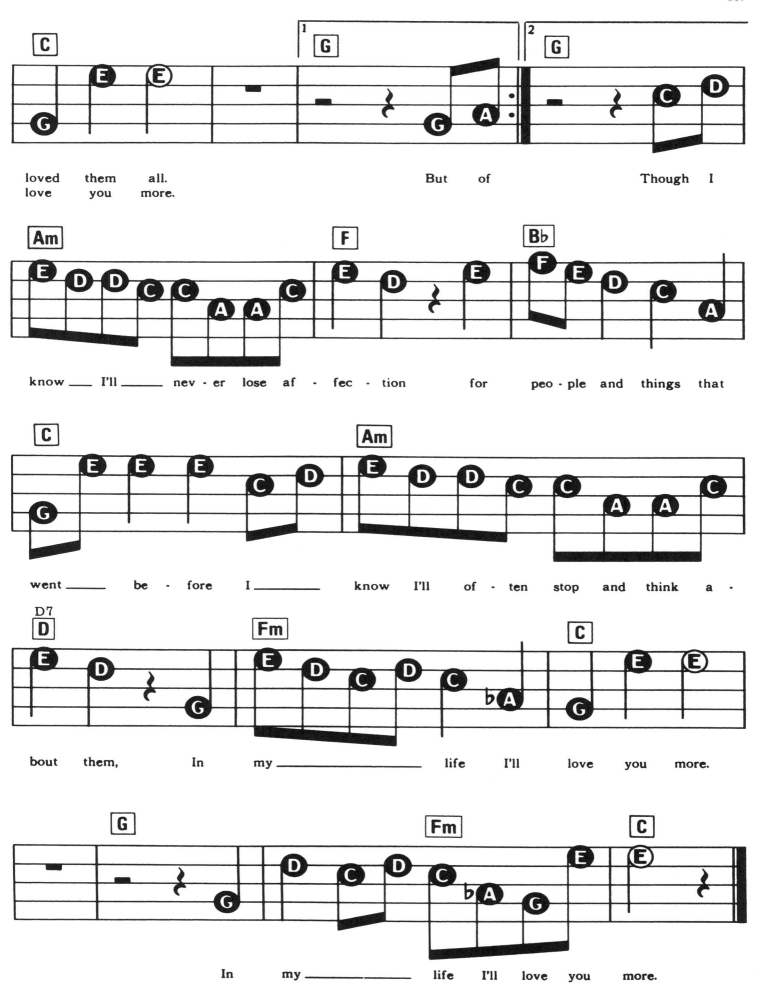

loved them all. But of Though I
love you all more.

know __ I'll __ nev-er lose af-fec-tion for peo-ple and things that

went __ be-fore I __ know I'll of-ten stop and think a-

bout them, In my __ life I'll love you more.

In my __ life I'll love you more.

108

Julia

Registration 9
Rhythm: Rock

Words and Music by John Lennon
and Paul McCartney

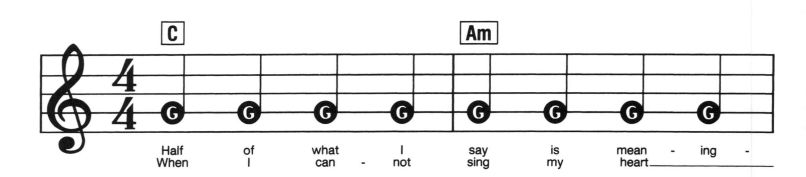

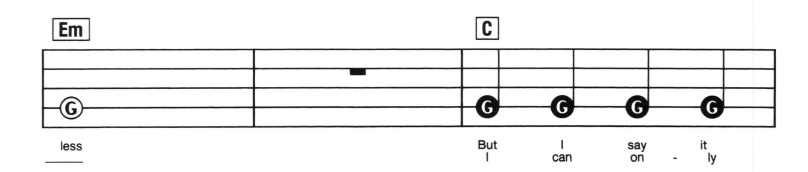

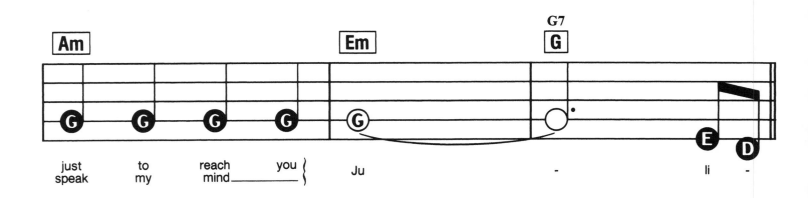

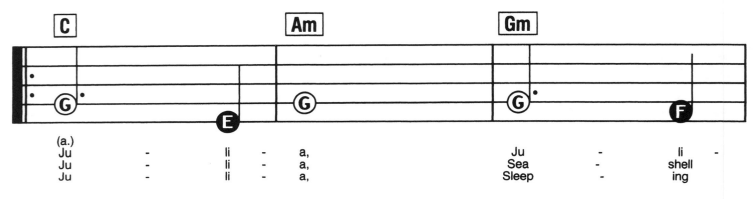

109

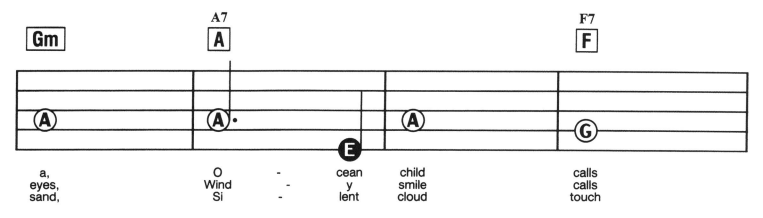

a, O - cean child calls
eyes, Wind - y smile calls
sand, Si - lent cloud touch

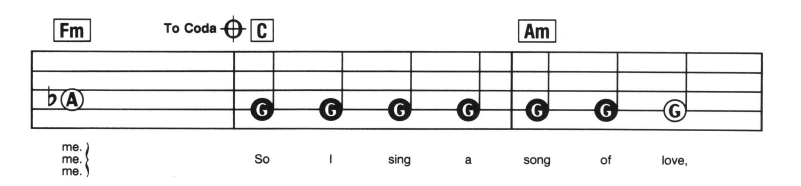

me.
me. So I sing a song of love,
me.

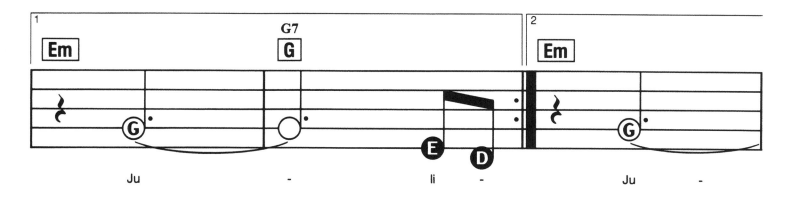

Ju - li - Ju -

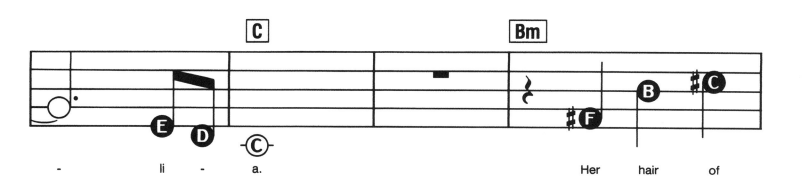

- li - a. Her hair of

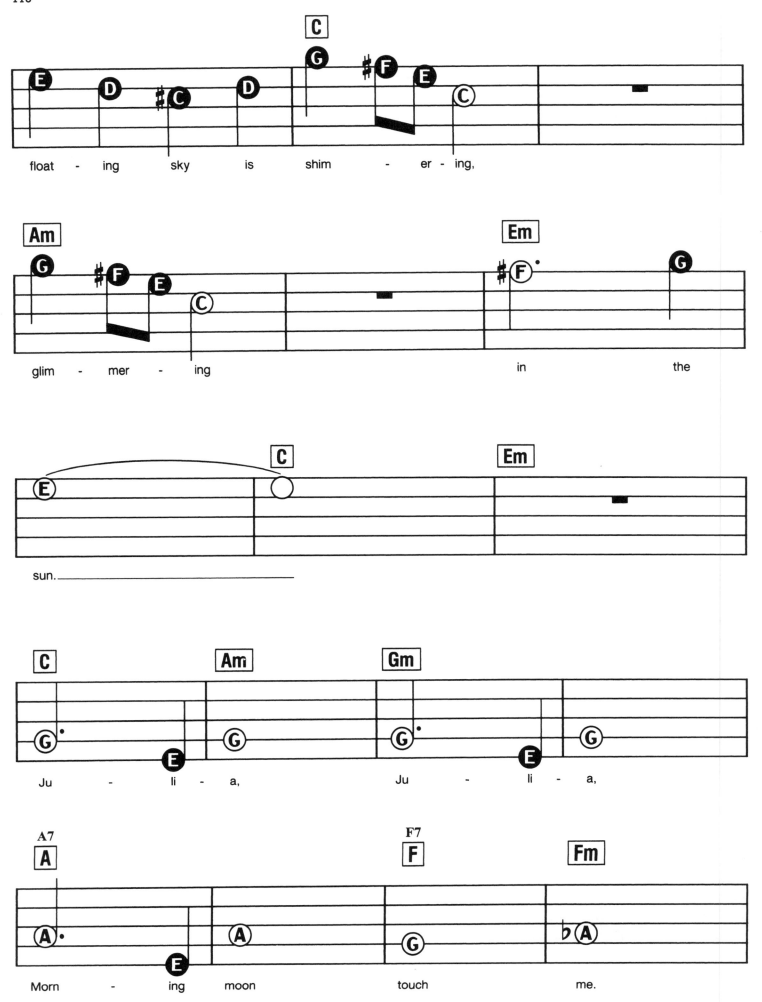

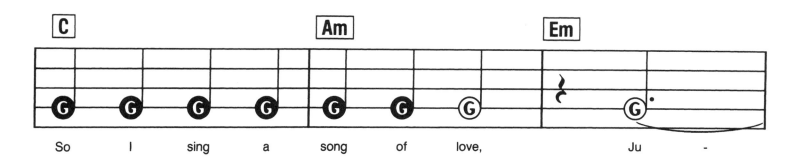

So I sing a song of love, Ju -

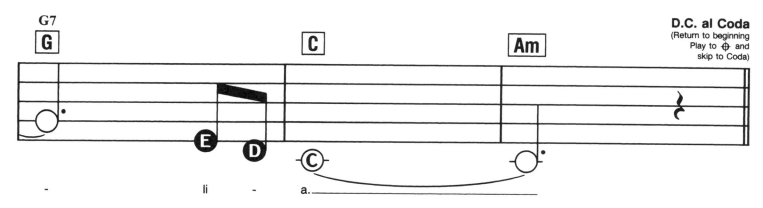

D.C. al Coda
(Return to beginning
Play to ⊕ and
skip to Coda)

- li - a.

CODA

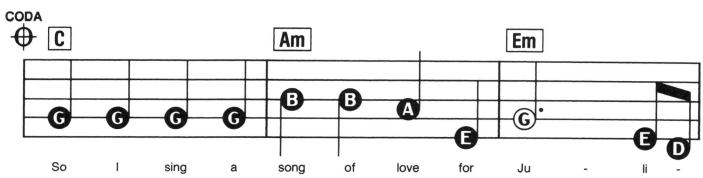

So I sing a song of love for Ju - li -

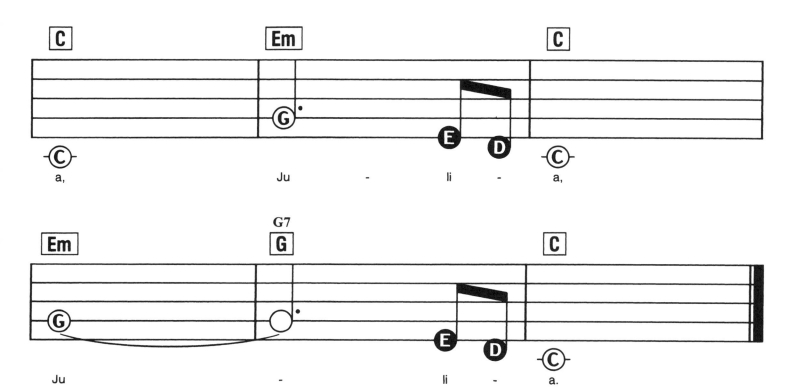

a, Ju - li - a,

Ju - li - a.

Lady Madonna

Registration 4
Rhythm: Rock

Words and Music by John Lennon
and Paul McCartney

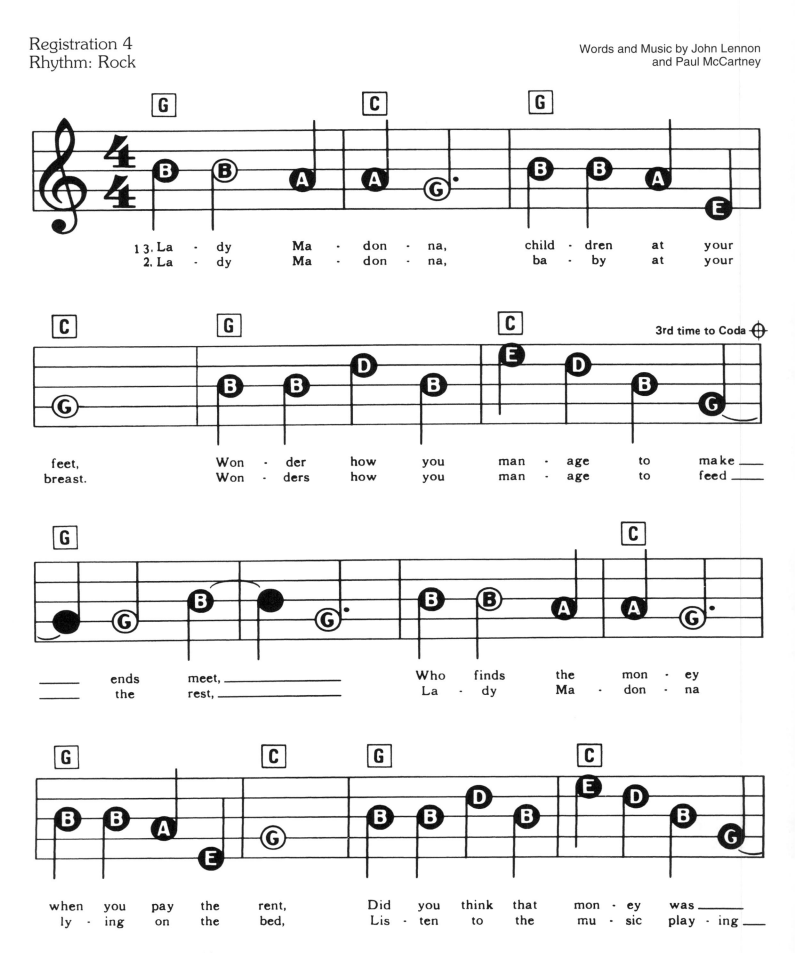

Let It Be

Registration 3
Rhythm: Rock

Words and Music by John Lennon
and Paul McCartney

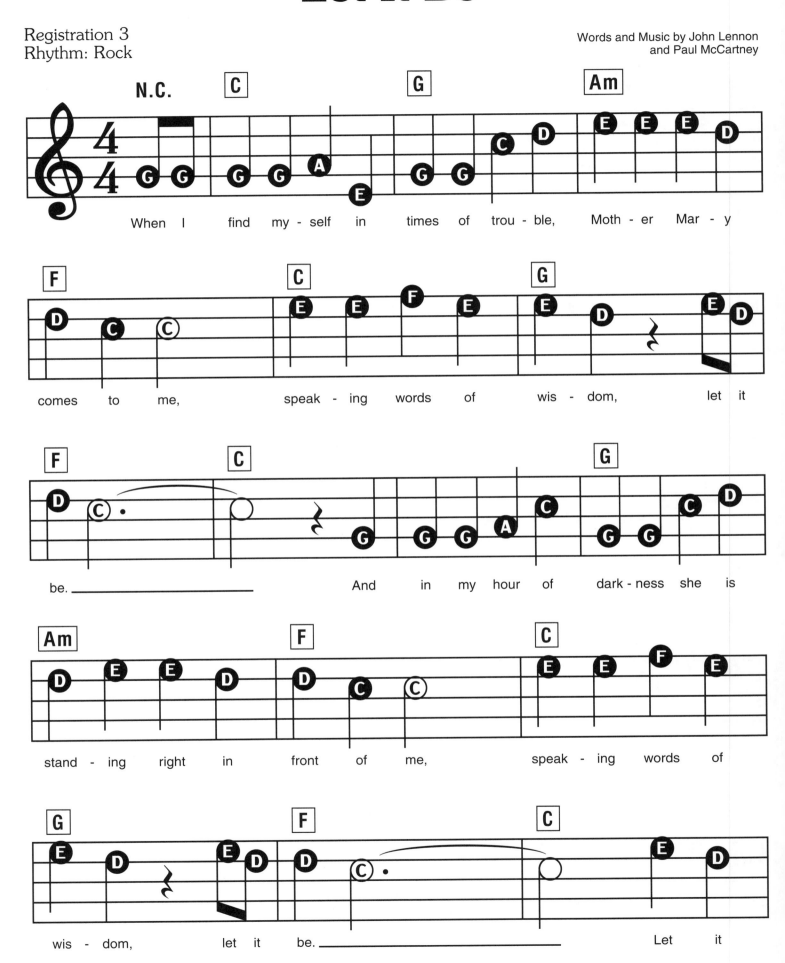

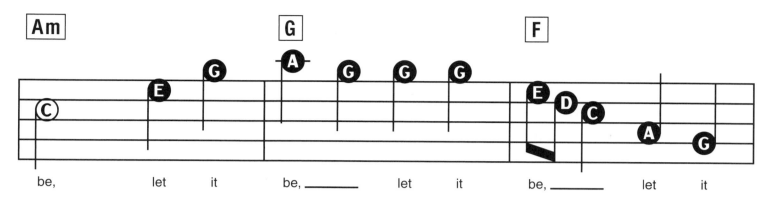

be, let it be, _____ let it be, _____ let it

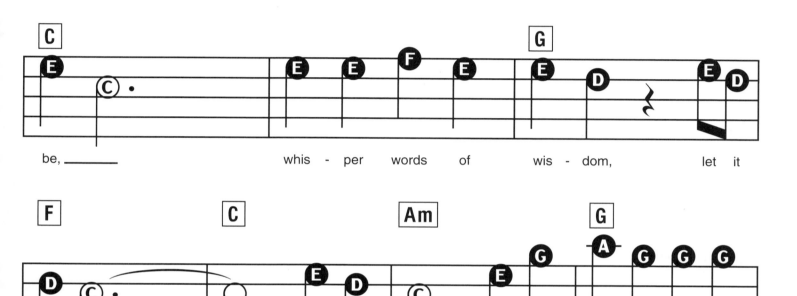

be, _____ whis - per words of wis - dom, let it

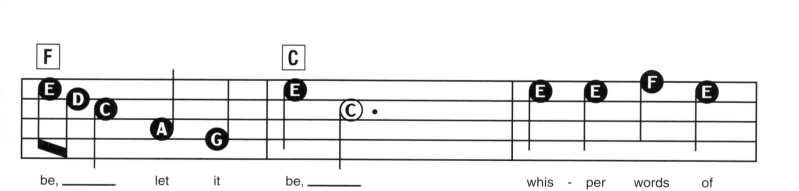

be. _____ Let it be, let it be, _____ let it

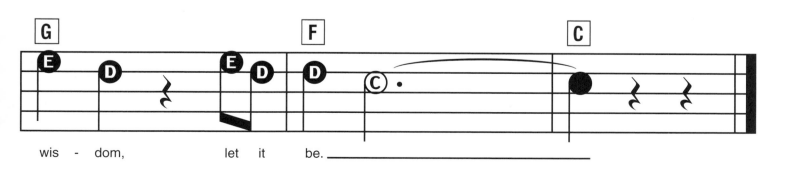

be, _____ let it be, _____ whis - per words of

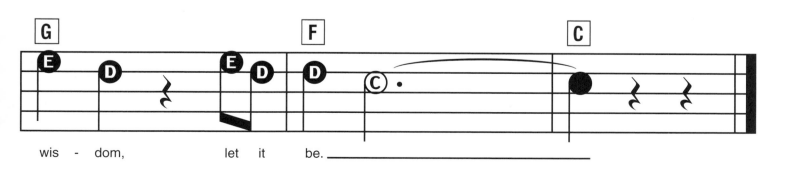

wis - dom, let it be. _____

The Long and Winding Road

Registration 1
Rhythm: Ballad

Words and Music by John Lennon
and Paul McCartney

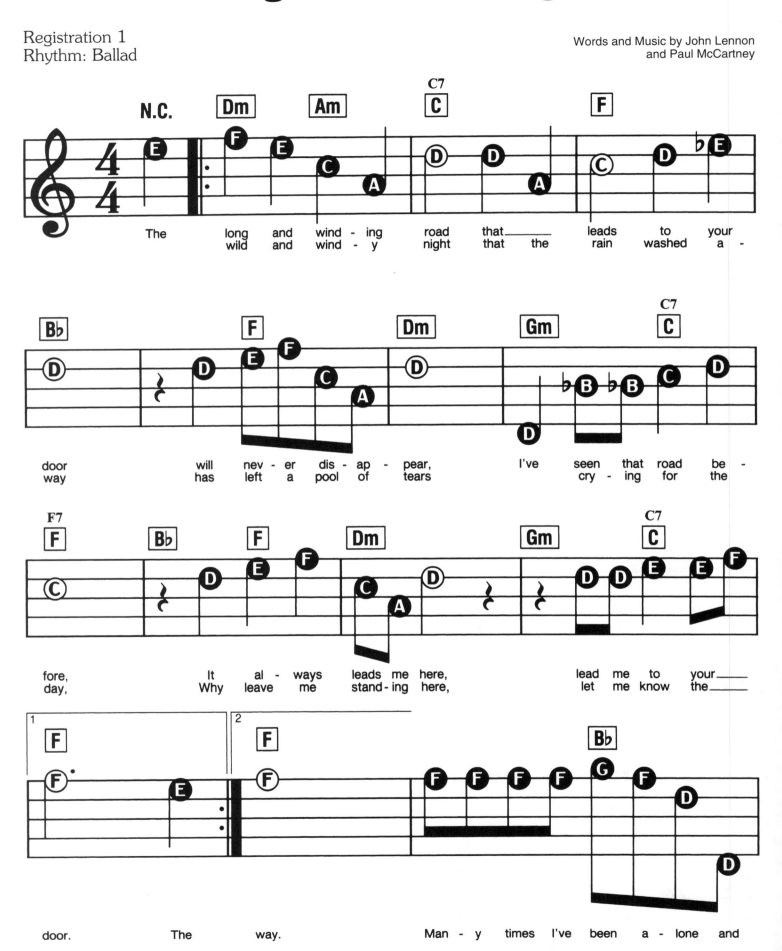

117

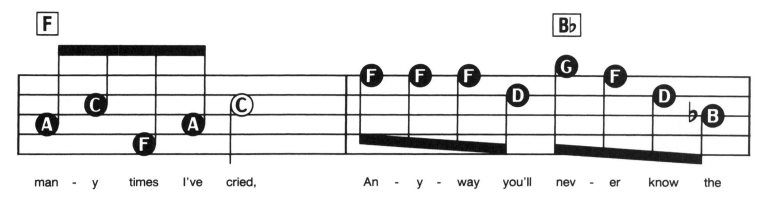

man - y times I've cried, An - y - way you'll nev - er know the

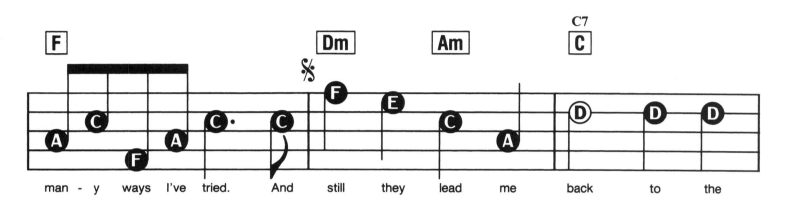

man - y ways I've tried. And still they lead me back to the

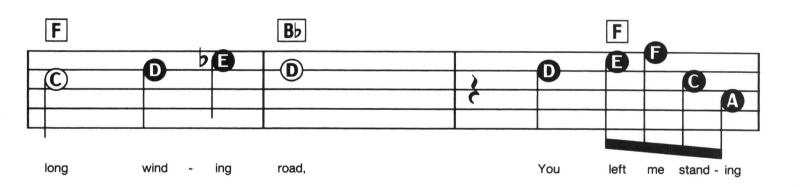

long wind - ing road, You left me stand - ing

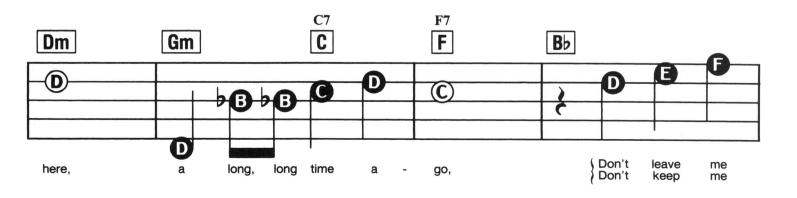

here, a long, long time a - go, { Don't leave me / Don't keep me } me

118

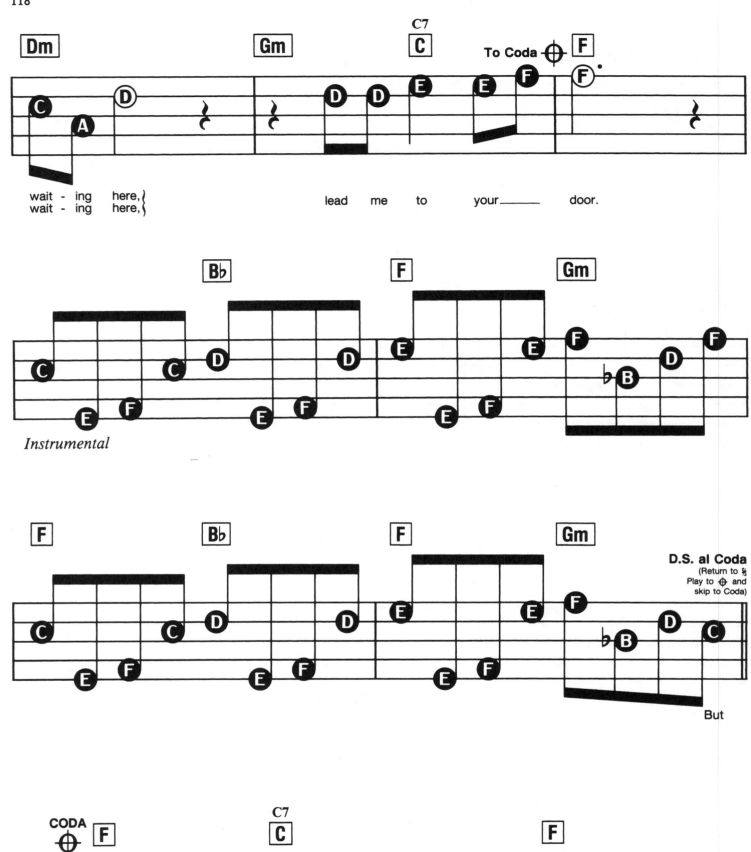

Instrumental

wait - ing here,
wait - ing here,   lead me to your ____ door.

But

door.   Yeah, yeah, yeah, yeah.

Martha My Dear

Registration 8
Rhythm: Swing or Shuffle

Words and Music by John Lennon
and Paul McCartney

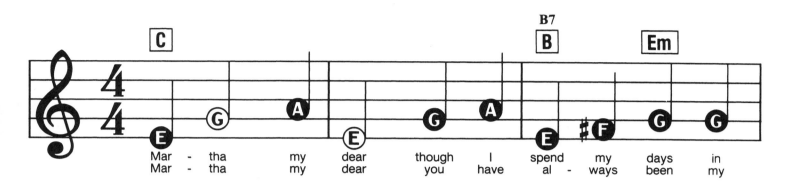

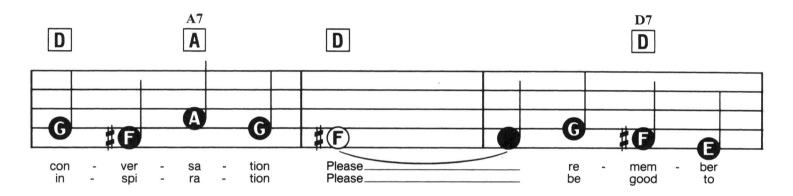

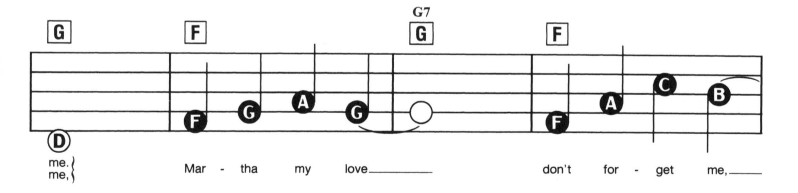

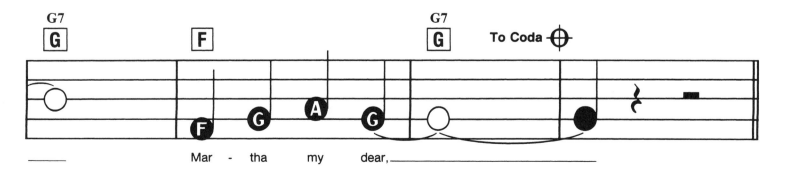

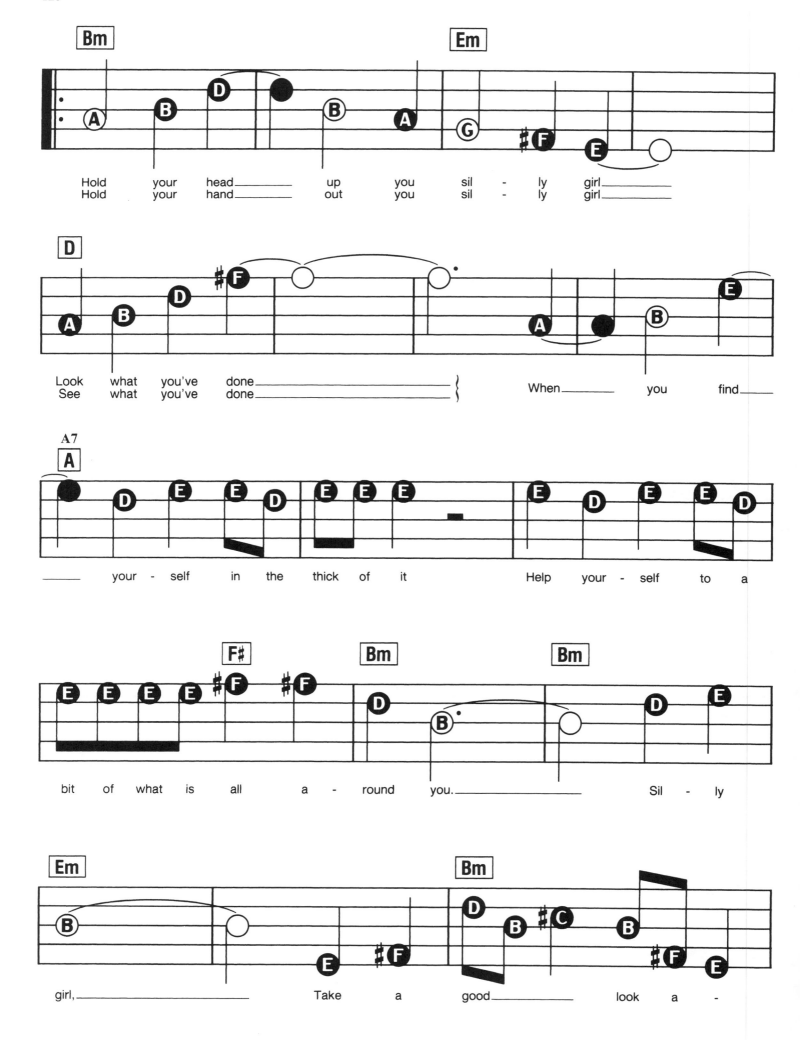

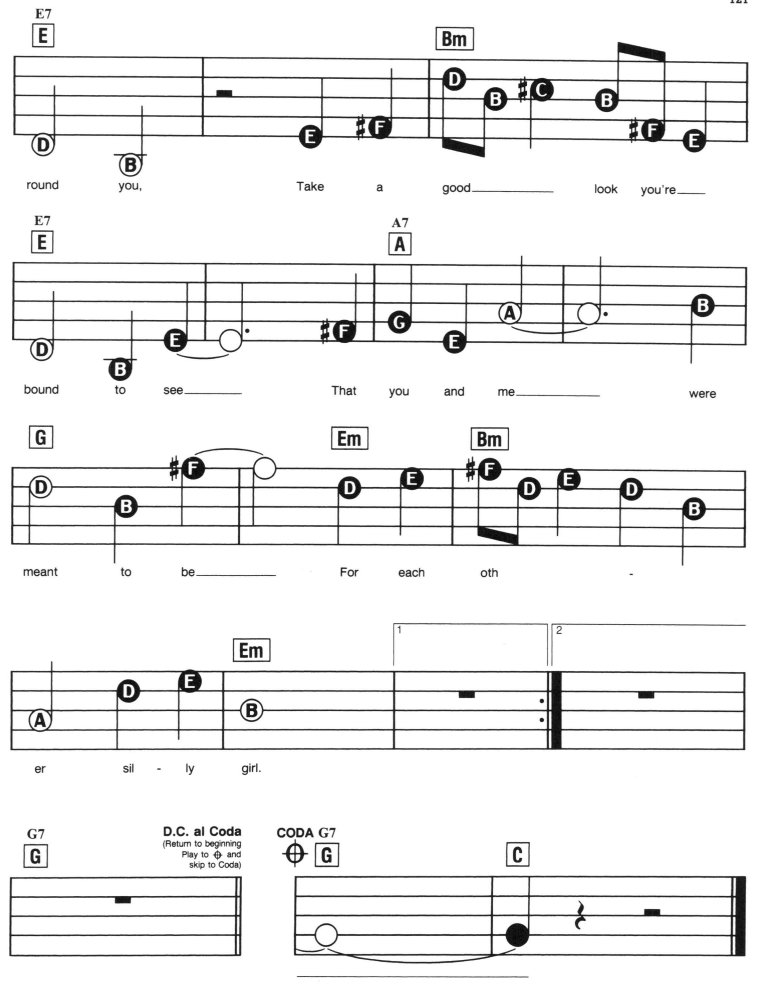

Love Me Do

Registration 8
Rhythm: Country Swing

Words and Music by John Lennon
and Paul McCartney

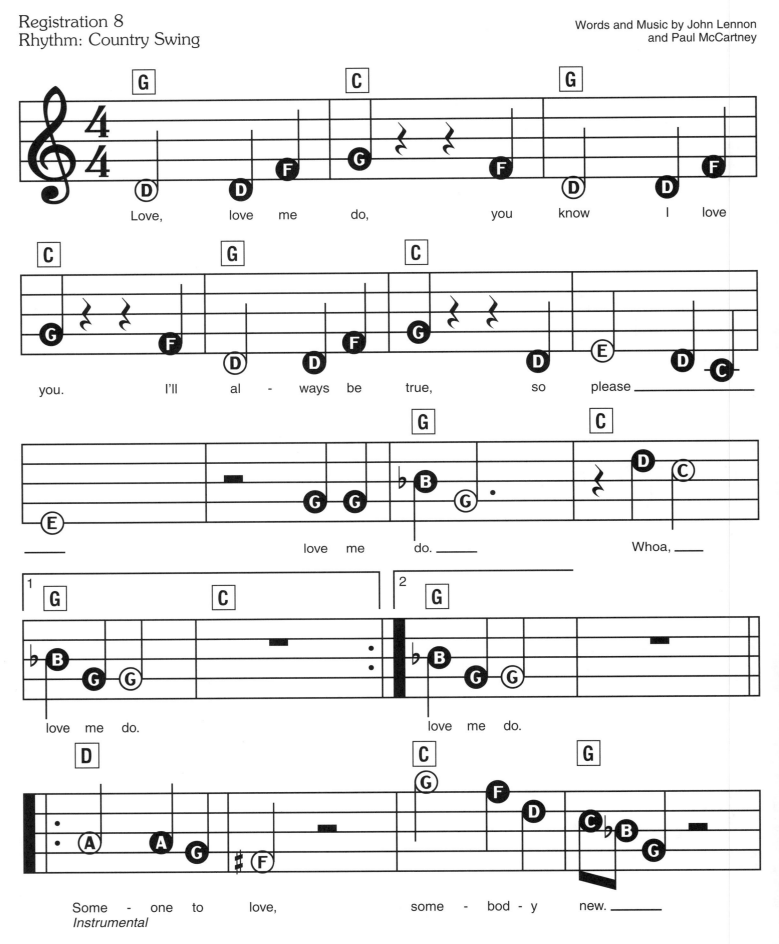

123

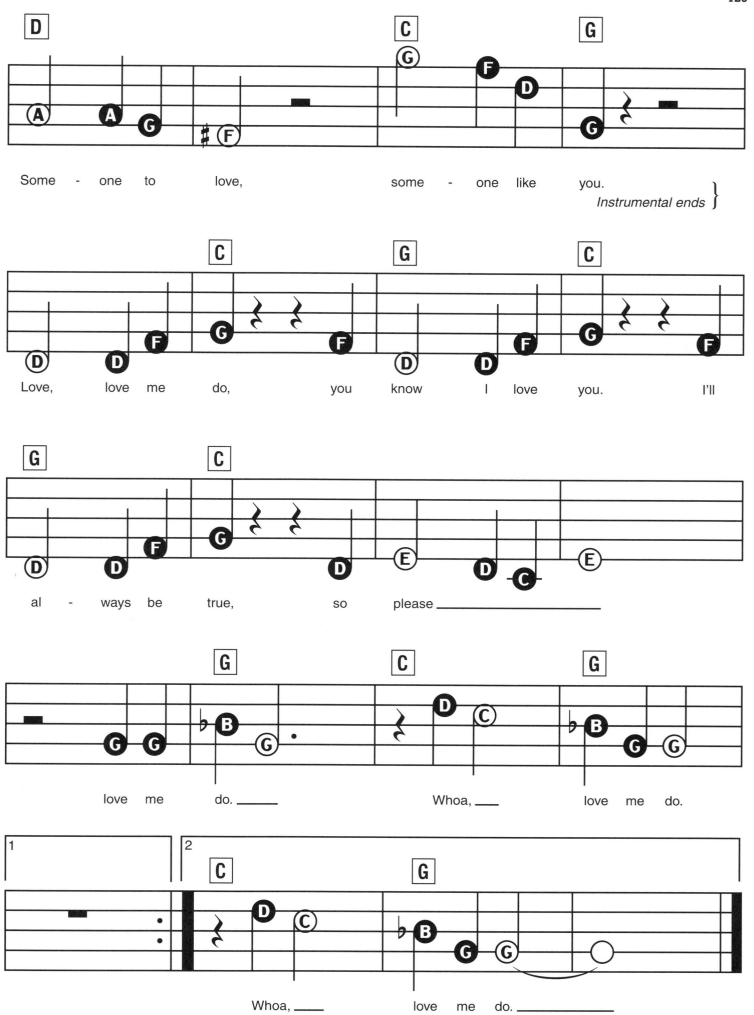

Lucy in the Sky with Diamonds

Registration 8
Rhythm: Waltz

Words and Music by John Lennon
and Paul McCartney

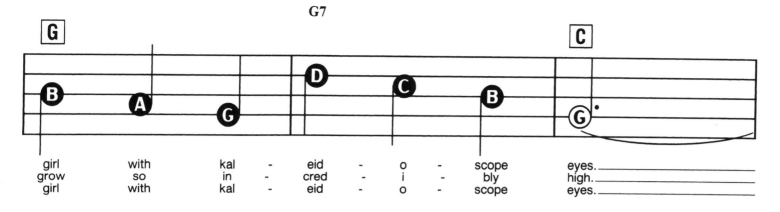

girl   with   kal - eid - o - scope   eyes. _____
grow   so   in - cred - i - bly   high. _____
girl   with   kal - eid - o - scope   eyes. _____

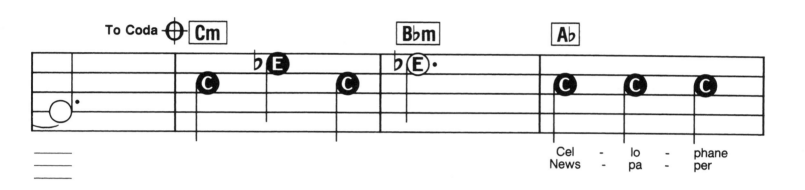

Cel - lo - phane
News - pa - per

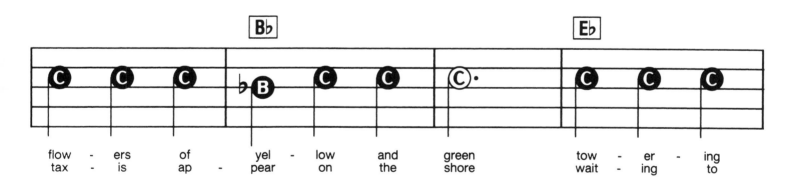

flow - ers   of   yel - low   and   green   tow - er - ing
tax - is   ap - pear   on   the   shore   wait - ing   to

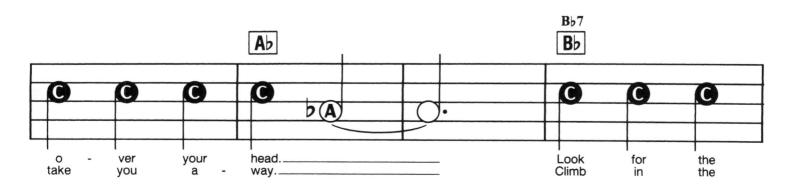

o - ver   your   head. _____   Look   for   the
take   you   a - way. _____   Climb   in   the

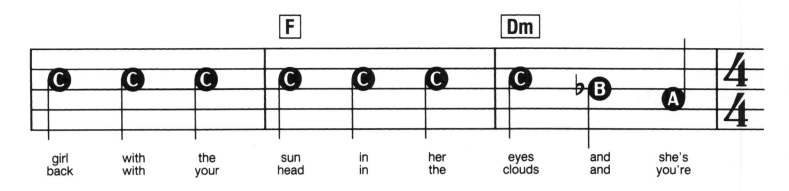

girl with the sun in her eyes and she's
back with your head in the clouds and you're

Rhythm: Rock

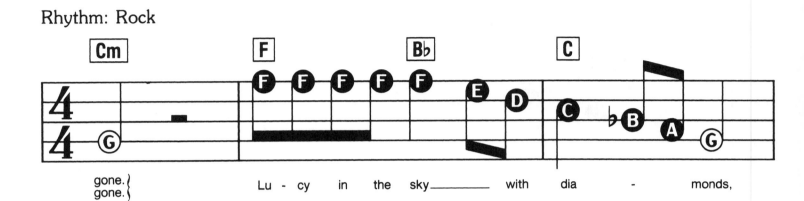

gone.
gone.
Lu - cy in the sky_____ with dia - monds,

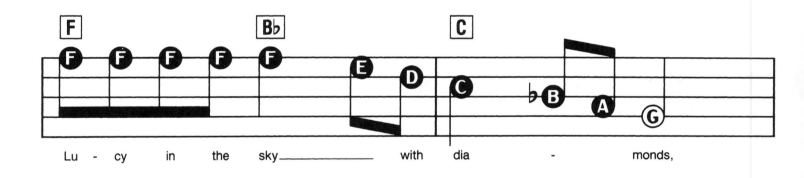

Lu - cy in the sky_____ with dia - monds,

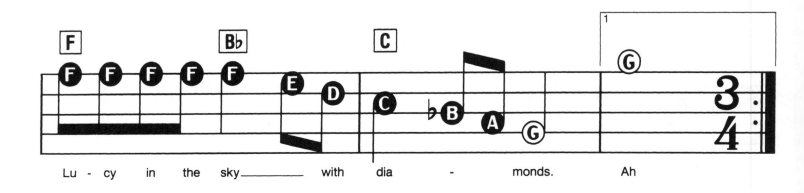

Lu - cy in the sky_____ with dia - monds. Ah

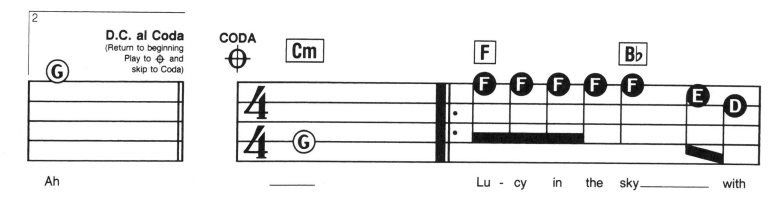

Ah _____ Lu - cy in the sky _____ with

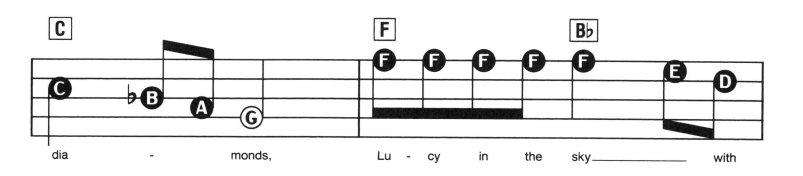

dia - monds, Lu - cy in the sky _____ with

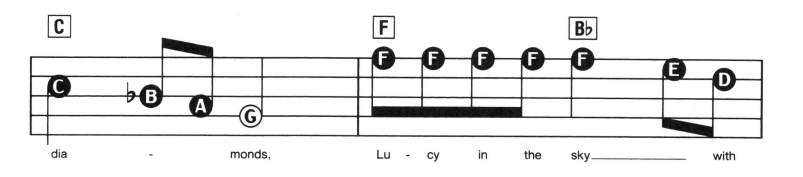

dia - monds, Lu - cy in the sky _____ with

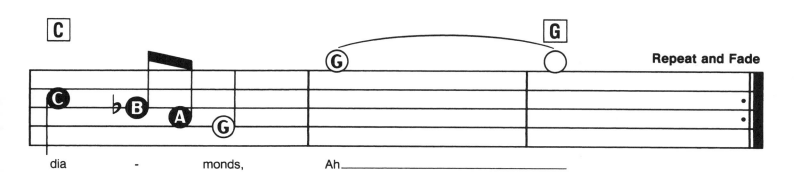

dia - monds, Ah _____

Magical Mystery Tour

Registration 2
Rhythm: Rock

Words and Music by John Lennon
and Paul McCartney

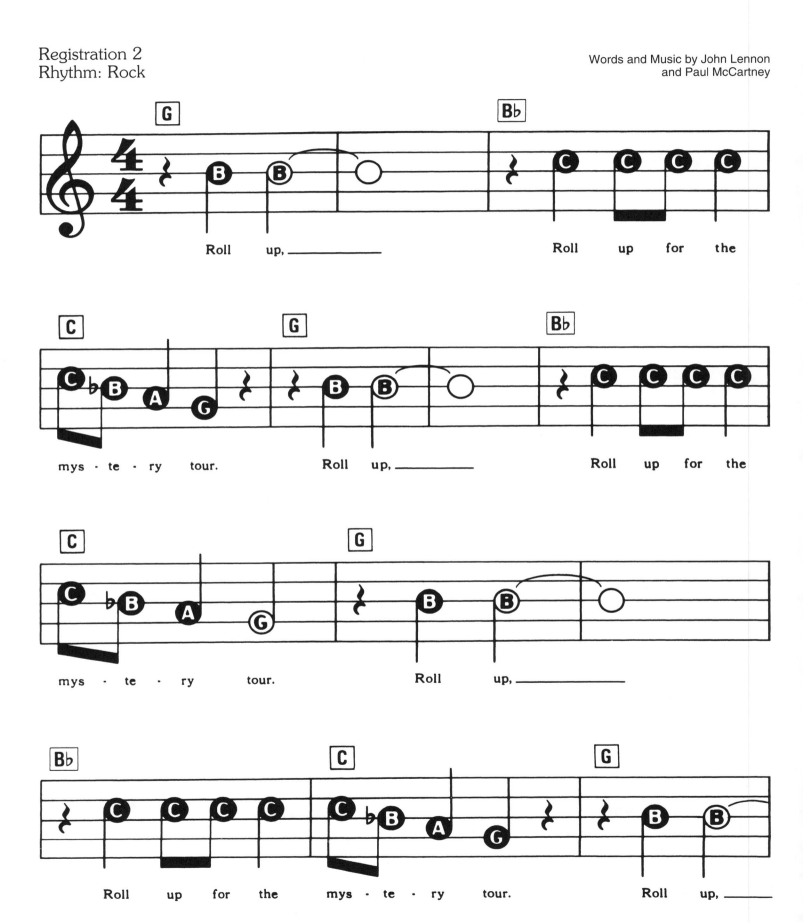

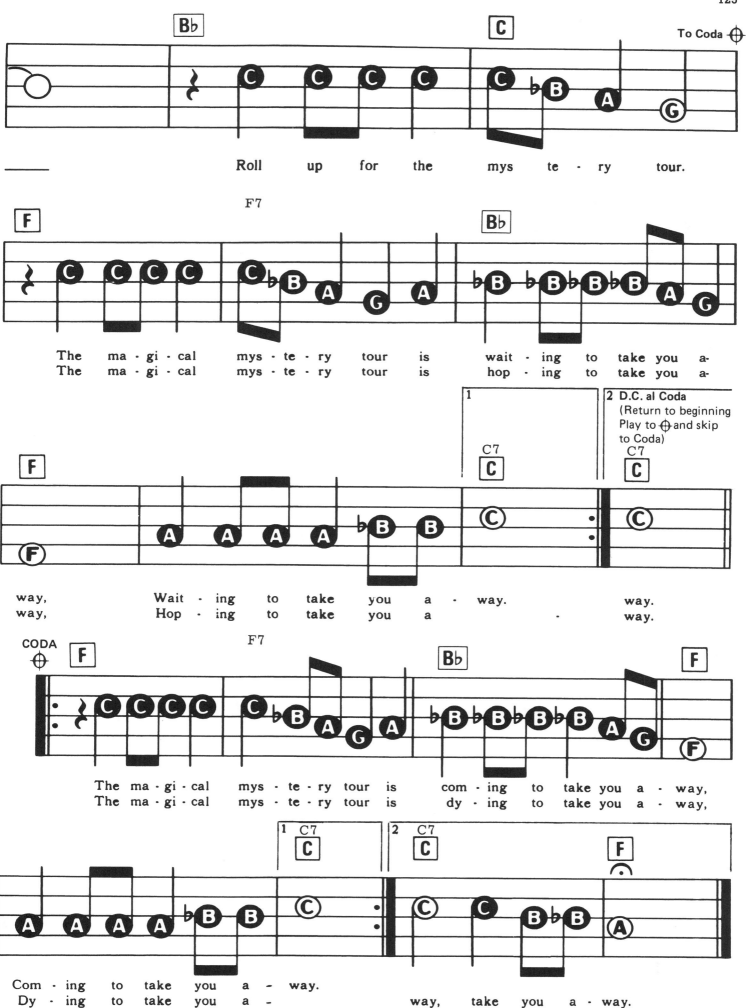

Michelle

Registration 1
Rhythm: Rock

Words and Music by John Lennon
and Paul McCartney

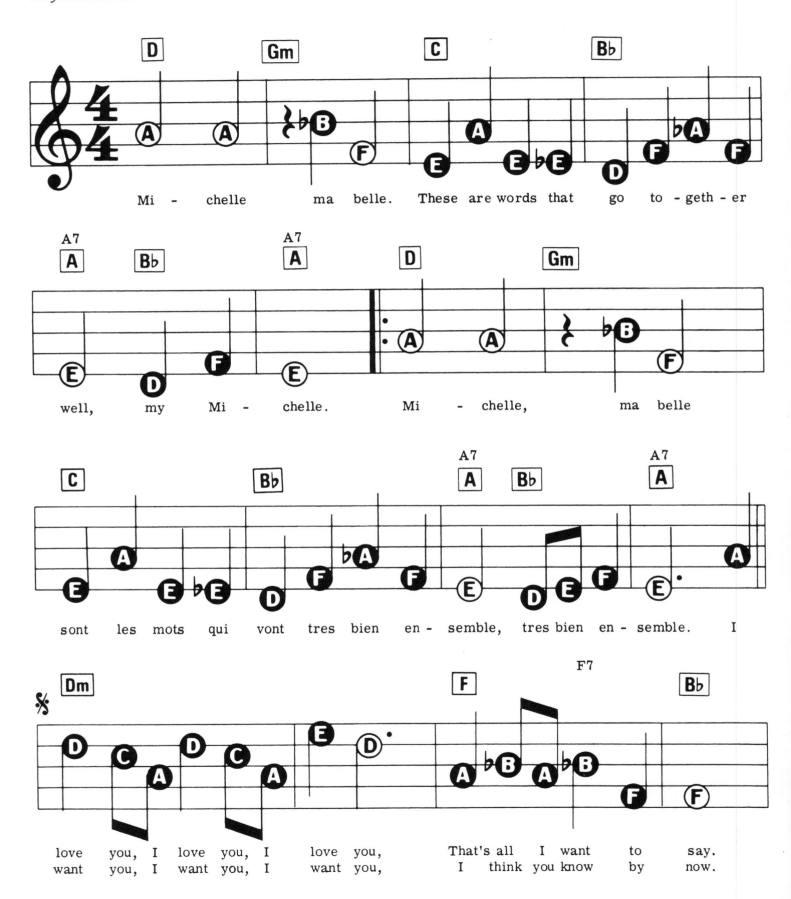

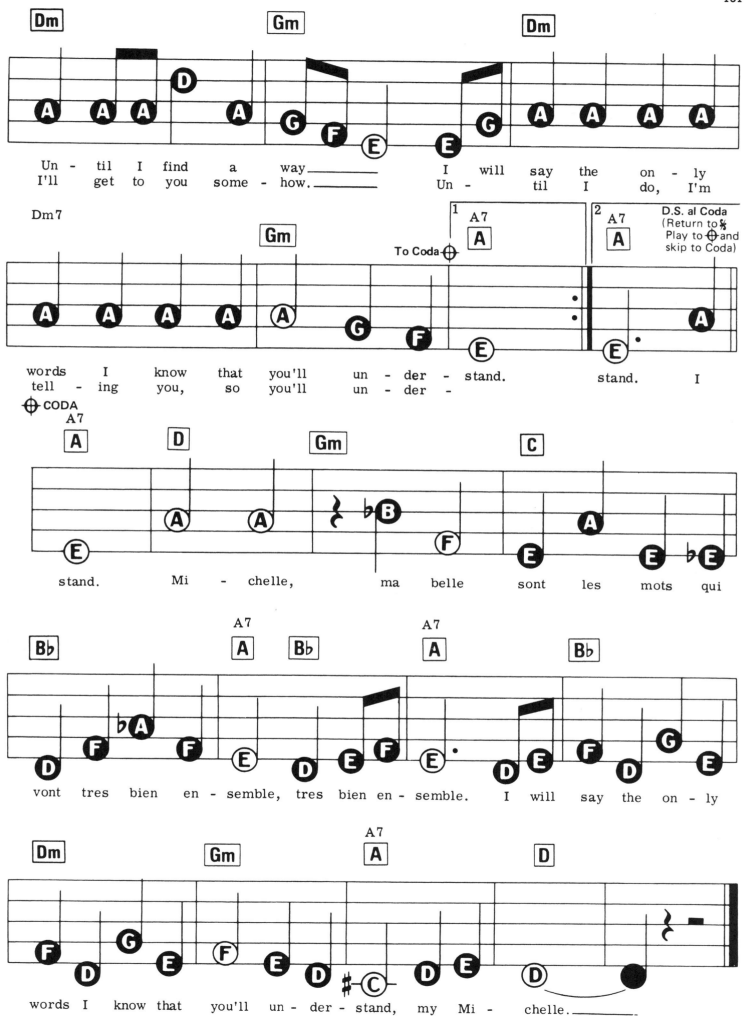

Mother Nature's Son

Registration 4
Rhythm: 8 Beat or Rock

Words and Music by John Lennon
and Paul McCartney

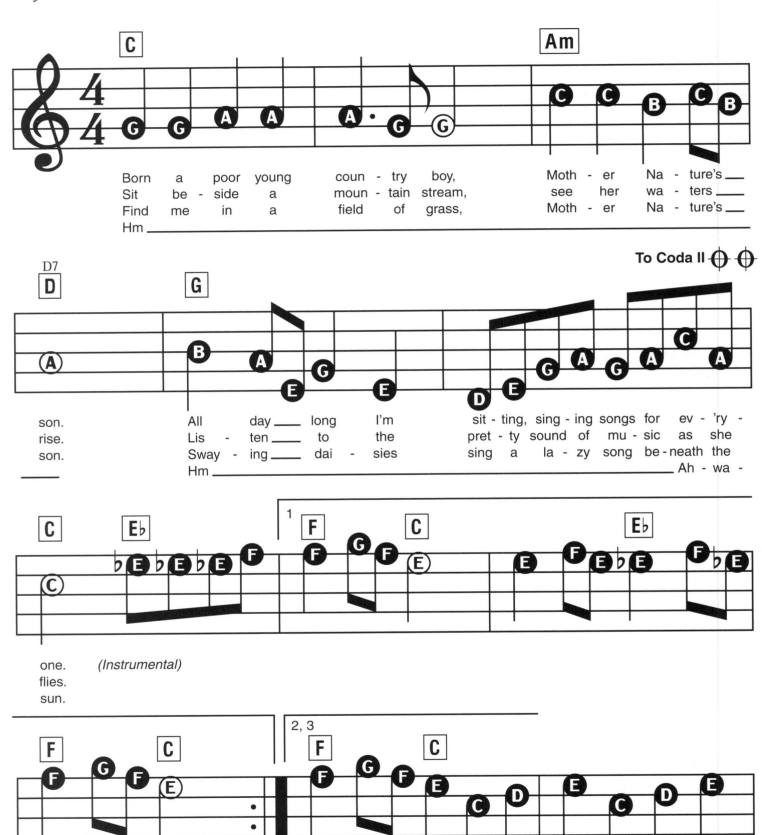

Born a poor young country boy, Moth-er Na-ture's ___
Sit be-side a moun-tain stream, see her wa-ters ___
Find me in a field of grass, Moth-er Na-ture's ___
Hm ___

To Coda II

son. All day ___ long I'm sit-ting, sing-ing songs for ev-'ry-
rise. Lis-ten ___ to the pret-ty sound of mu-sic as she
son. Sway-ing ___ dai-sies sing a la-zy song be-neath the
Hm ___ Ah - wa-

one. *(Instrumental)*
flies.
sun.

Du du du du du du

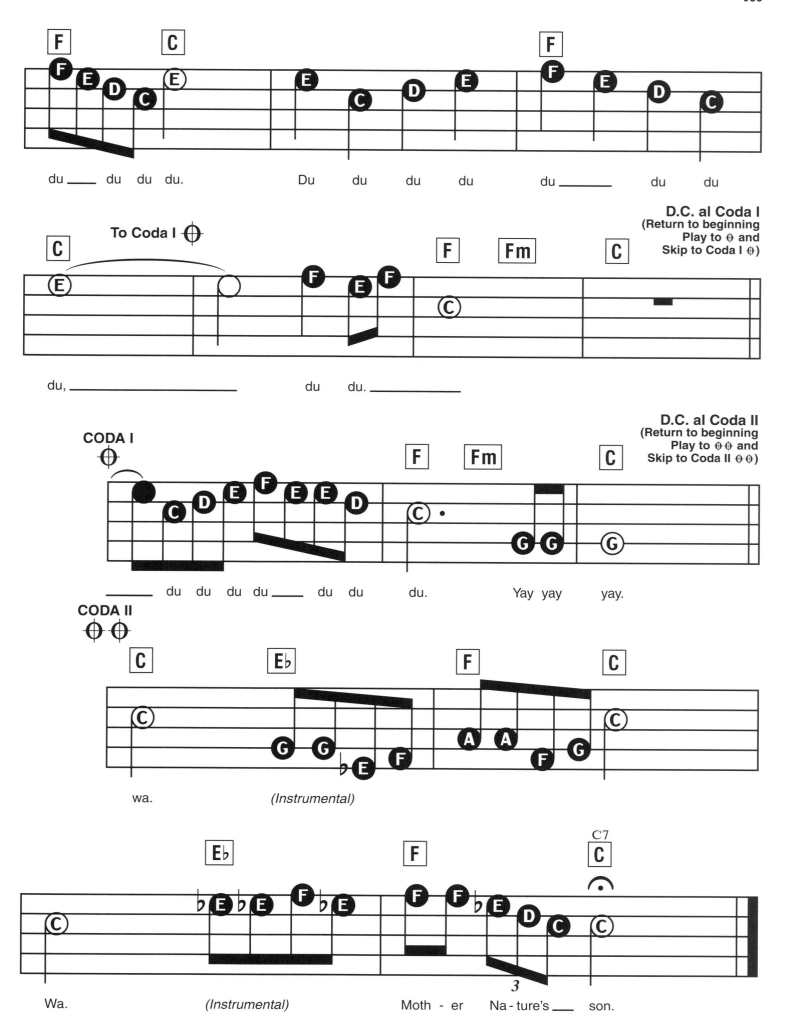

Norwegian Wood
(This Bird Has Flown)

Registration 8
Rhythm: Waltz

Words and Music by John Lennon
and Paul McCartney

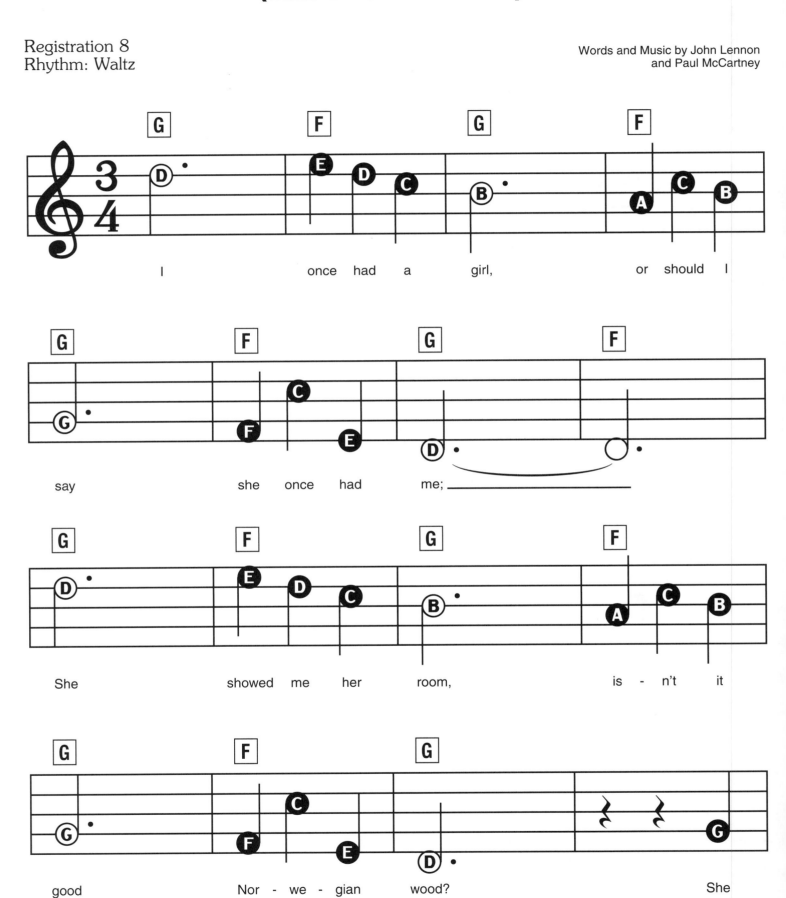

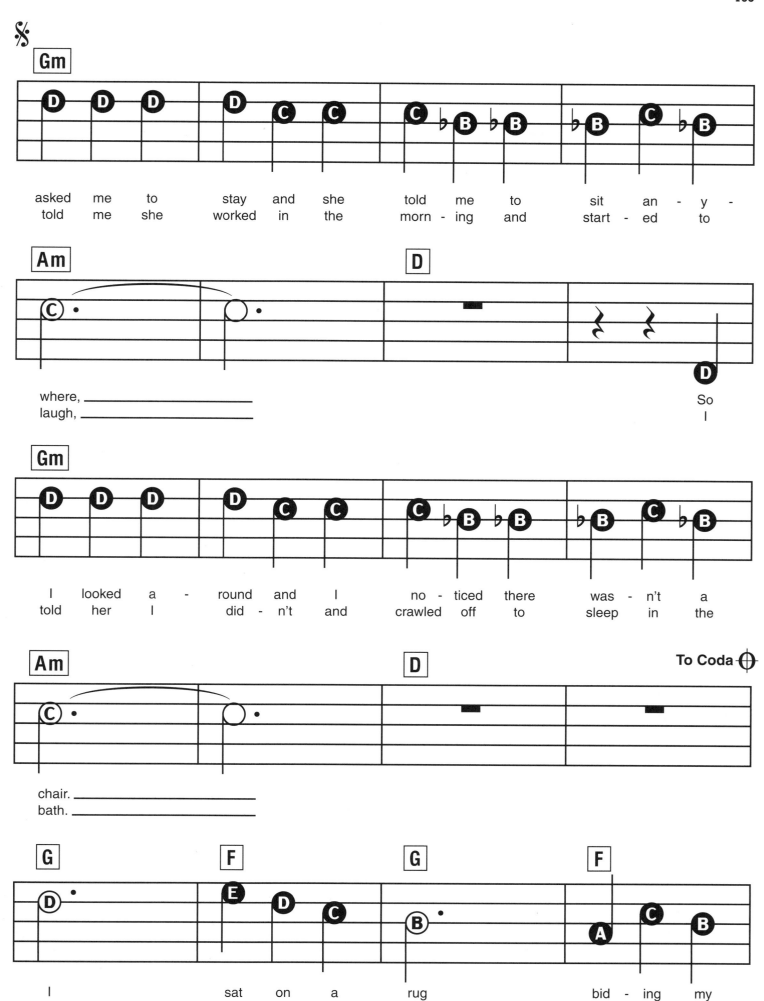

136

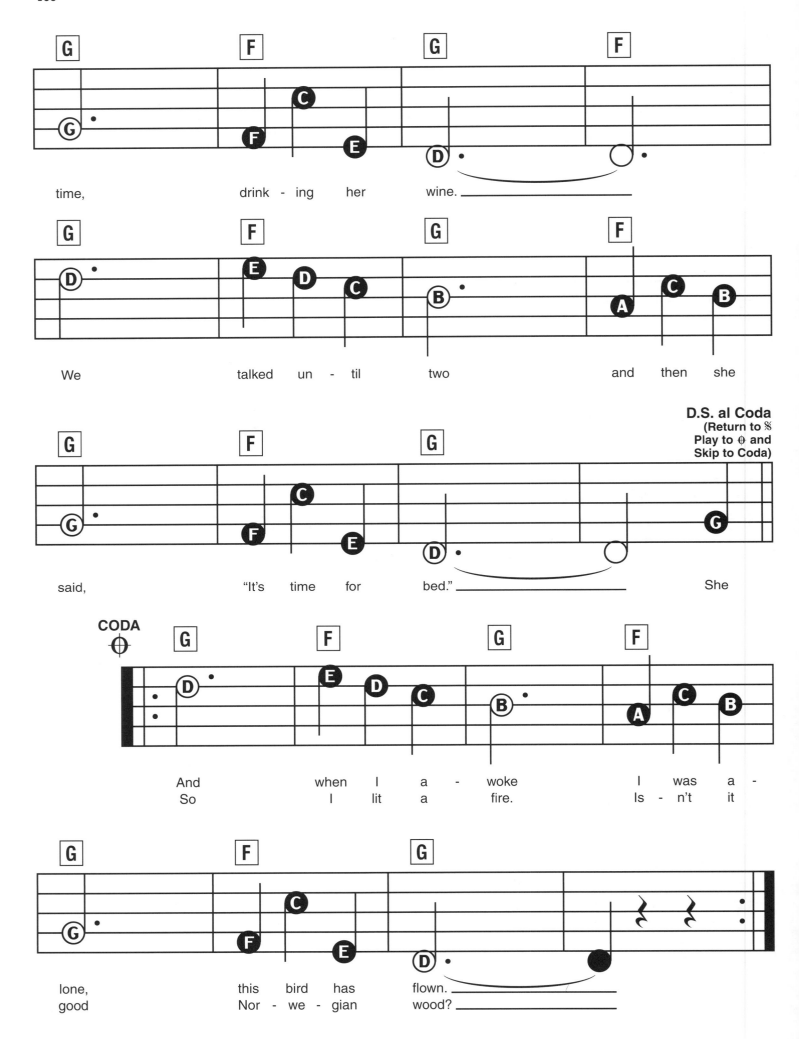

She Loves You

Registration 1
Rhythm: Rock

Words and Music by John Lennon
and Paul McCartney

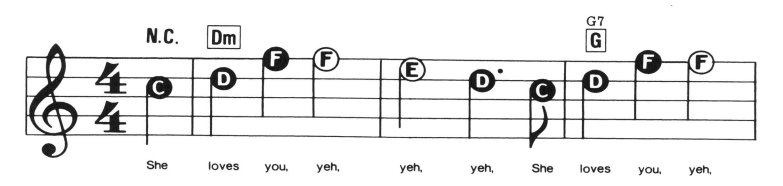

She loves you, yeh, yeh, yeh, She loves you, yeh,

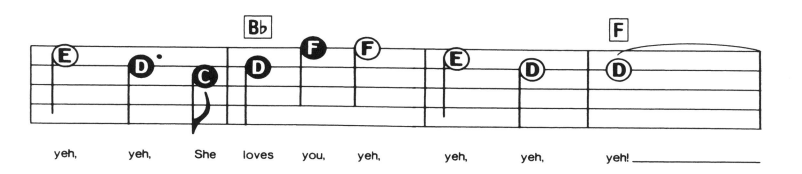

yeh, yeh, She loves you, yeh, yeh, yeh, yeh!

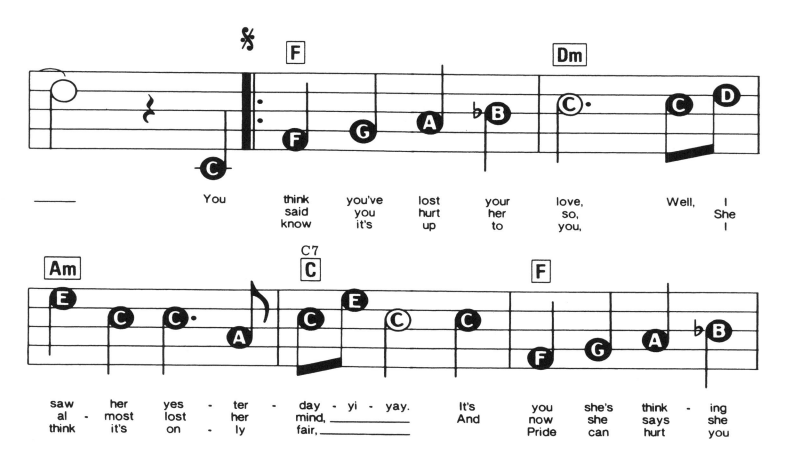

You think you've lost your love, Well, I
think said you it's hurt her so, She
know it's up to you, I

saw her yes - ter - day - yi - yay. It's you she's think - ing
al - most lost her mind, And you now she says she
think it's on - ly fair, Pride can hurt you

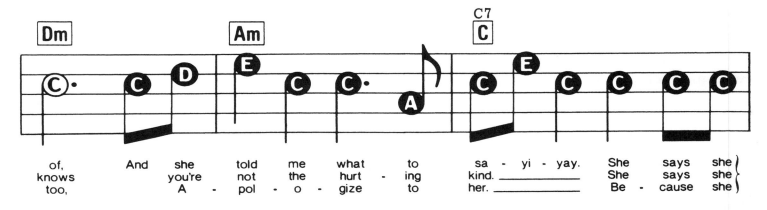

of, And she told me what to sa - yi - yay. She says she
knows you're not the hurt - ing kind. _____ She says she
too, A - pol - o - gize to her. _____ Be - cause she

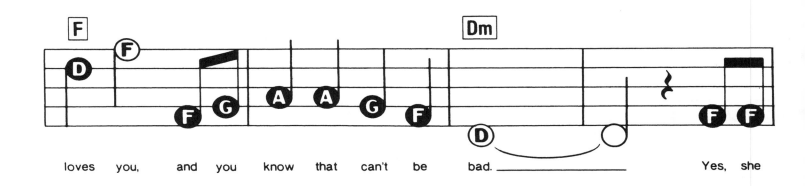

loves you, and you know that can't be bad. _____ Yes, she

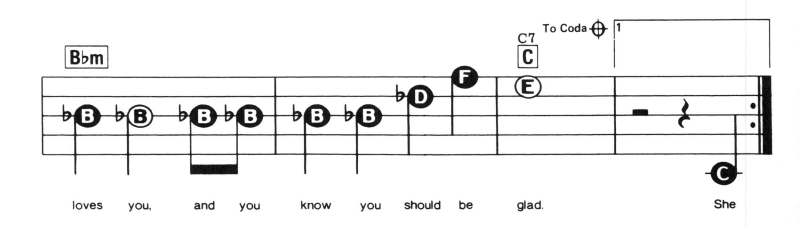

loves you, and you know you should be glad. She

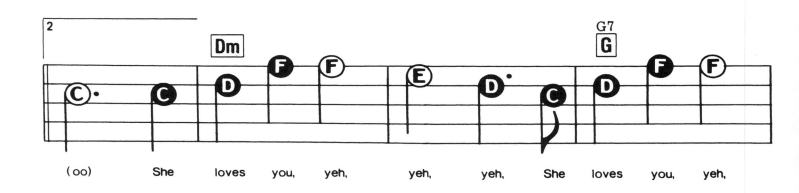

(oo) She loves you, yeh, yeh, yeh, She loves you, yeh,

139

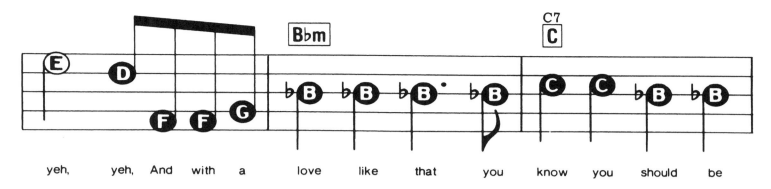

yeh, yeh, And with a love like that you know you should be

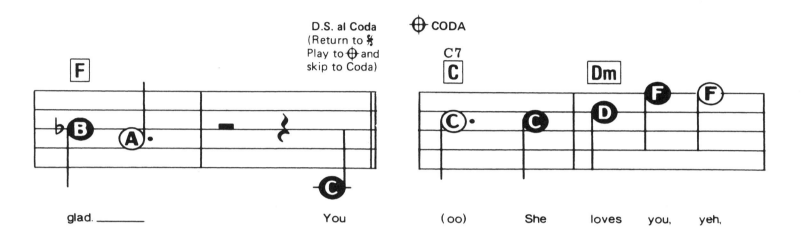

D.S. al Coda
(Return to 𝄋
Play to ⊕ and
skip to Coda)

⊕ CODA

glad. _____ You

(oo) She loves you, yeh,

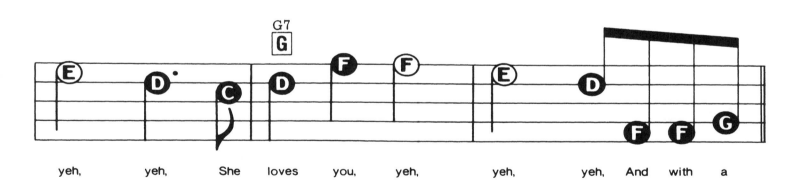

yeh, yeh, She loves you, yeh, yeh, yeh, And with a

Repeat and Fade

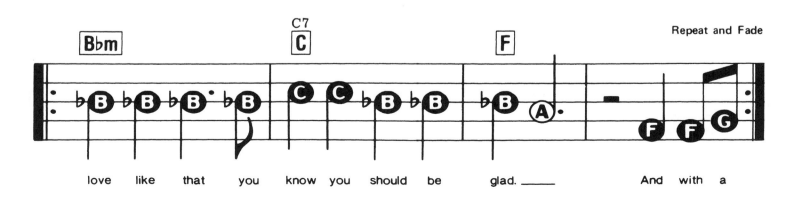

love like that you know you should be glad. _____ And with a

Nowhere Man

Registration 2
Rhythm: Rock

Words and Music by John Lennon
and Paul McCartney

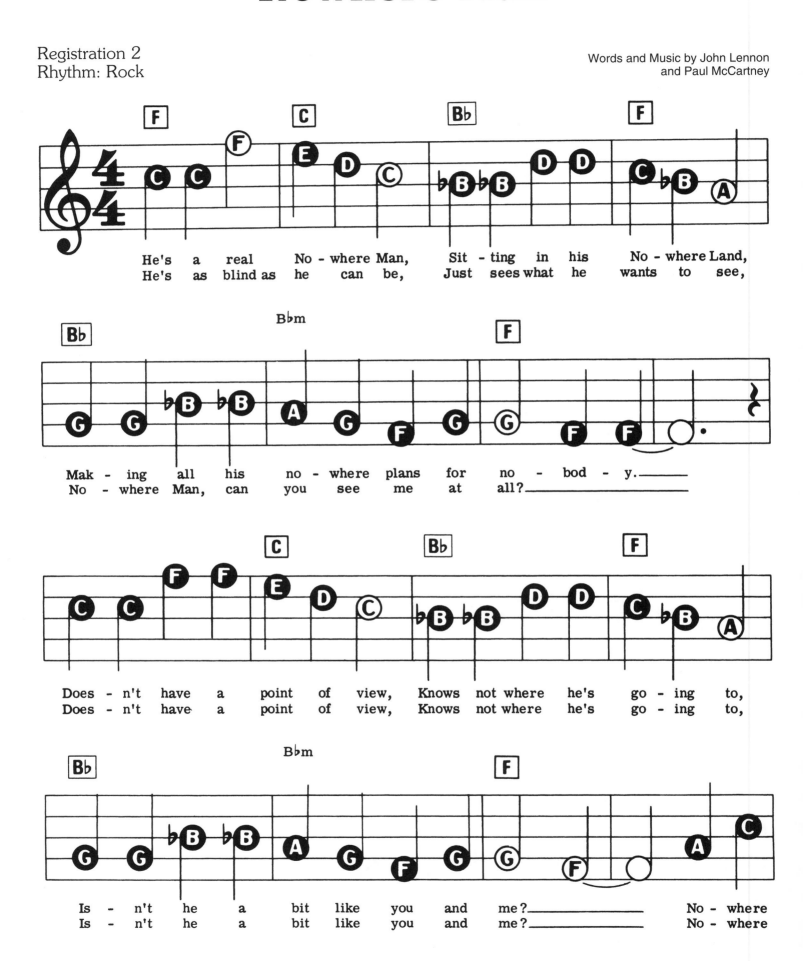

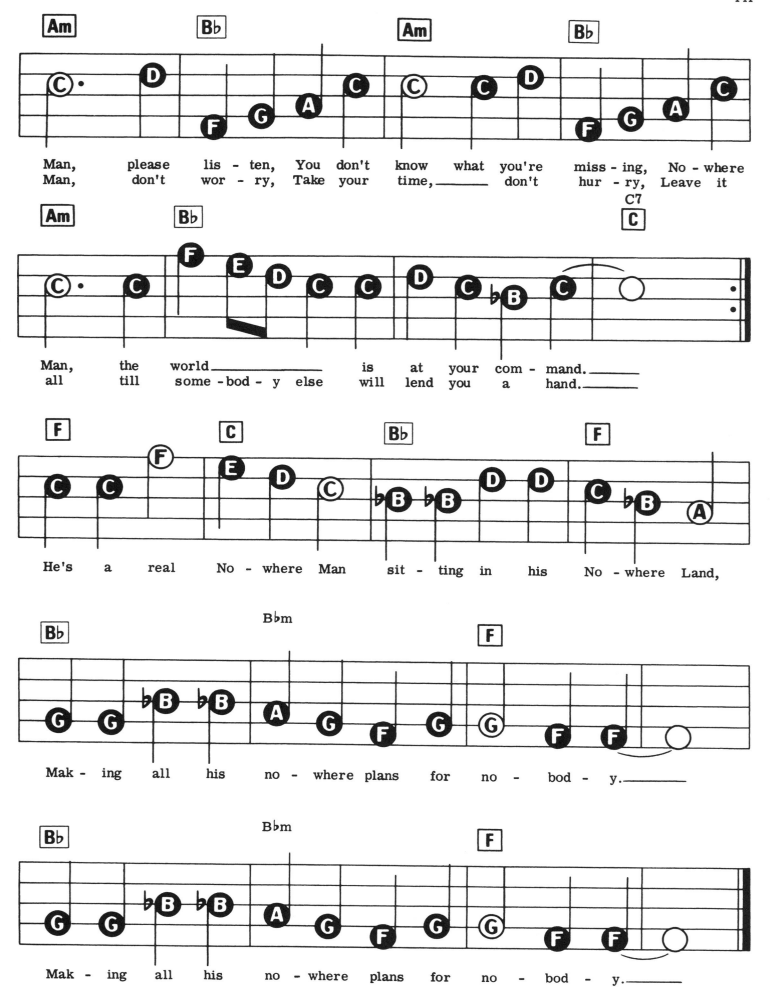

Ob-La-Di, Ob-La-Da

Registration 9
Rhythm: Rock

Words and Music by John Lennon
and Paul McCartney

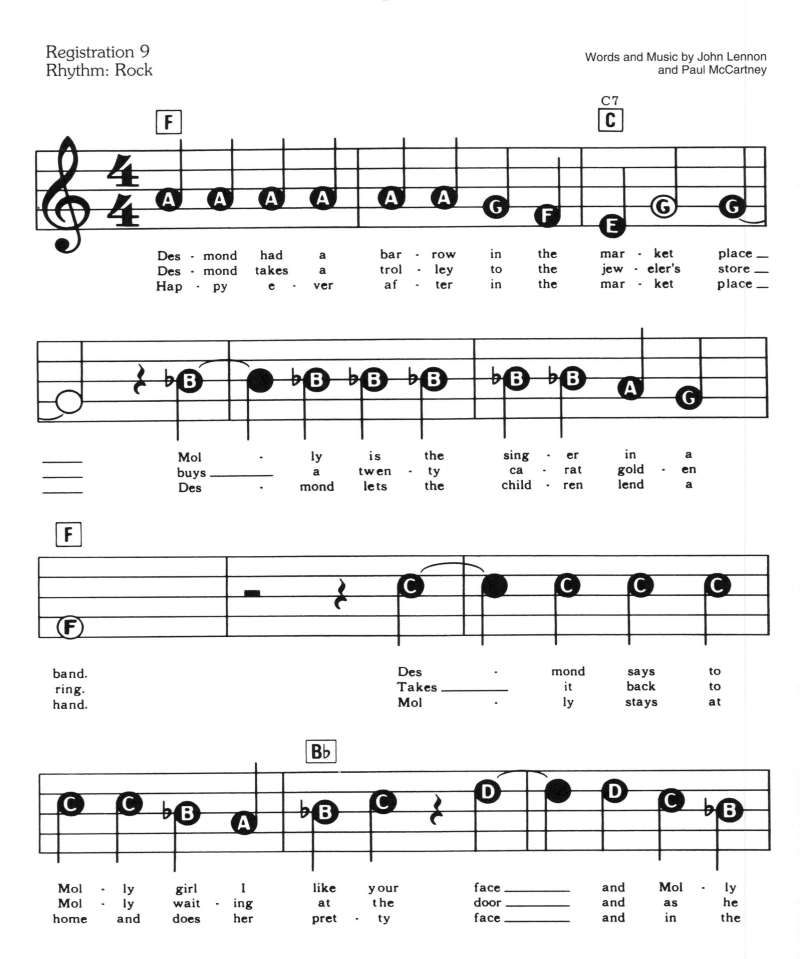

143

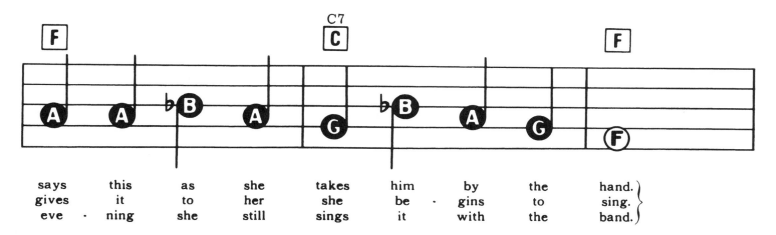

says | this | as | she | takes | him | by | the | hand.
gives | it | to | her | she | be-gins | to | sing.
eve-ning | to | she | still | sings | it | with | to | the | band.

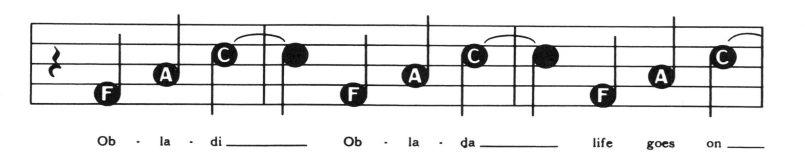

Ob - la - di _____ Ob - la - da _____ life goes on _____

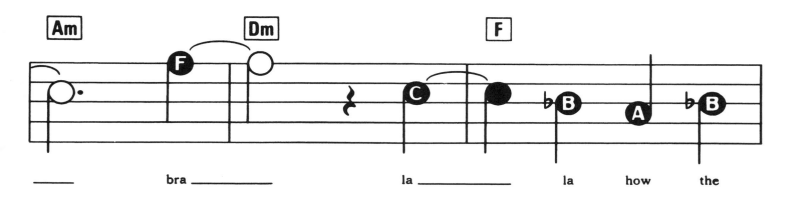

_____ bra _____ la _____ la how the

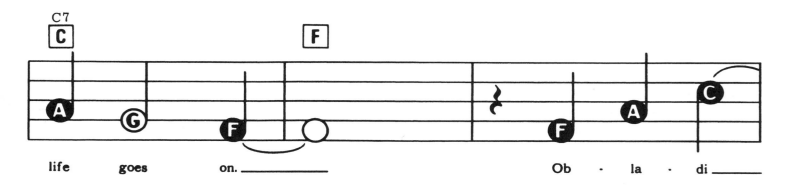

life goes on. _____ Ob - la - di _____

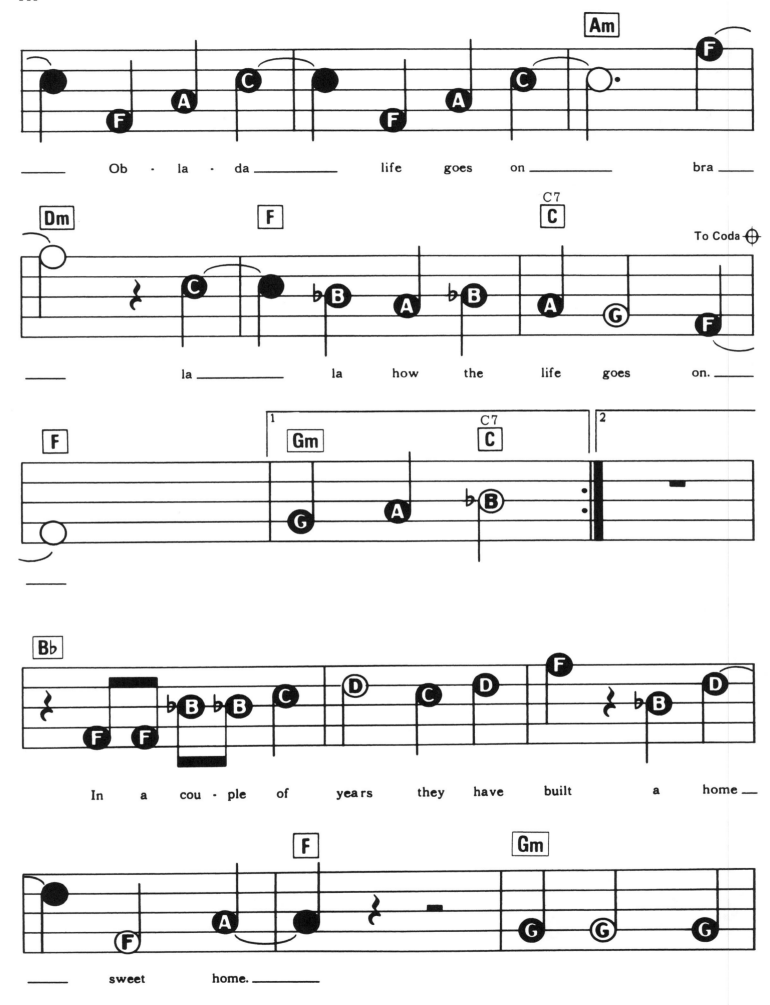

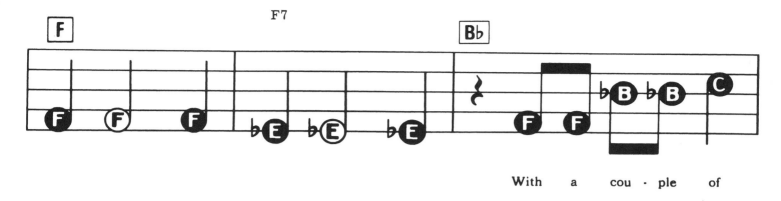

With a cou - ple of

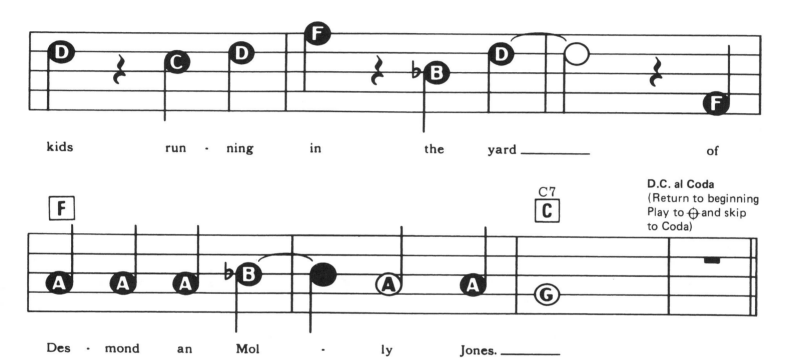

kids run - ning in the yard _____ of

Des - mond an Mol - ly Jones. _____

D.C. al Coda
(Return to beginning
Play to ⊕ and skip
to Coda)

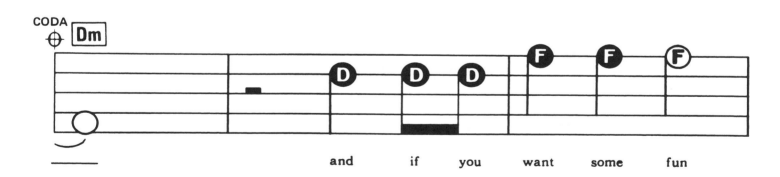

_____ and if you want some fun

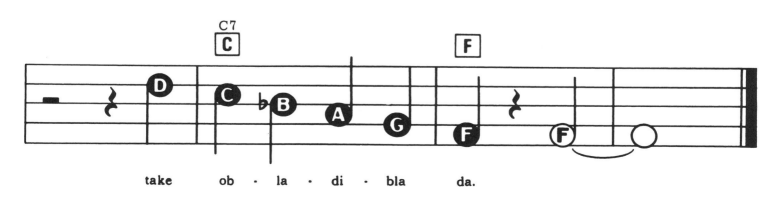

take ob - la - di - bla - da.

Paperback Writer

Registration 4
Rhythm: Rock

Words and Music by John Lennon
and Paul McCartney

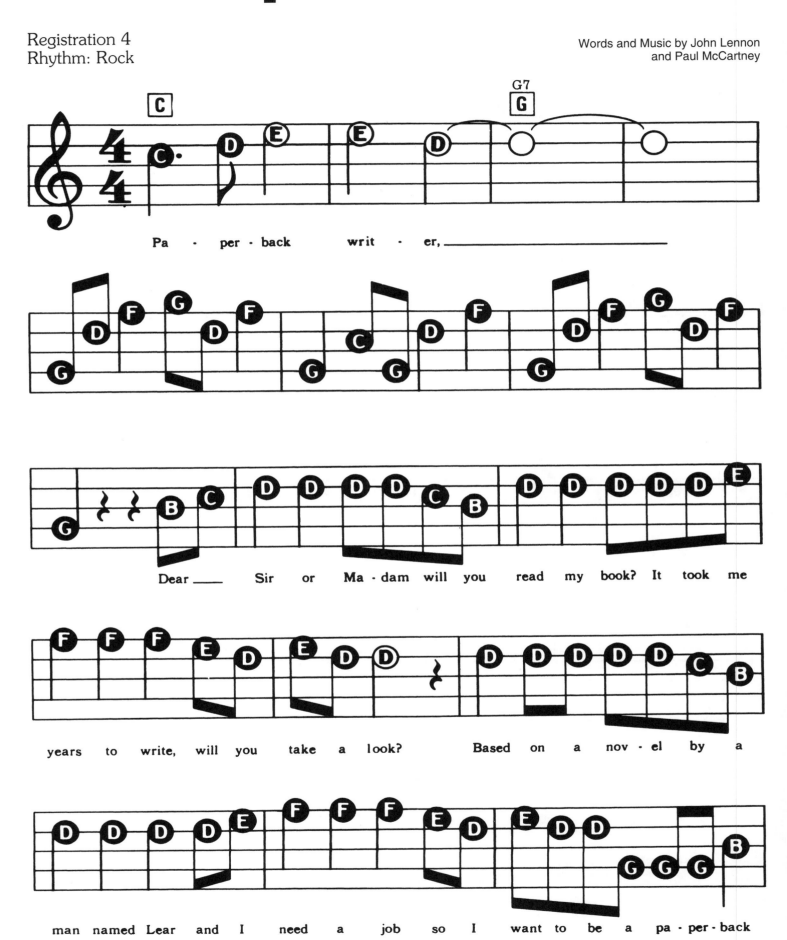

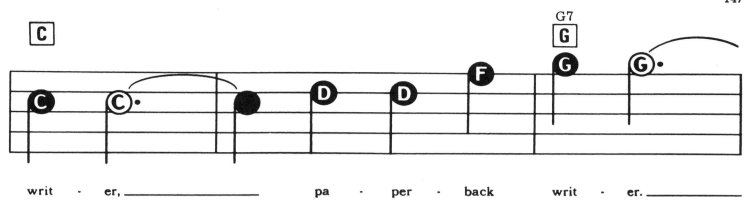

writ - er, _____ pa - per - back writ - er. _____

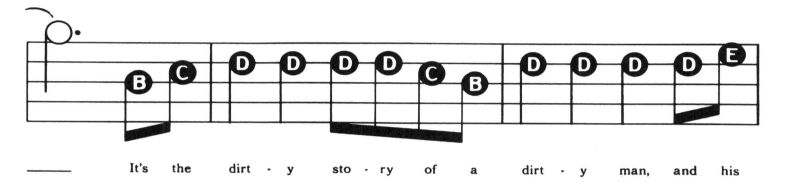

_____ It's the dirt - y sto - ry of a dirt - y man, and his

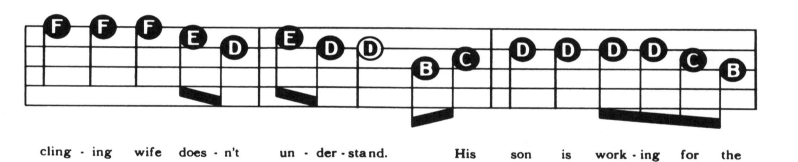

cling - ing wife does - n't un - der - stand. His son is work - ing for the

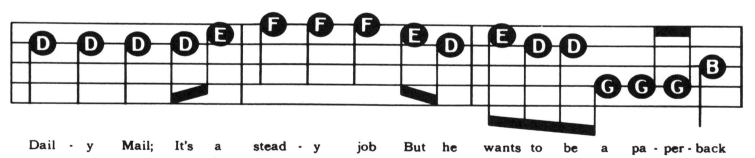

Dai - ly Mail; It's a stead - y job But he wants to be a pa - per - back

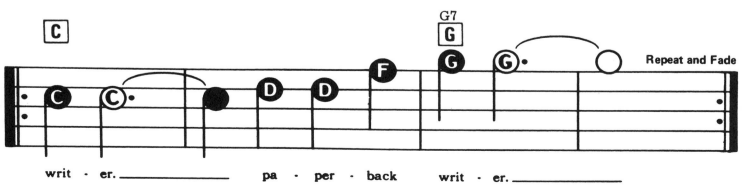

writ - er. _____ pa - per - back writ - er. _____

Penny Lane

Registration 2
Rhythm: Rock

Words and Music by John Lennon
and Paul McCartney

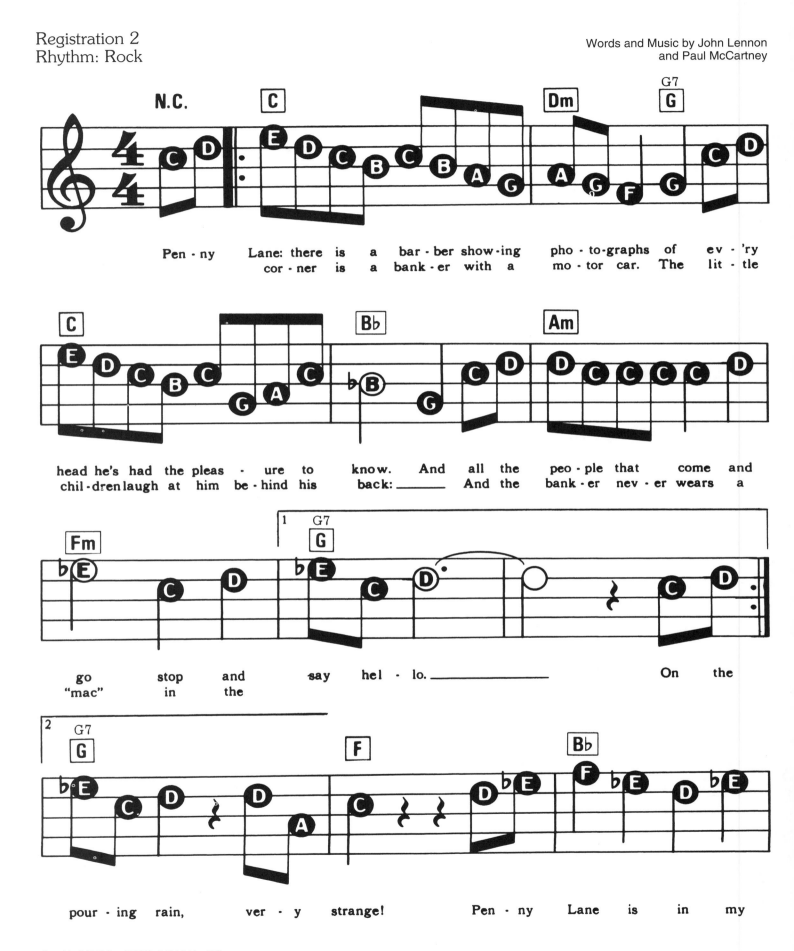

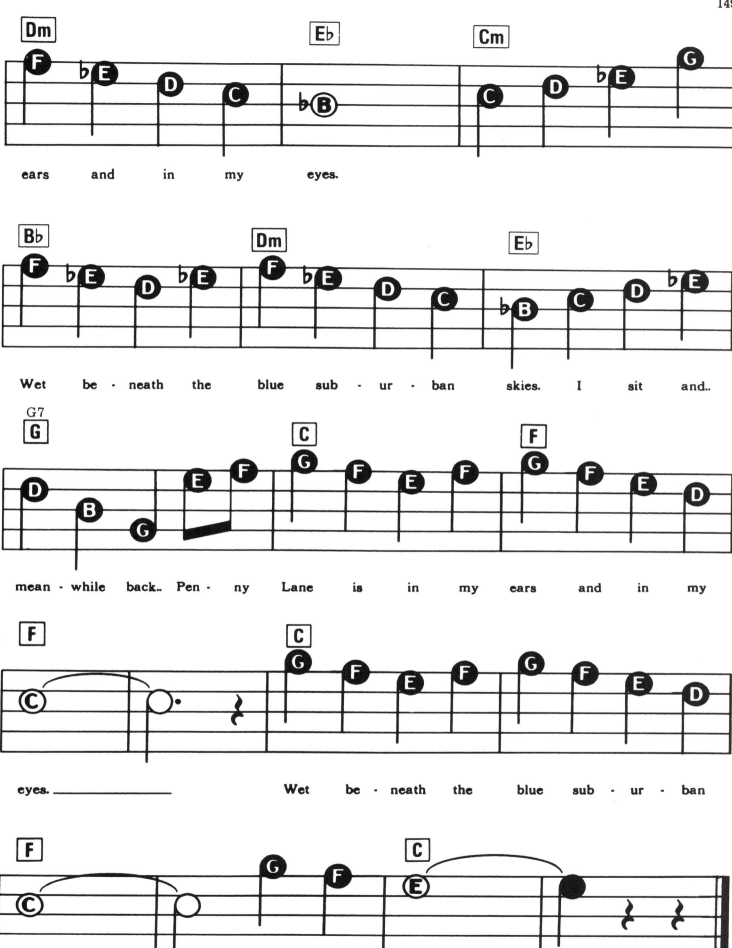

ears   and   in   my   eyes.

Wet   be · neath   the   blue   sub · ur · ban   skies.   I   sit   and..

mean · while   back..   Pen · ny   Lane   is   in   my   ears   and   in   my

eyes. _____   Wet   be · neath   the   blue   sub · ur · ban

skies _____   Pen · ny   Lane. _____

149

Please Please Me

Registration 8
Rhythm: Rock

Words and Music by John Lennon
and Paul McCartney

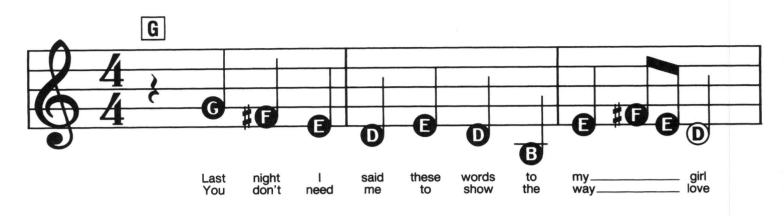

Last night I said these words to my _____ girl
You don't need me to show the way _____ love

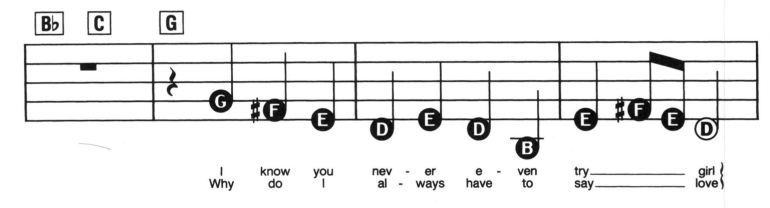

I know you nev - er e - ven try _____ girl
Why do I al - ways have to say _____ love

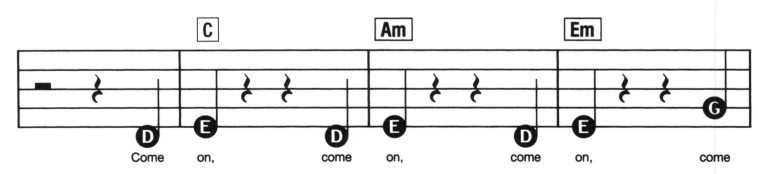

Come on, come on, come on, come

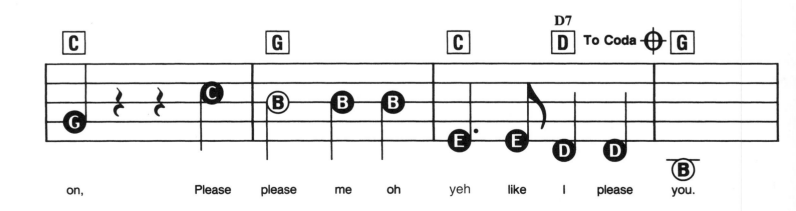

on, Please please me oh yeh like I please you.

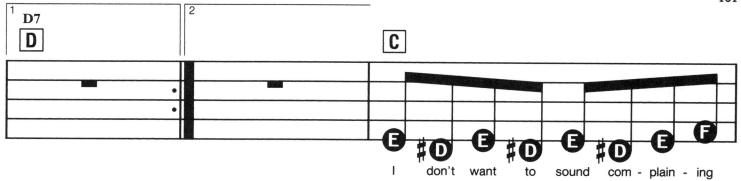

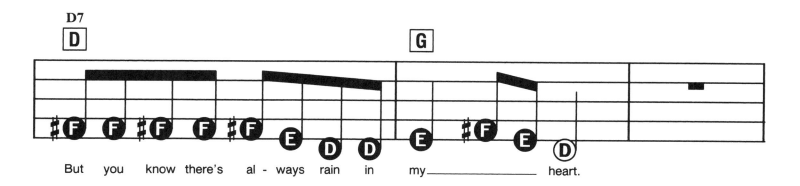

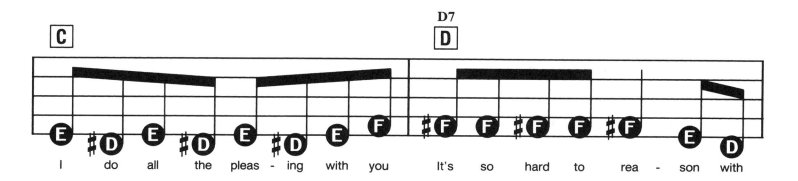

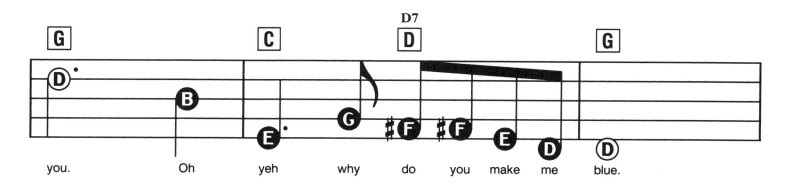

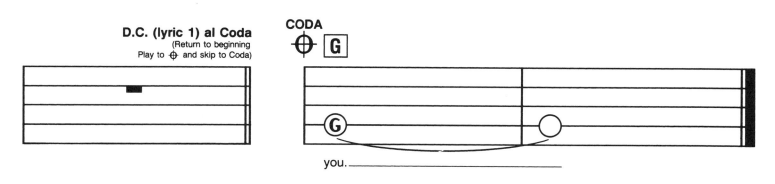

151

Rocky Raccoon

Registration 5
Rhythm: Fox Trot or Swing

Words and Music by John Lennon
and Paul McCartney

153

Run for Your Life

Registration 3
Rhythm: Rock

Words and Music by John Lennon
and Paul McCartney

Well I'd rath - er see you dead lit - tle girl than to
know that I'm a wick - ed guy and I was

be with an - oth - er man
born with a jeal - ous mind

You'd bet - ter keep your
And I can't keep spend my

head lit - tle girl or I won't know where I am
whole life tryin' just to make you toe the line

You'd bet - ter

run for your life if you can lit - tle girl _____ Hide your head in the

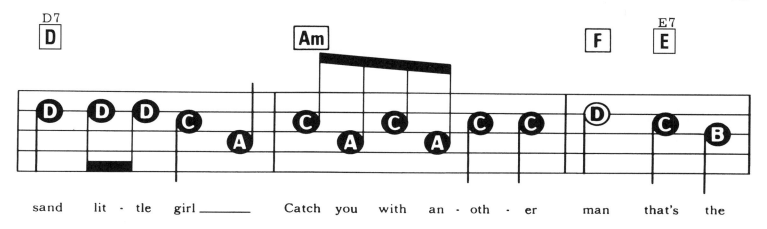

sand lit - tle girl _____ Catch you with an - oth - er man that's the

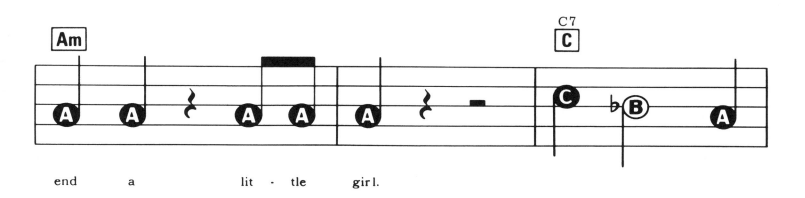

end a lit - tle girl.

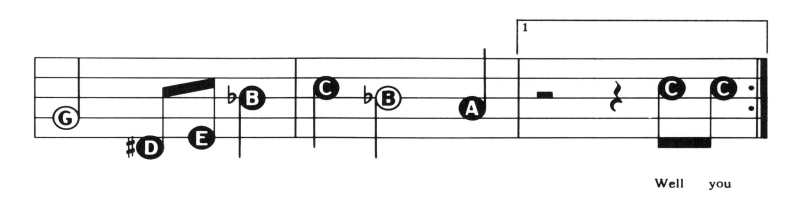

Well you

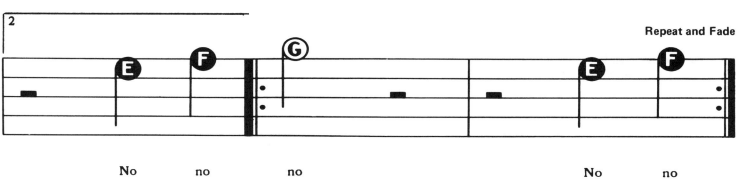

No no no   No no

Sgt. Pepper's Lonely Hearts Club Band

Registration 4
Rhythm: Rock

Words and Music by John Lennon
and Paul McCartney

It was twen-ty years a-go to-day that Ser-geant

Pep-per taught the band to play. They've been go-ing in and out of

style, but they're guar-an-teed to raise a smile. So

may I in-tro-duce to you the act you've known for all these

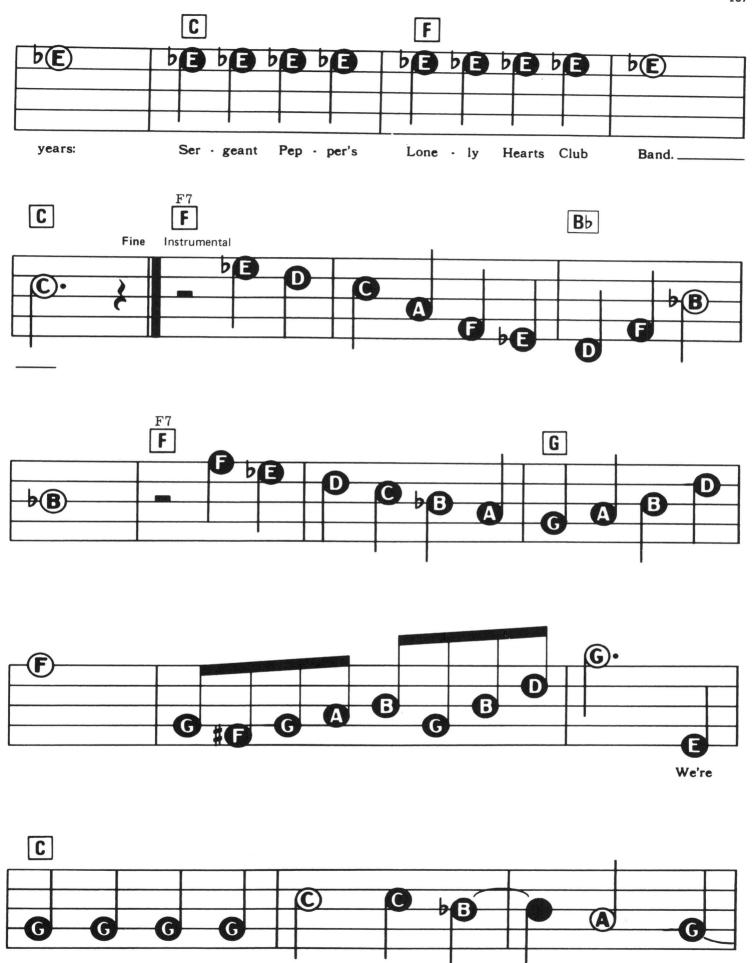

years: Ser · geant Pep · per's Lone · ly Hearts Club Band. _____

Fine   Instrumental

We're

Ser · geant Pep · per's Lone - ly Hearts _____ Club Band, ___

158

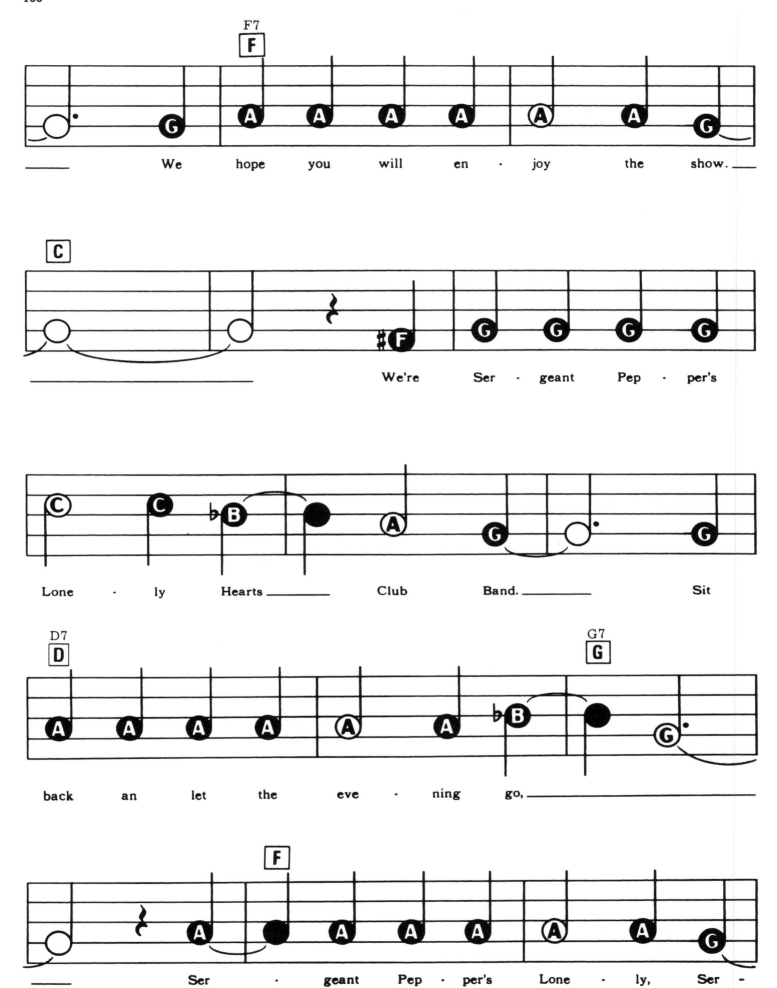

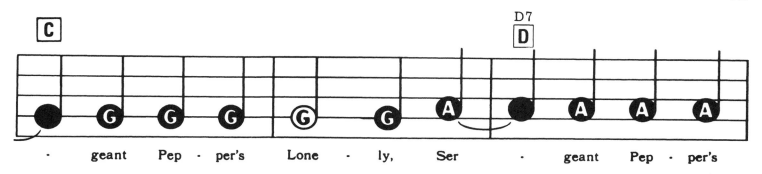

- geant Pep - per's Lone - ly, Ser - geant Pep - per's

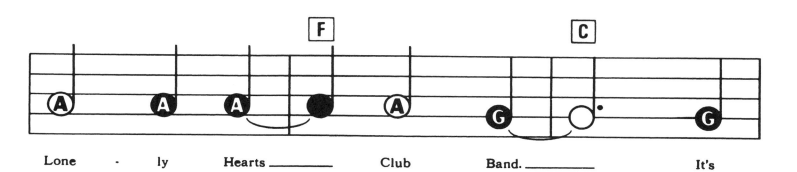

Lone - ly Hearts _____ Club Band. _____ It's

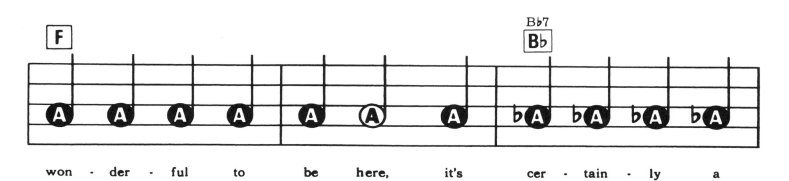

won - der - ful to be here, it's cer - tain - ly a

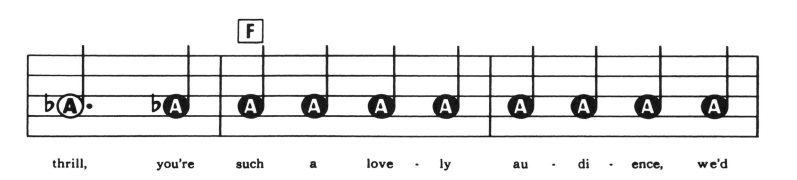

thrill, you're such a love - ly au - di - ence, we'd

D.S. al Fine
(Return to 𝄋
Play to fine)

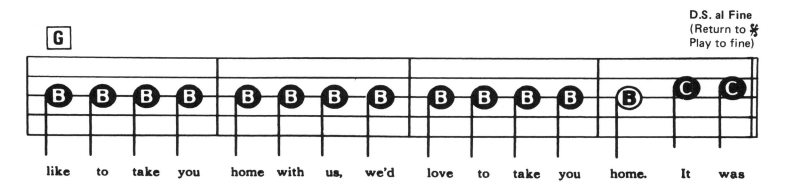

like to take you home with us, we'd love to take you home. It was

She's a Woman

Registration 3
Rhythm: Rock

Words and Music by John Lennon
and Paul McCartney

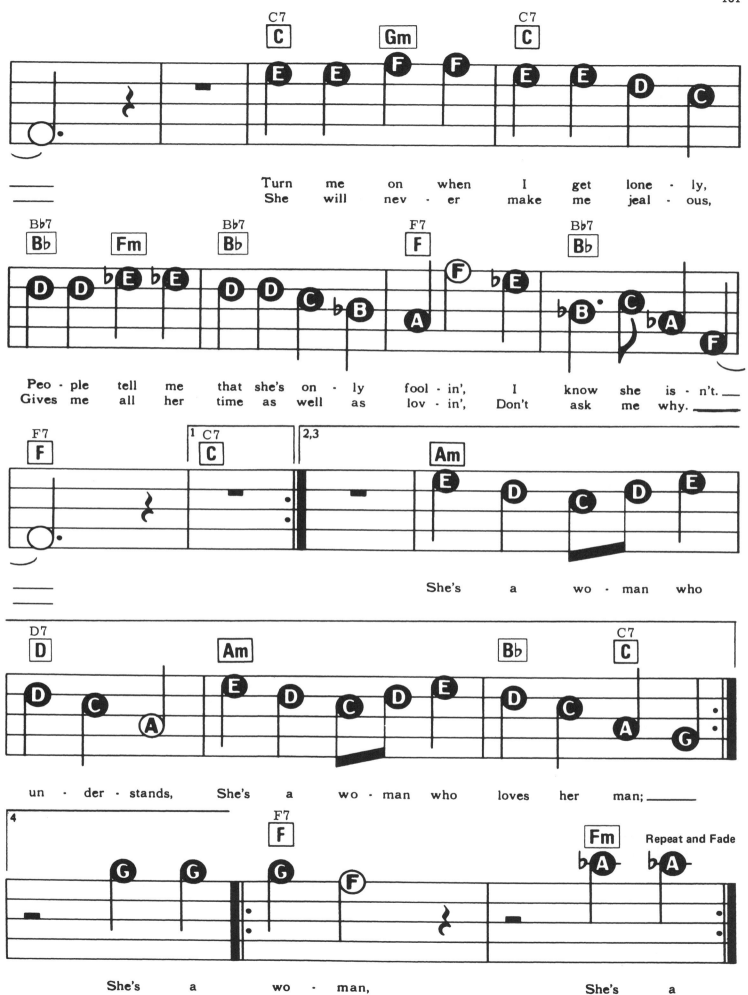

Turn me on when I get lone‑ly,
She will nev‑er make me jeal‑ous,

Peo‑ple tell me that she's on‑ly fool‑in', I know she is‑n't.
Gives me all her time as well as lov‑in', Don't ask me why.

She's a wo‑man who

un‑der‑stands, She's a wo‑man who loves her man;

She's a wo‑man, She's a

Something

Registration 4
Rhythm: Rock

Words and Music by
George Harrison

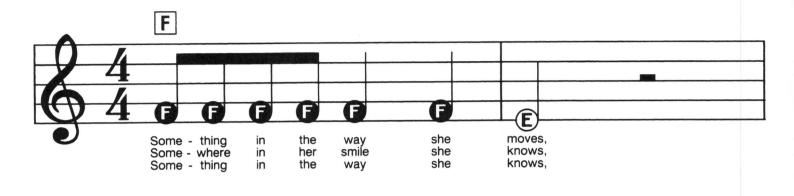

Some - thing in the way she moves,
Some - where in her smile she knows,
Some - thing in the way she knows,

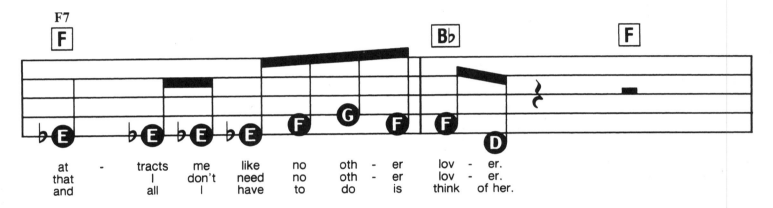

at - tracts me like no oth - er lov - er.
that I don't need no oth - er lov - er.
and all I need have to do is think of her.

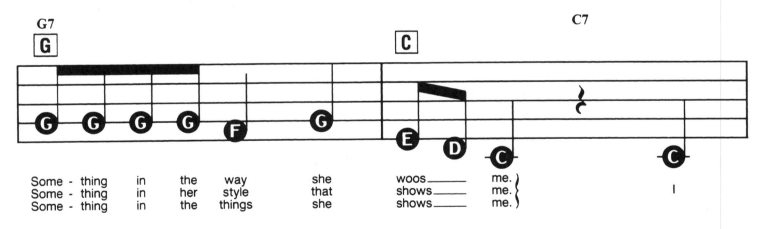

Some - thing in the way she woos_____ me.
Some - thing in her way style that shows_____ me.
Some - thing in the things that she shows_____ me.

I

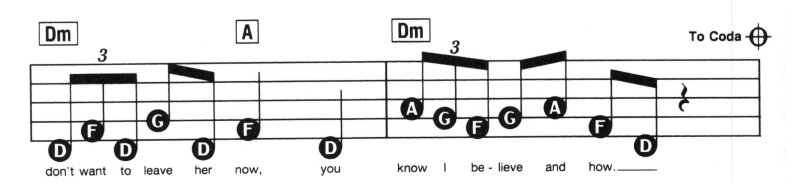

don't want to leave her now, you know I be - lieve and how._____

To Coda ⊕

163

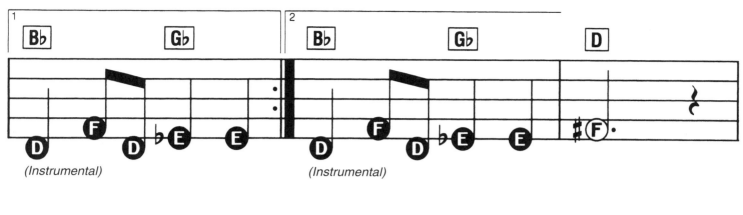

(Instrumental)   (Instrumental)

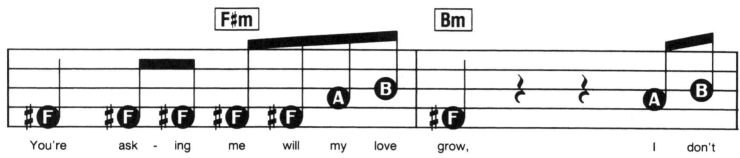

You're ask - ing me will my love grow, I don't

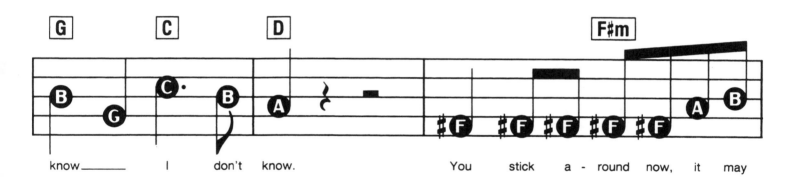

know_____ I don't know.   You stick a - round now, it may

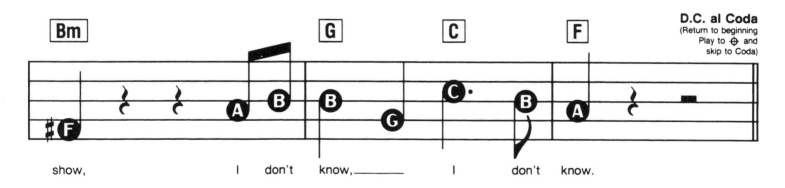

D.C. al Coda
(Return to beginning
Play to ⊕ and
skip to Coda)

show, I don't know,_____ I don't know.

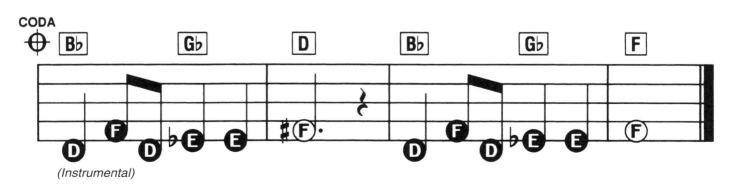

(Instrumental)

Strawberry Fields Forever

Registration 2
Rhythm: Rock

Words and Music by John Lennon
and Paul McCartney

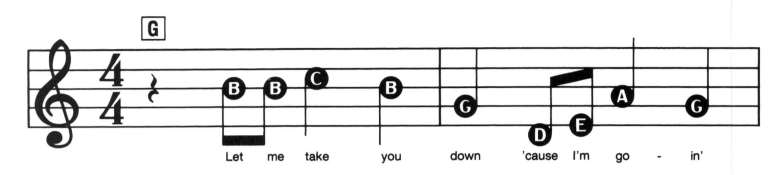

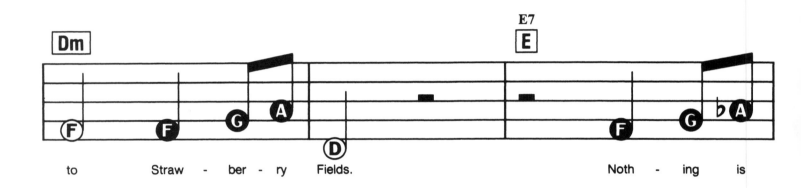

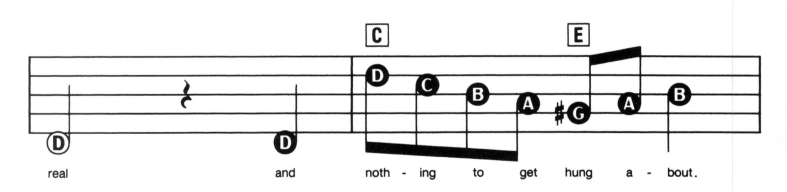

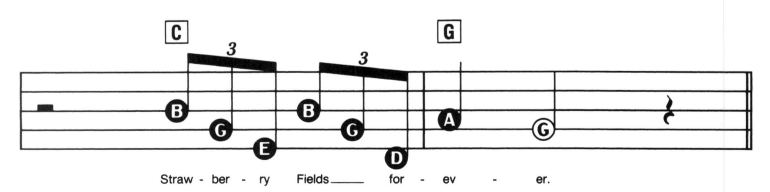

165

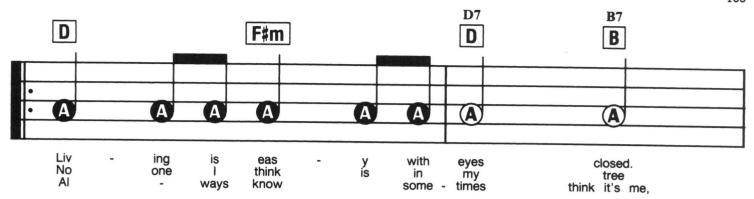

Liv - ing is eas - y with eyes closed.
No one I think is in my tree
Al - ways know some - times think it's me,

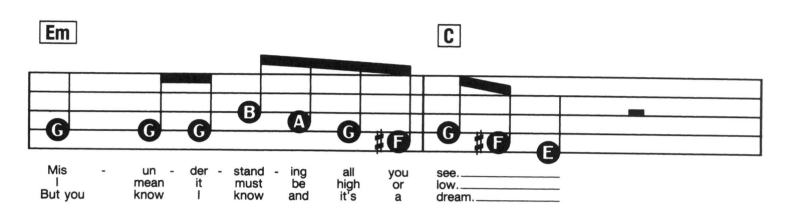

Mis - un - der - stand - ing all you see._____
I mean it must be high or low._____
But you know I know and it's a dream._____

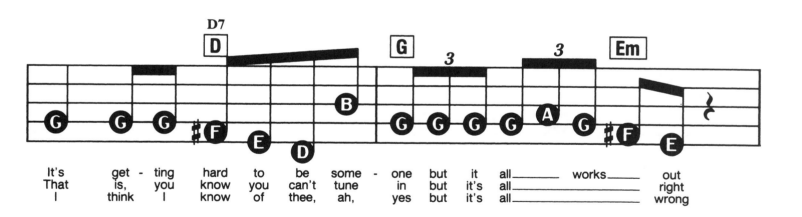

It's get - ting hard to be some - one but it all_____ works_____ out
That is, you know you can't tune in but it's all_____ right
I think I know of thee, ah, yes but it's all_____ wrong

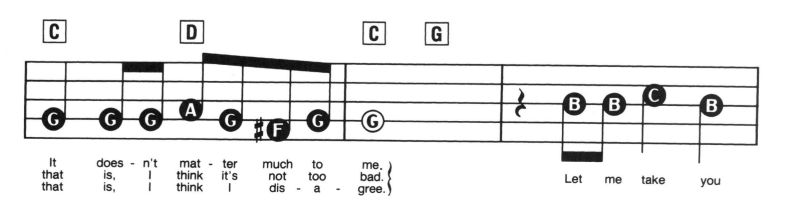

It does - n't mat - ter much to me.
that is, I think it's not too bad.
that is, I think I dis - a - gree.

Let me take you

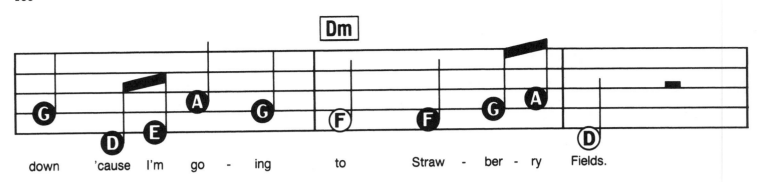

down 'cause I'm go - ing to Straw - ber - ry Fields.

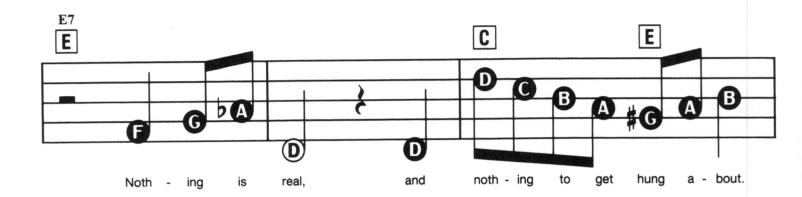

Noth - ing is real, and noth - ing to get hung a - bout.

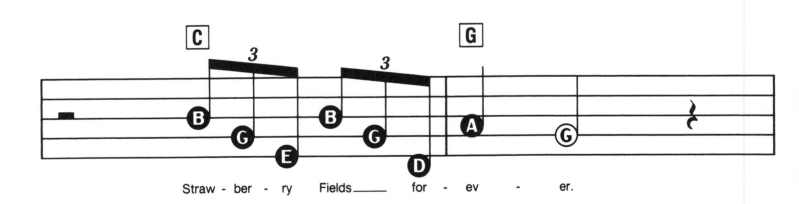

Straw - ber - ry Fields_____ for - ev - er.

Repeat and Fade

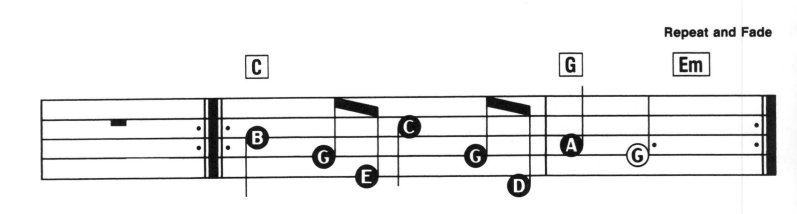

Twist and Shout

Registration 4
Rhythm: Rock

Words and Music by Bert Russell
and Phil Medley

Well, shake it up ba - by, _____ now, *Shake it up baby* Twist and

shout. _____ *Twist and* Come shout on, come on, _____ come on, come on,

ba - by, _____ now, *Come on ba - by* Come on and work it on out. _____ *Work it on out*

Well, work it on out, _____ (Work it on out) You know you look so
You know you twist lit - tle girl, _____ (Twist little girl) You know you twist so

168

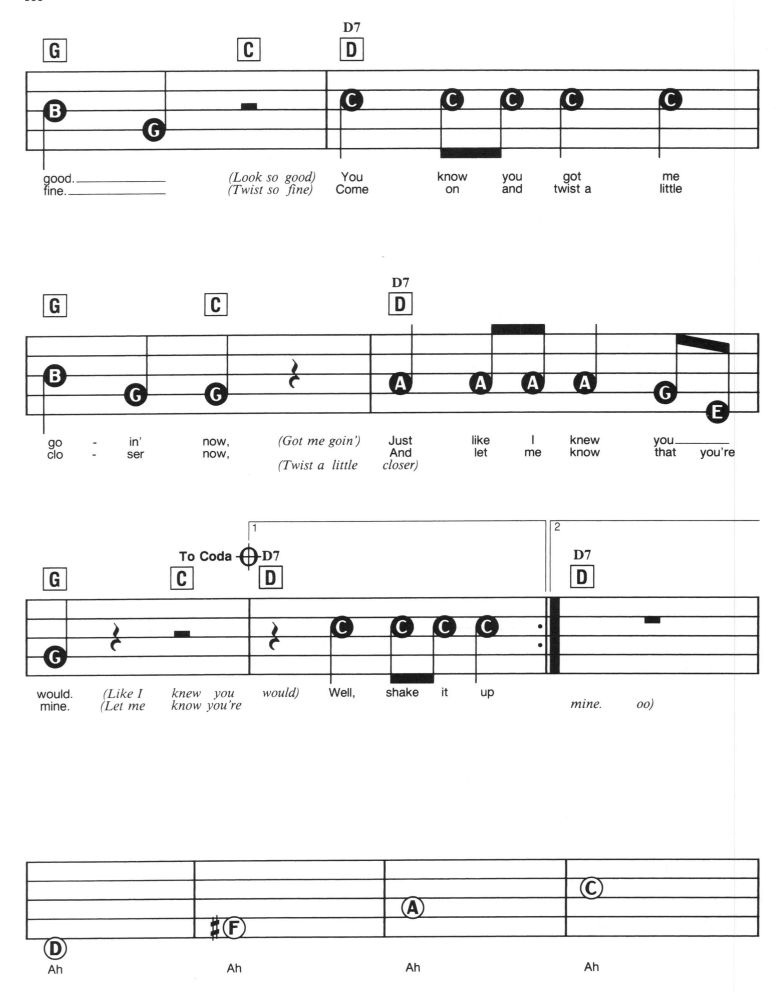

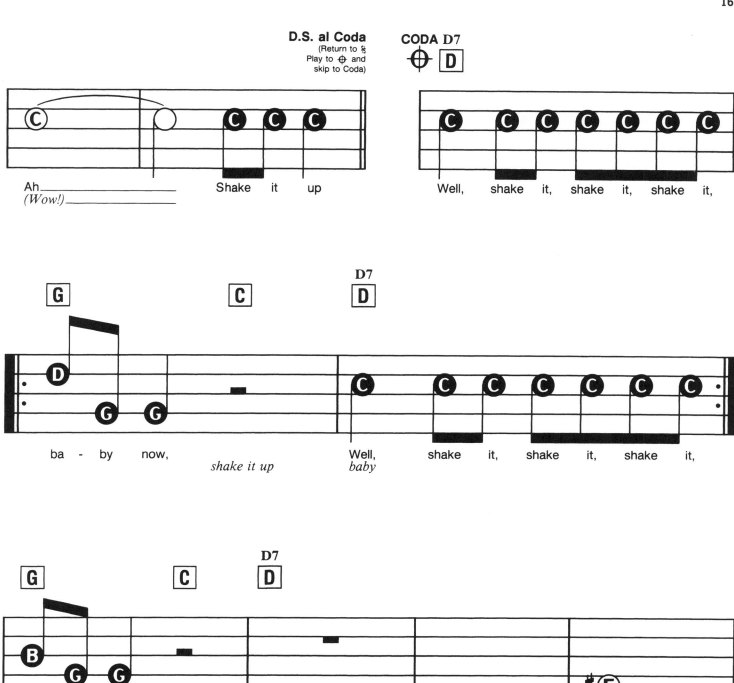

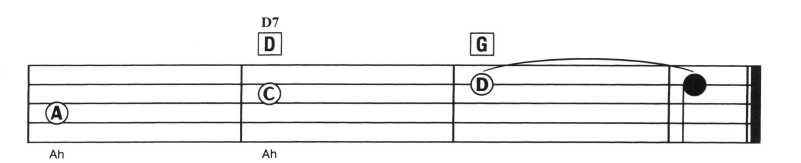

Taxman

Registration 2
Rhythm: Rock

Words and Music by
George Harrison

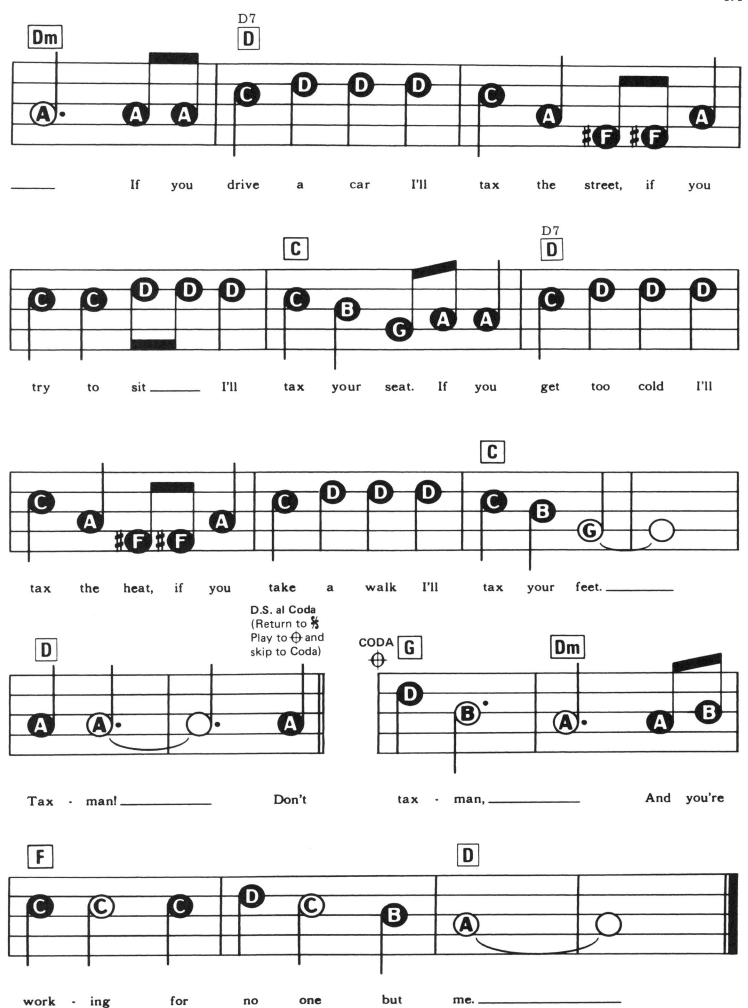

If you drive a car I'll tax the street, if you

try to sit _____ I'll tax your seat. If you get too cold I'll

tax the heat, if you take a walk I'll tax your feet. _____

Tax - man! _____ Don't tax - man, _____ And you're

work - ing for no one but me. _____

This Boy
(Ringo's Theme)

Registration 5
Rhythm: Slow Rock or Shuffle

Words and Music by John Lennon
and Paul McCartney

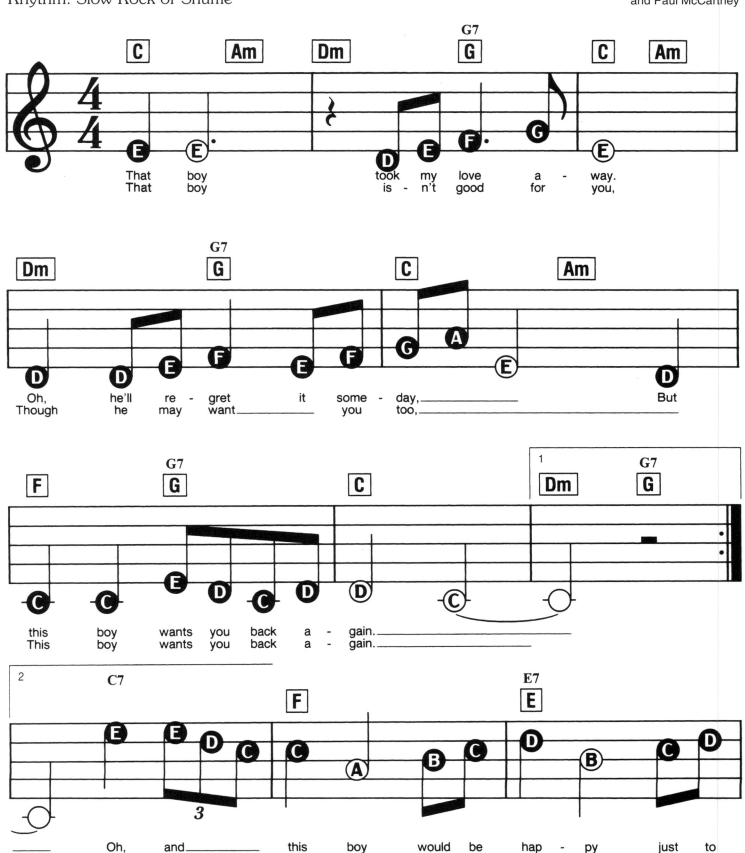

173

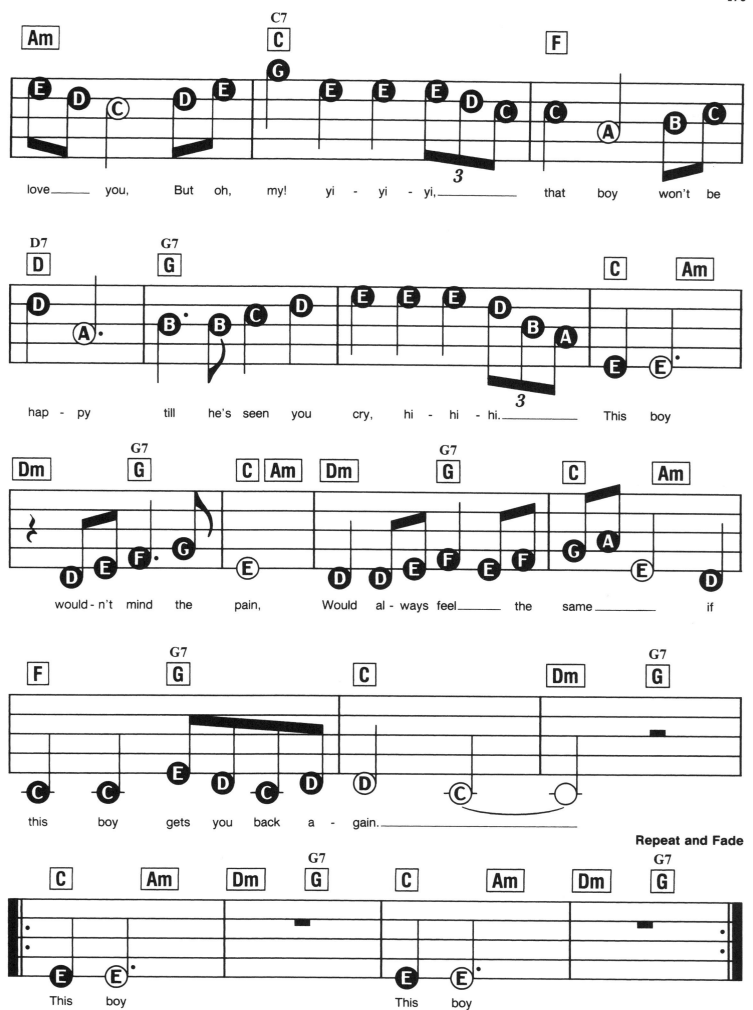

Ticket to Ride

Registration 4
Rhythm: Rock

Words and Music by John Lennon
and Paul McCartney

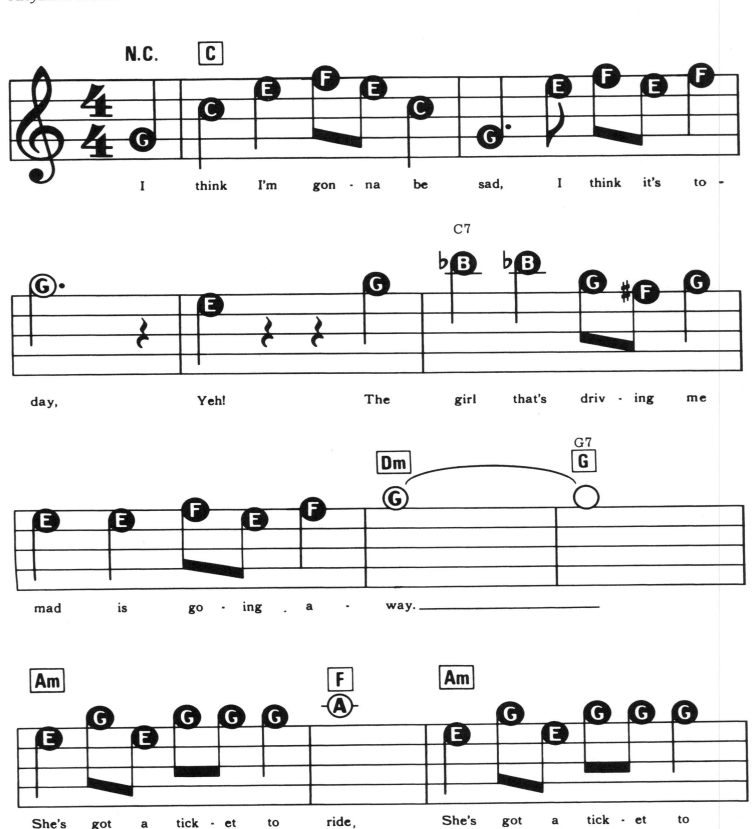

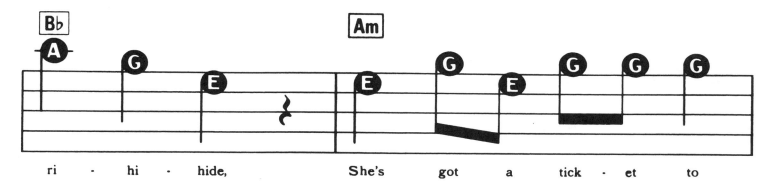

ri - hi - hide, She's got a tick - et to

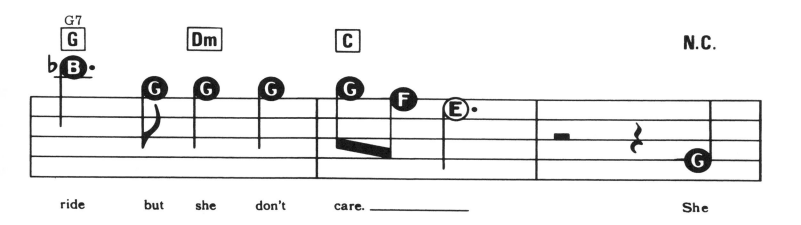

ride but she don't care. _____ She

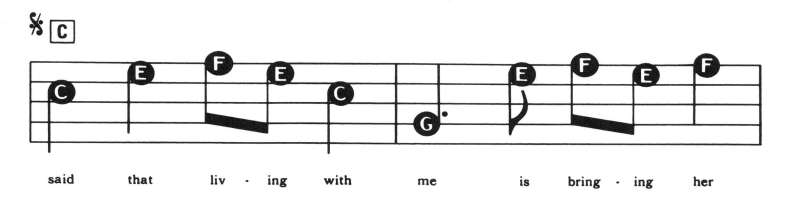

said that liv - ing with me is bring - ing her

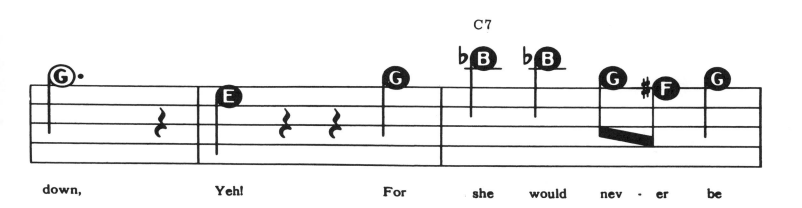

down, Yeh! For she would nev - er be

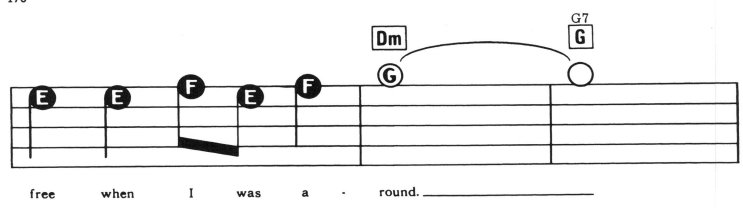

free when I was a - round. _____

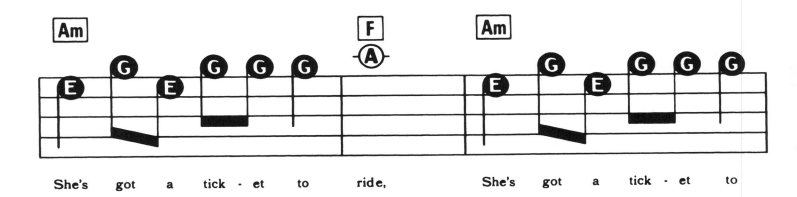

She's got a tick - et to ride,   She's got a tick - et to

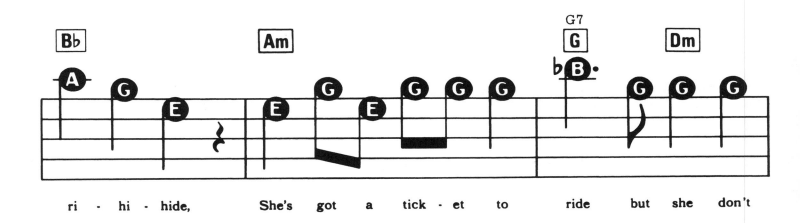

ri - hi - hide,   She's got a tick - et to ride but she don't

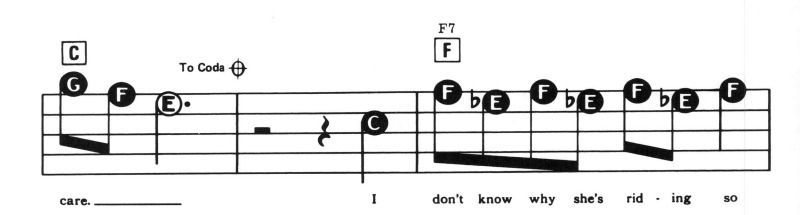

care. _____   I don't know why she's rid - ing so

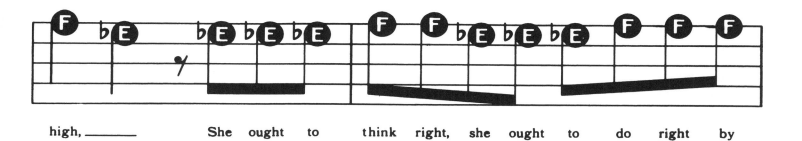

high, _____ She ought to think right, she ought to do right by

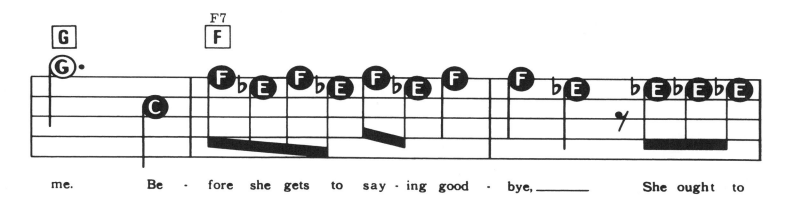

me. Be - fore she gets to say - ing good - bye, _____ She ought to

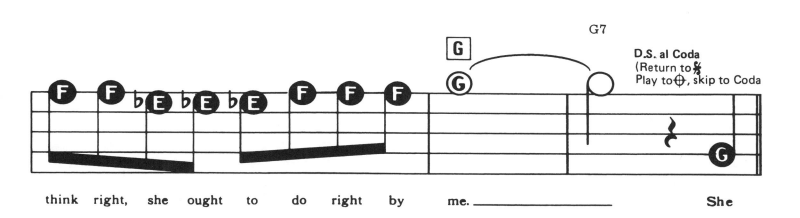

think right, she ought to do right by me. _____ She

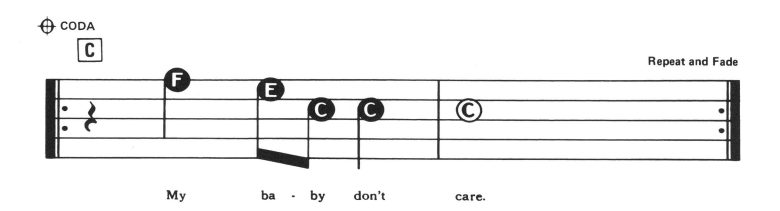

My ba - by don't care.

We Can Work It Out

Registration 9
Rhythm: Rock

Words and Music by John Lennon
and Paul McCartney

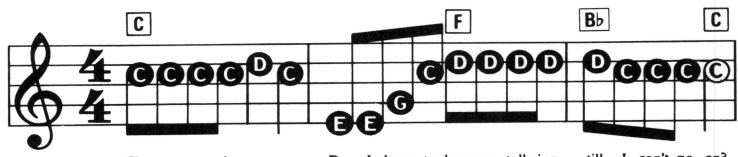

Try to see it my way, Do I have to keep on talk-ing till I can't go on?

To Coda ⊕

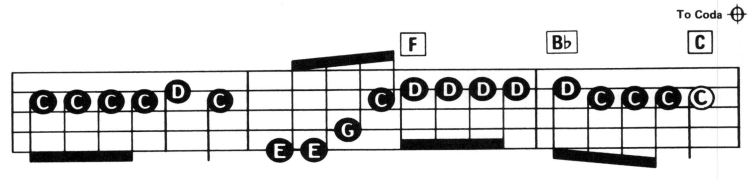

While you see it your way, Run the risk of know-ing that our love may soon be gone.

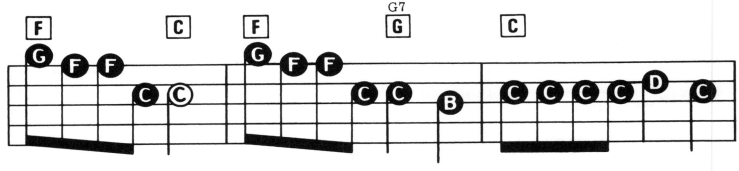

We can work it out. We can work it out.____ Think of whatyou're say - ing,

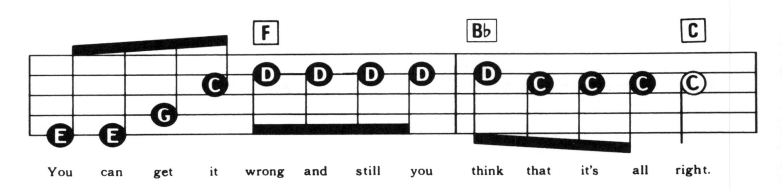

You can get it wrong and still you think that it's all right.

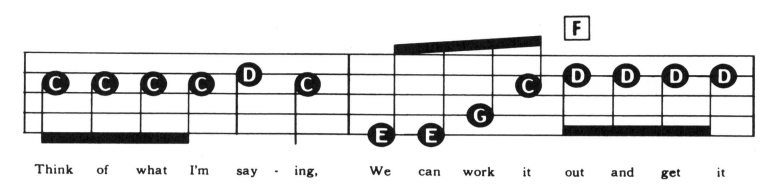

Think of what I'm say-ing, We can work it out and get it

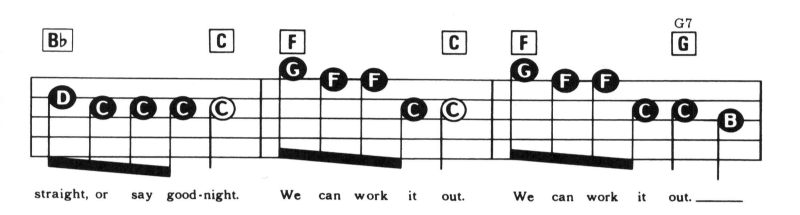

straight, or say good-night. We can work it out. We can work it out.

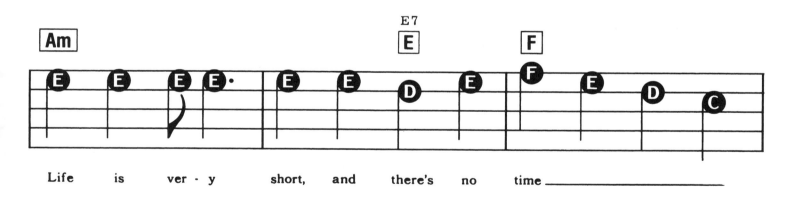

Life is ver-y short, and there's no time

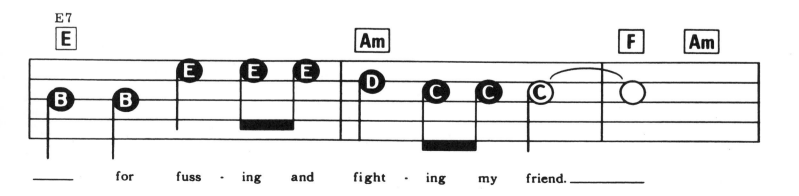

for fuss-ing and fight-ing my friend.

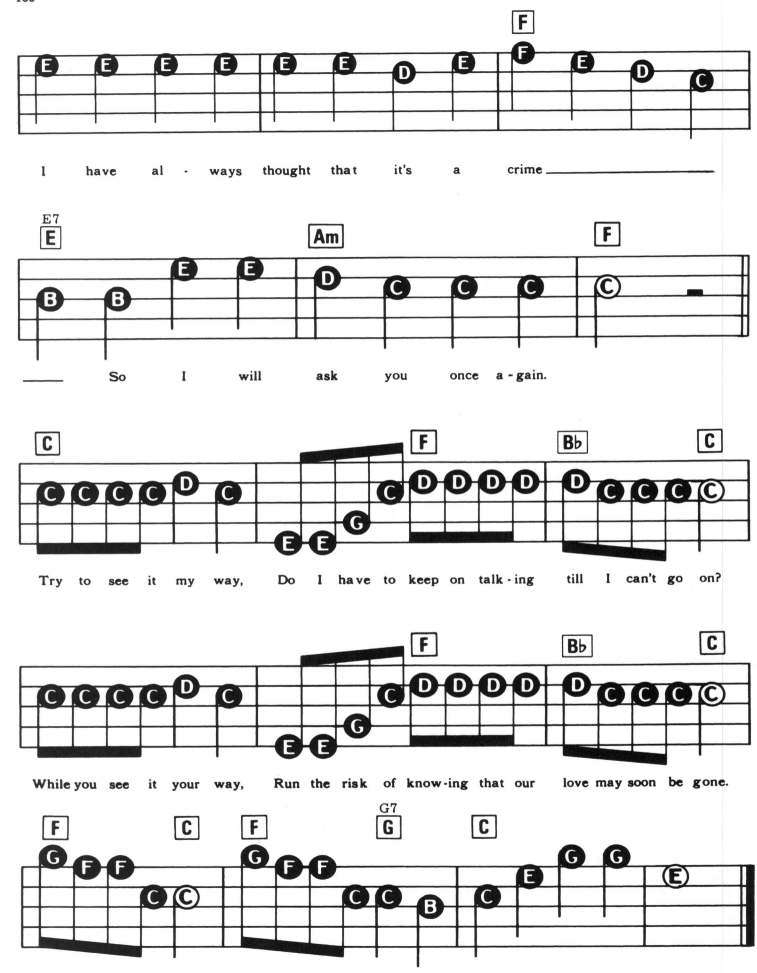

When I'm Sixty-Four

Registration 3
Rhythm: Rock

Words and Music by John Lennon
and Paul McCartney

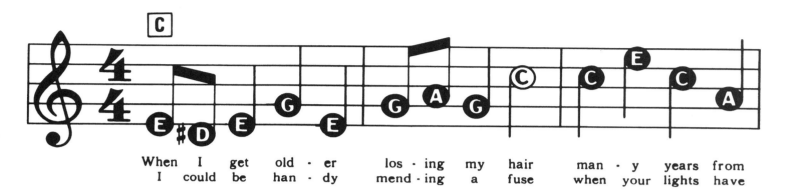

When I get old - er los - ing my hair man - y years from
I could be han - dy mend - ing a fuse when your lights have

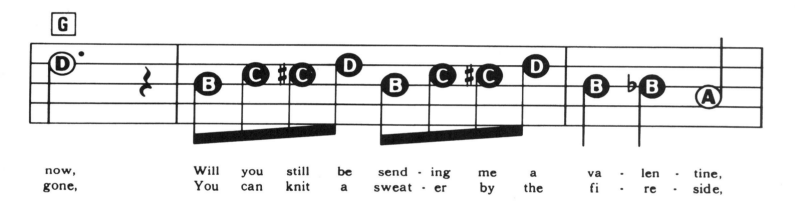

now, Will you still be send - ing me a va - len - tine,
gone, You can knit a sweat - er by the fi - re - side,

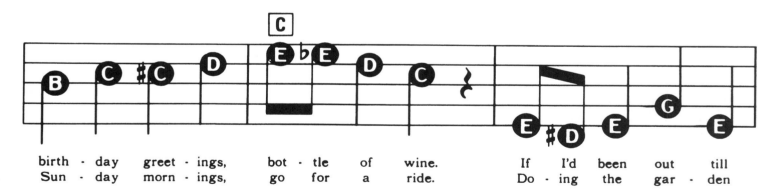

birth - day greet - ings, bot - tle of wine. If I'd been out till
Sun - day morn - ings, go for a ride. Do - ing the gar - den

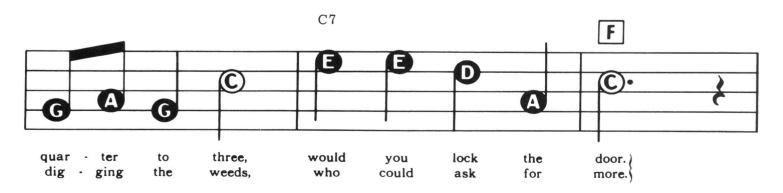

quar - ter to three, would you lock the door.
dig - ging the weeds, who could ask for more.

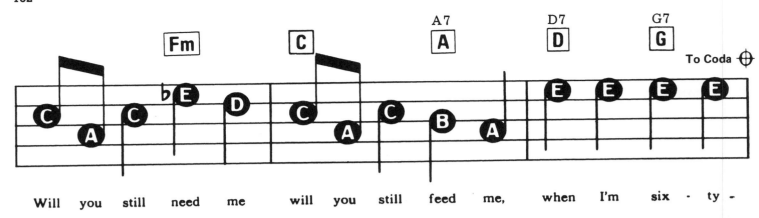

Will you still need me will you still feed me, when I'm six - ty -

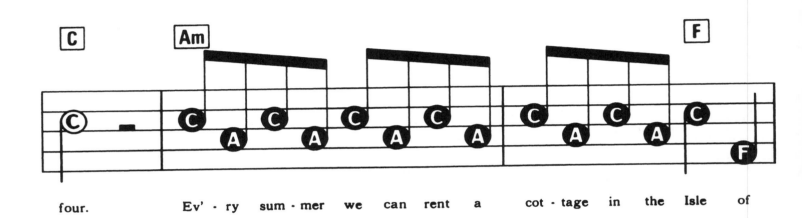

four. Ev' - ry sum - mer we can rent a cot - tage in the Isle of

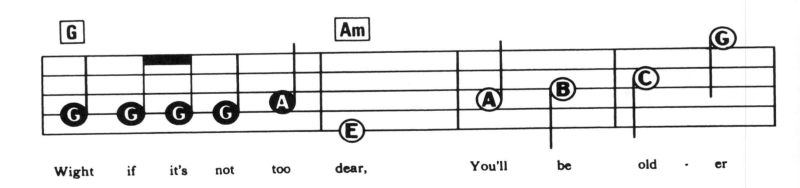

Wight if it's not too dear, You'll be old - er

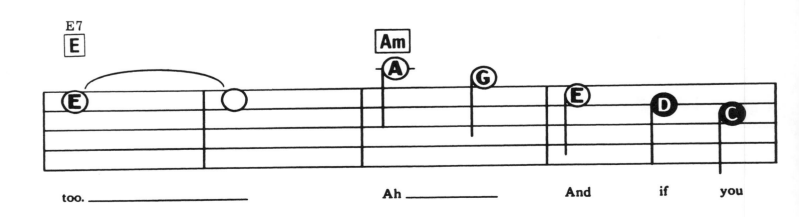

too. _____ Ah _____ And if you

183

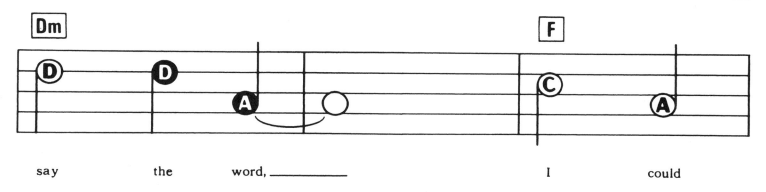

say   the   word, _____   I   could

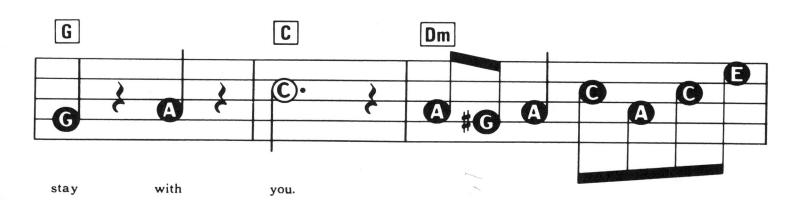

stay   with   you.

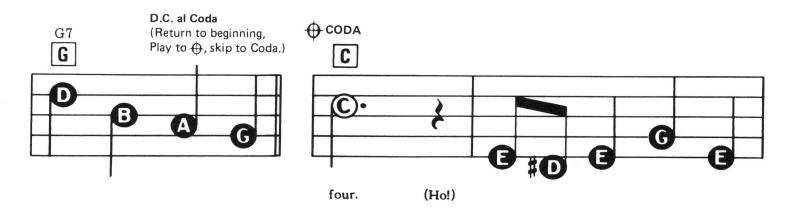

four.   (Ho!)

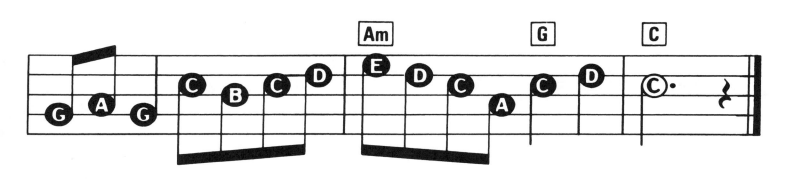

While My Guitar Gently Weeps

Registration 7
Rhythm: Rock or Latin

Words and Music by
George Harrison

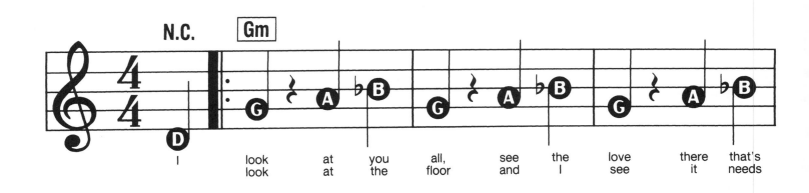

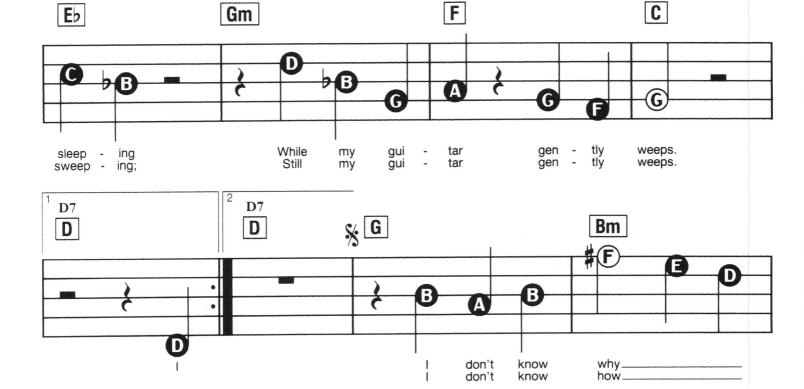

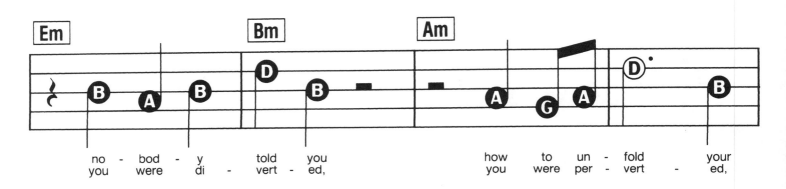

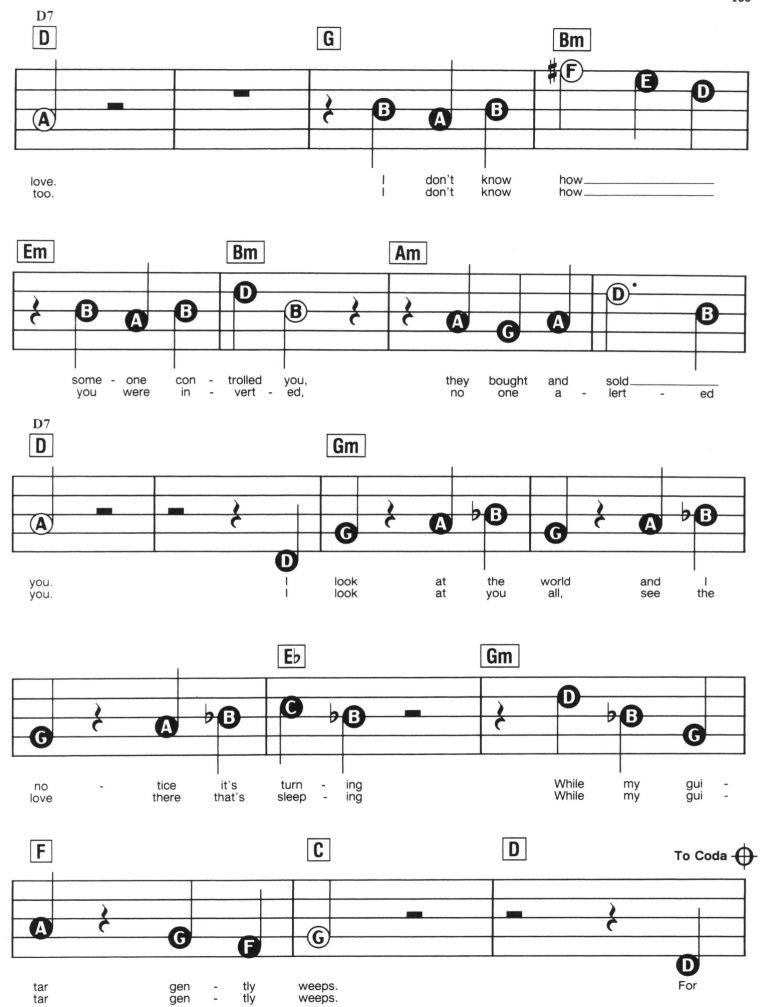

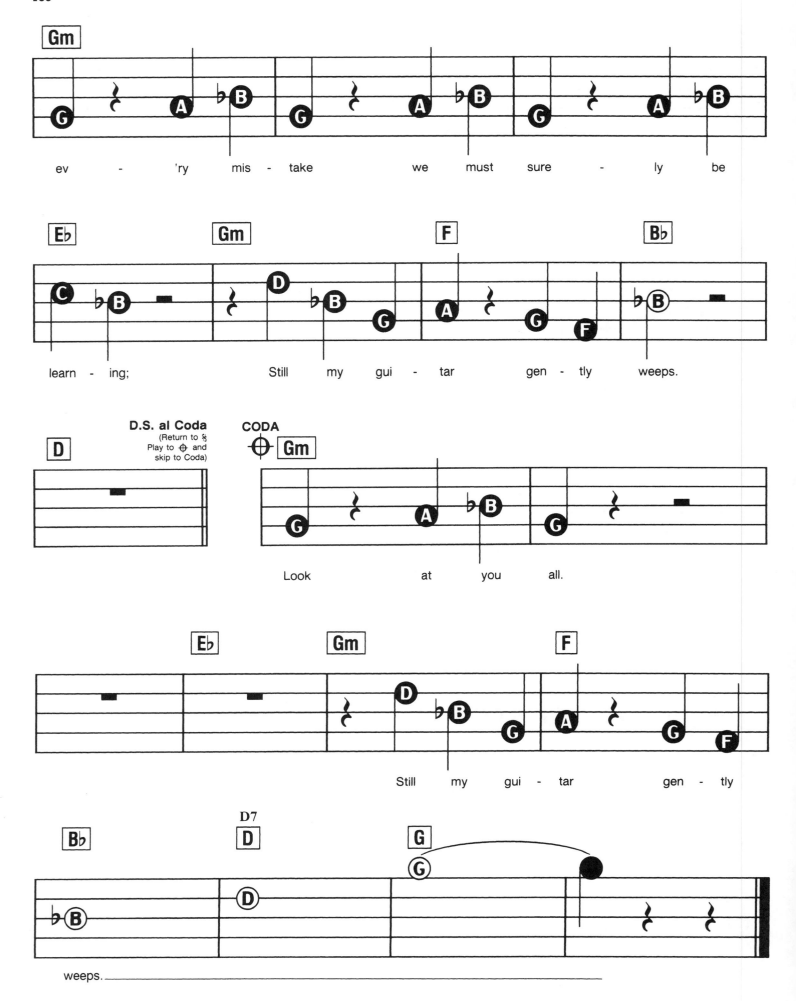

With a Little Help from My Friends

Registration 5
Rhythm: Swing or Shuffle

Words and Music by John Lennon
and Paul McCartney

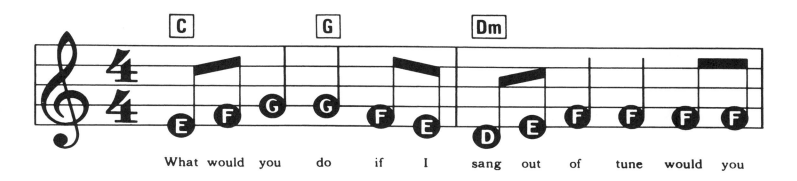

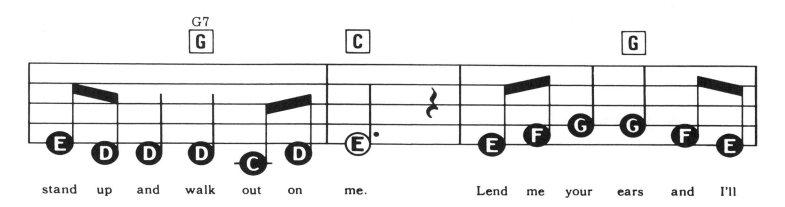

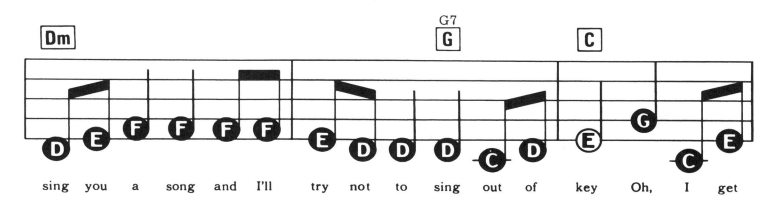

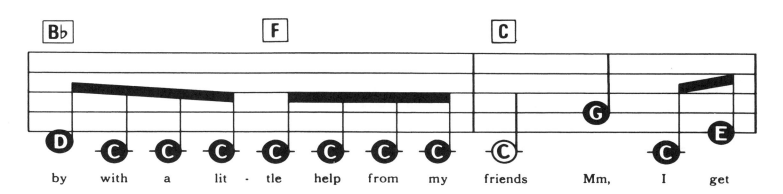

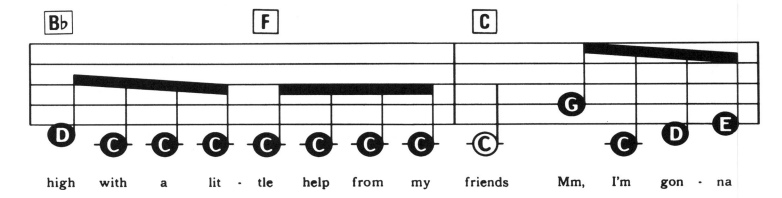

high with a lit·tle help from my friends Mm, I'm gon·na

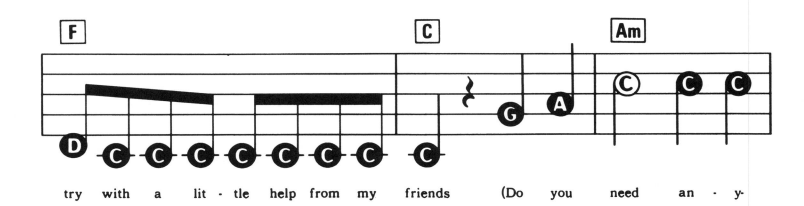

try with a lit·tle help from my friends (Do you need an·y-

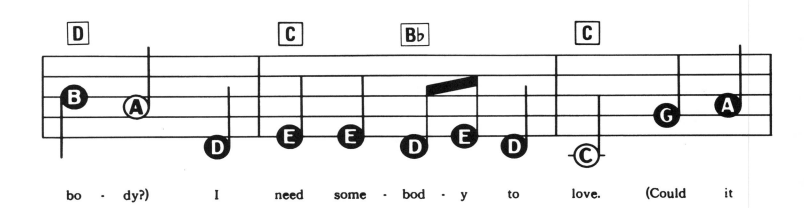

bo·dy?) I need some·bod·y to love. (Could it

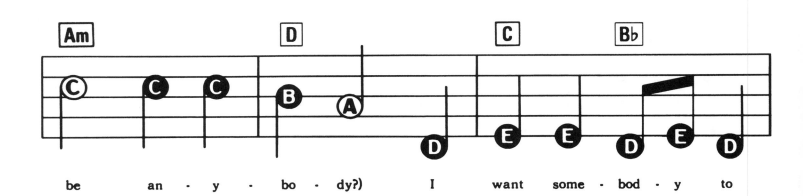

be an·y·bo·dy?) I want some·bod·y to

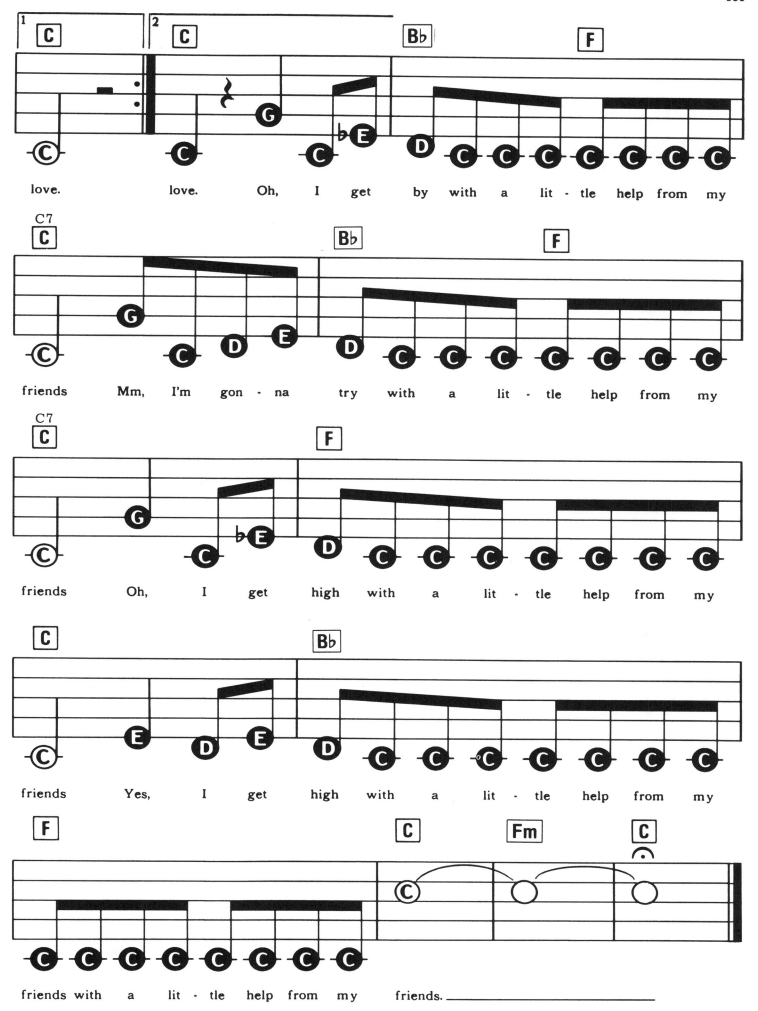

Yellow Submarine

Registration 2
Rhythm: 8 Beat or Rock

Words and Music by John Lennon
and Paul McCartney

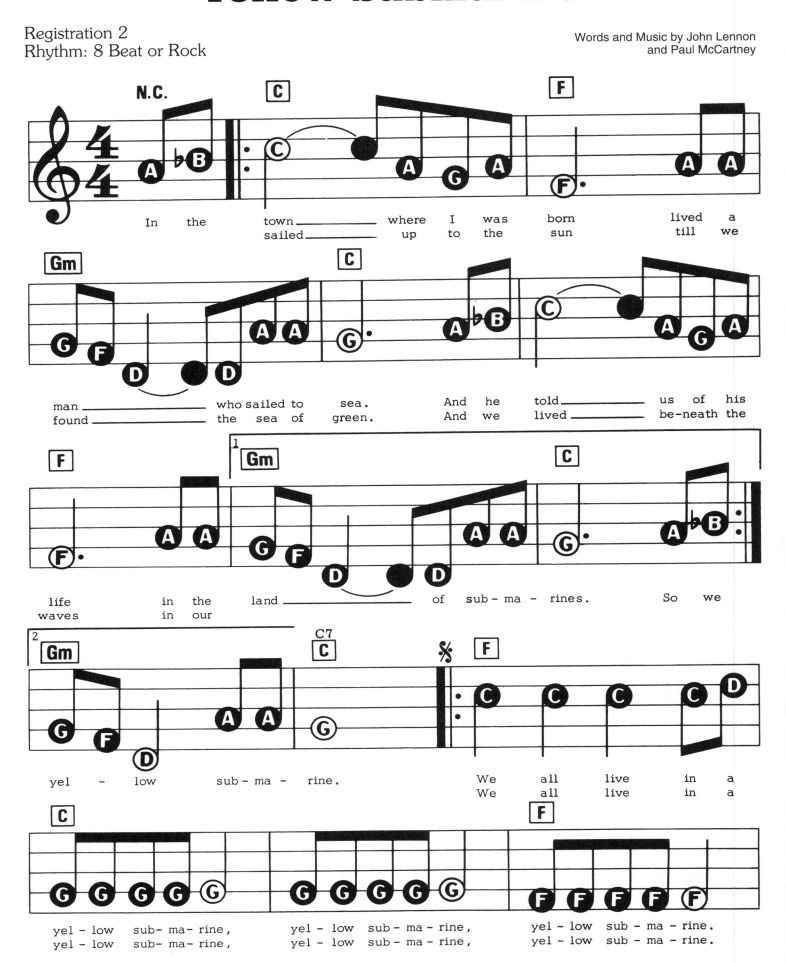

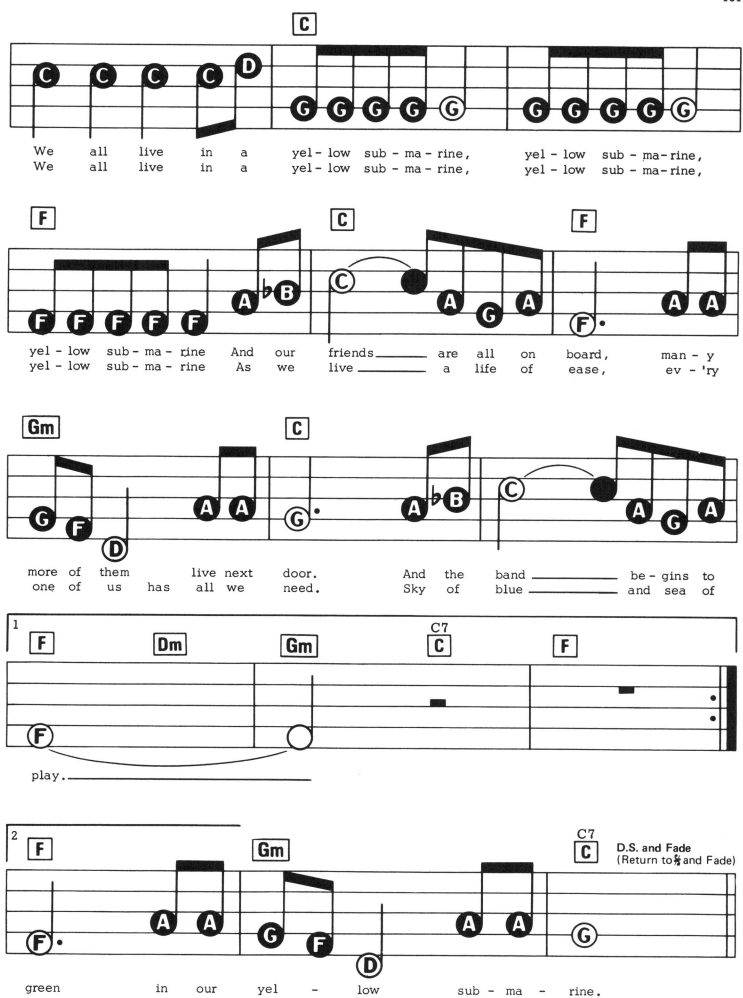

We all live in a yel-low sub-ma-rine, yel-low sub-ma-rine,
We all live in a yel-low sub-ma-rine, yel-low sub-ma-rine,

yel-low sub-ma-rine And our friends_____ are all on board, man-y
yel-low sub-ma-rine As we live_____ a life of ease, ev-'ry

more of them live next door. And the band_____ be-gins to
one of us has all we need. Sky of blue_____ and sea of

play._____

C7

D.S. and Fade
(Return to 𝄋 and Fade)

green in our yel - low sub-ma-rine.

Yesterday

Registration 2
Rhythm: Rock or Ballad

Words and Music by John Lennon
and Paul McCartney

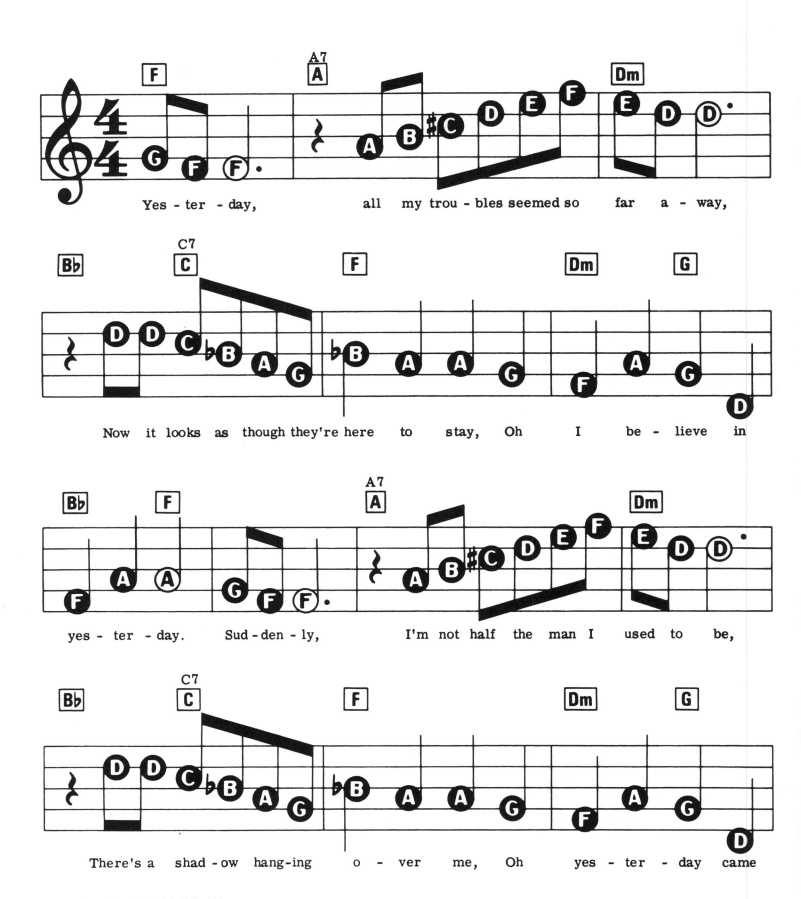

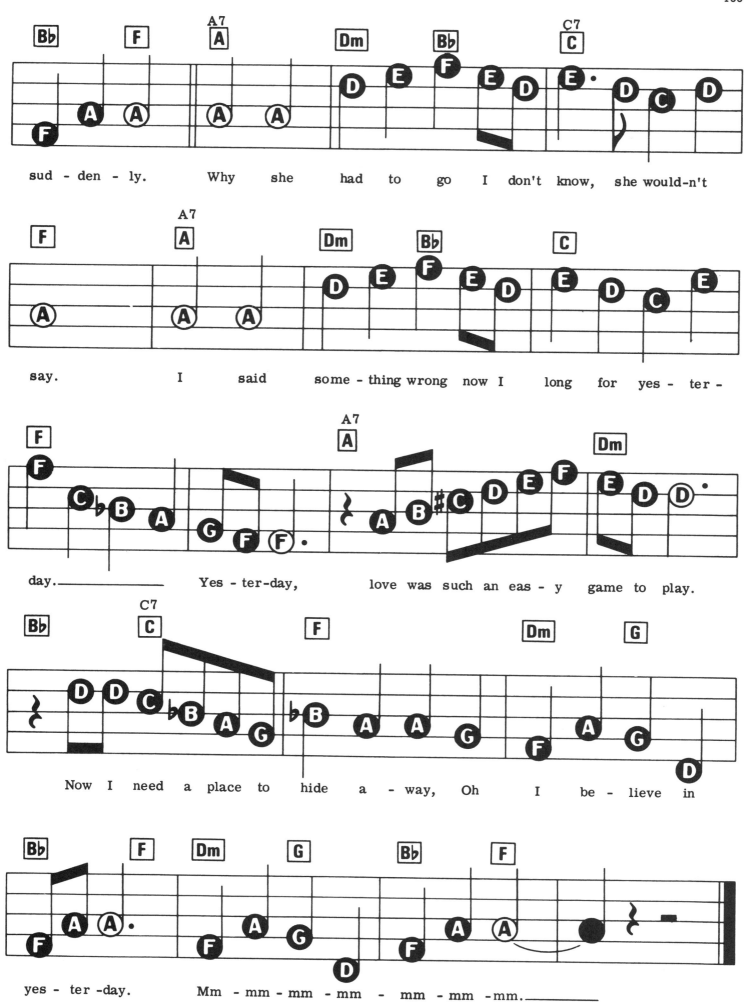

You Like Me Too Much

Registration 5
Rhythm: Rock

Words and Music by
George Harrison

N.C. / **Gm**

Though you're gone a - way this morn - ing, you'll be
tried be - fore to leave me you'll but you
I will fol - low you and bring you

B♭ / **F** / **Gm**

back a - gain to - night, tell - ing me there'll be no
have - n't got the nerve to walk out and make me
back where you be - long 'Cause I could - n't real - ly

B♭ / **F**

next time if I just don't treat you right. You'll
lone - ly if which is all that I de - serve. You'll
stand it, I ad - mit that I was wrong, I

Am / **C7 C**

nev - er leave me and you know it's true, _____
nev - er leave me and you know it's true, _____
would - n't let you leave me 'cause it's true, _____

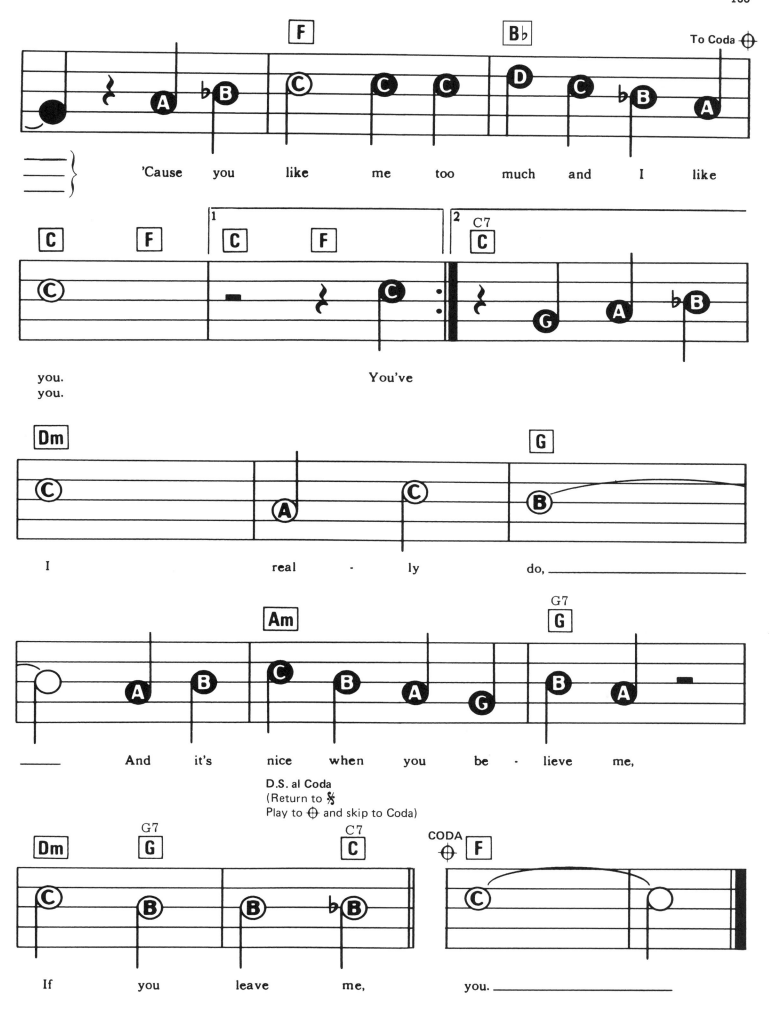

You Won't See Me

Registration 2
Rhythm: Rock

Words and Music by John Lennon
and Paul McCartney

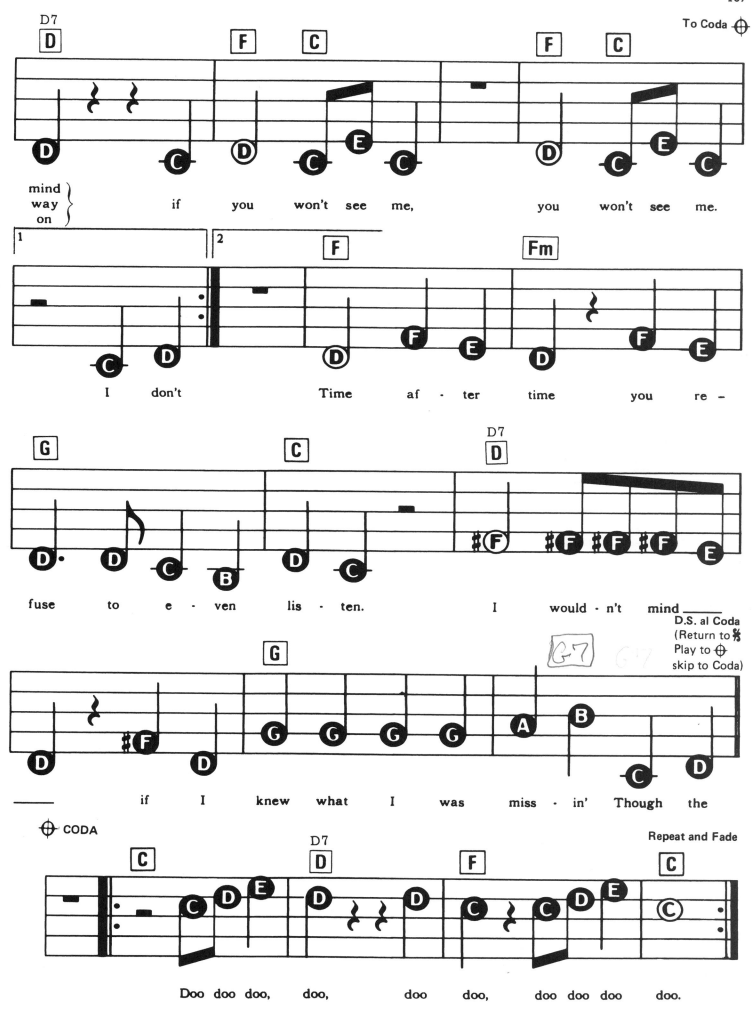

You're Going to Lose That Girl

Registration 4
Rhythm: Rock

Words and Music by John Lennon
and Paul McCartney

199

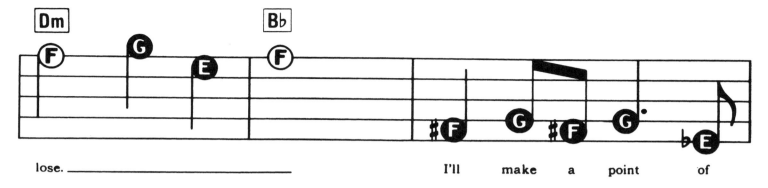

lose. _____ I'll make a point of

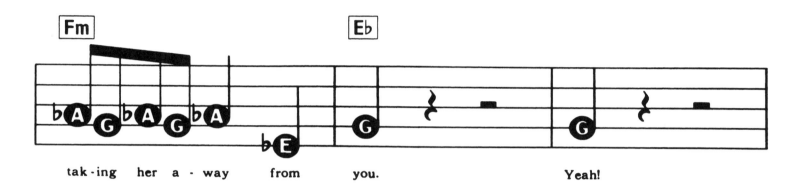

tak-ing her a - way from you. Yeah!

D.C. al Coda
(Return to the beginning
Play to ⊕ and skip to Coda)

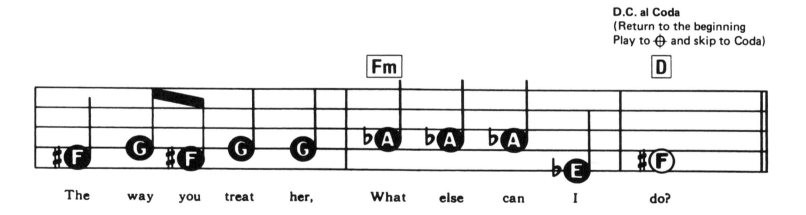

The way you treat her, What else can I do?

⊕ CODA

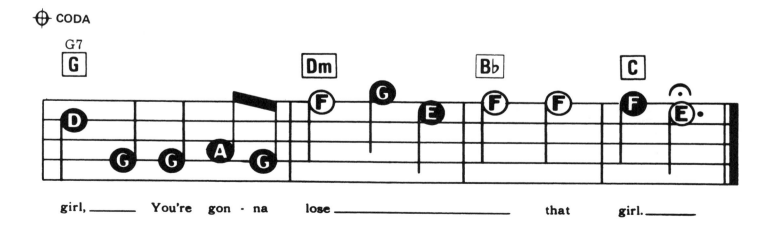

girl, ____ You're gon - na lose _____ that girl. ____

Your Mother Should Know

Registration 2
Rhythm: Rock or Shuffle

Words and Music by John Lennon
and Paul McCartney

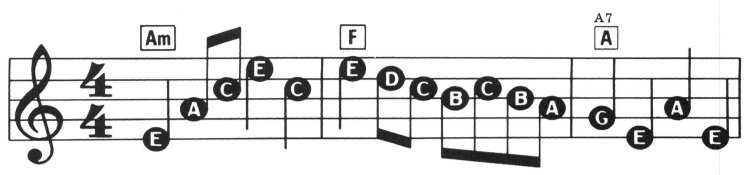

Let's all get up and dance to a song that was a hit be-fore your

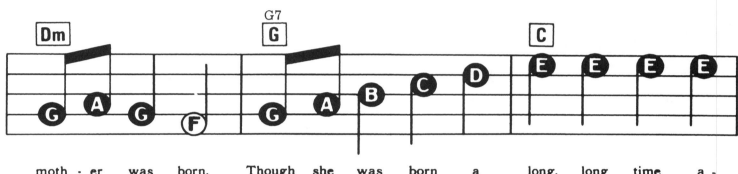

moth-er was born. Though she was born a long, long time a-

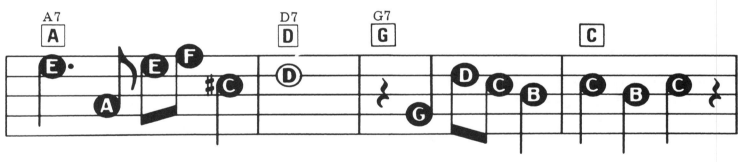

go, your moth-er should know, your moth-er should know._____

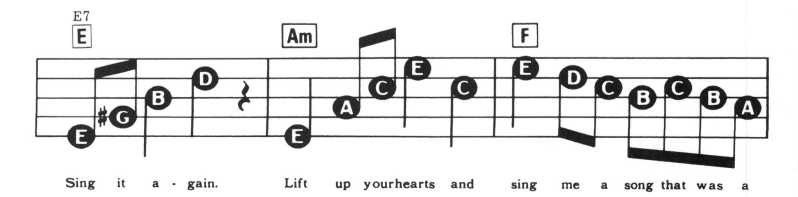

Sing it a-gain. Lift up yourhearts and sing me a song that was a

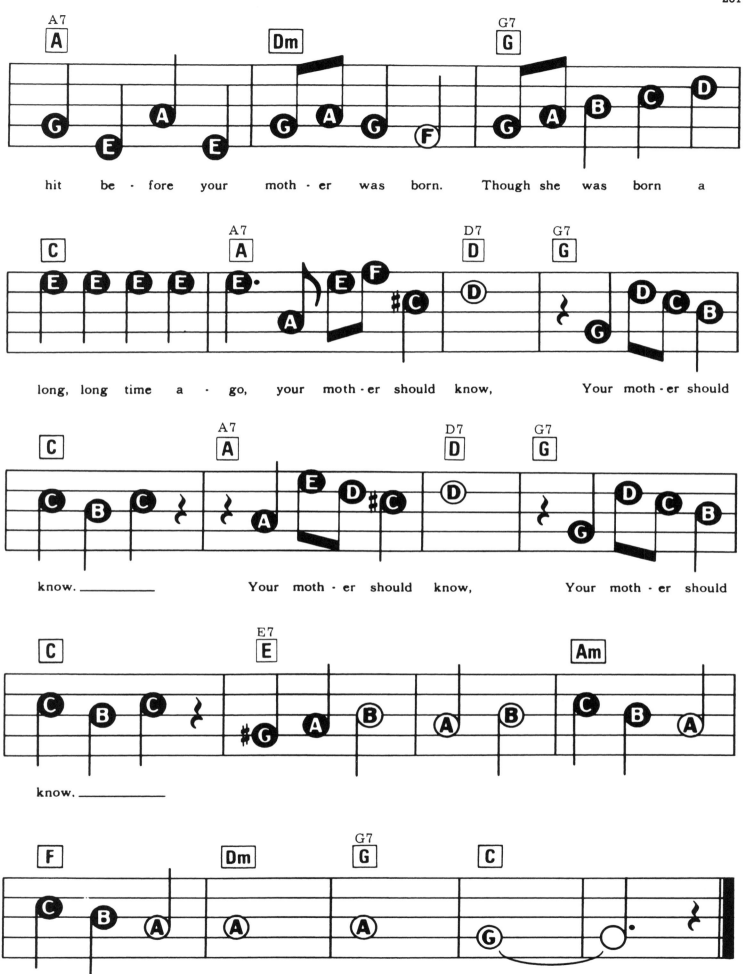

201

You've Got to Hide Your Love Away

Registration 4
Rhythm: Waltz

Words and Music by John Lennon
and Paul McCartney

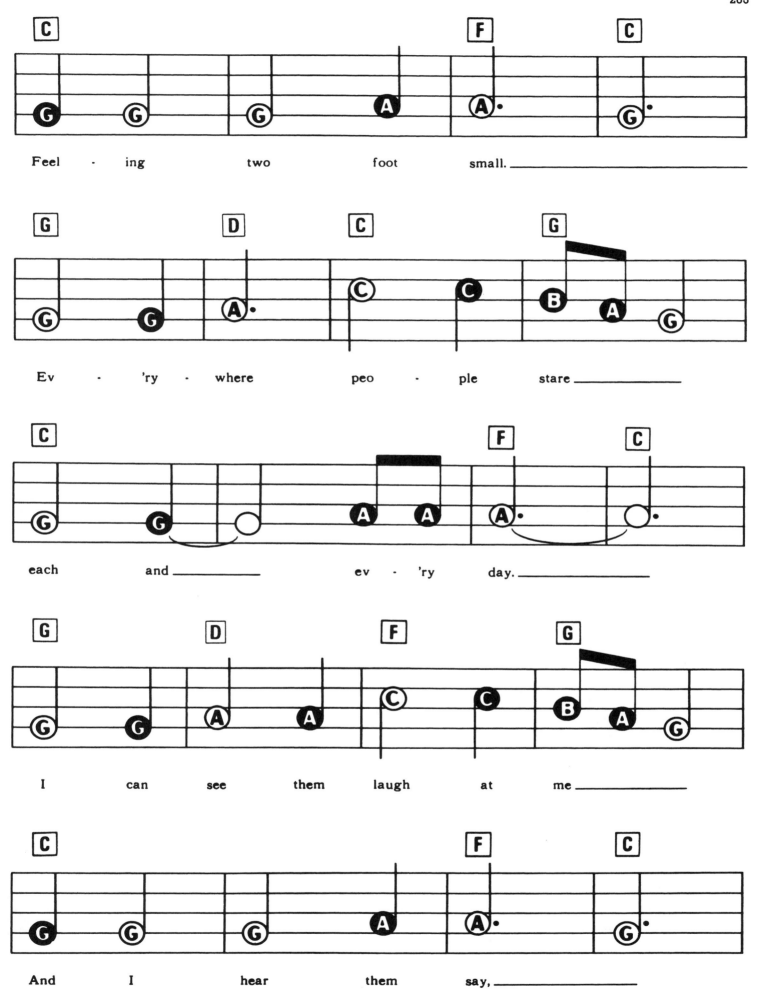

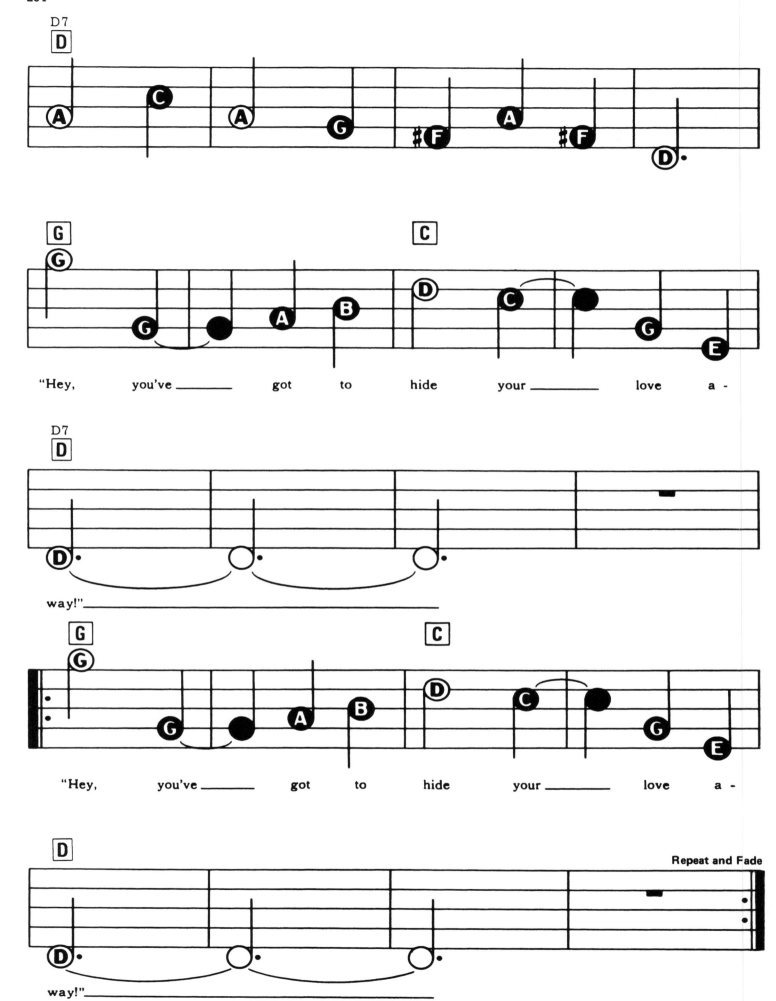

"Hey, you've _____ got to hide your _____ love a -

way!" _____

"Hey, you've _____ got to hide your _____ love a -

Repeat and Fade

way!" _____